Teaching Reading
with
Multicultural Books
Kids Love

CAROL J. FUHLER

fulcrum resources
golden, colorado

Dedication

*To my husband, Richard, who has reminded me that
every single day is to be treasured, and to my sons, Eric
and Patrick, who are so eagerly passing on the love of
reading to their own precious children.*

Library of Congress Cataloging-in-Publication Data
Fuhler, Carol J.
  Teaching reading with multicultural books kids love / Carol J. Fuhler.
    p. cm.
Includes bibliographical references and index.
  ISBN 1-55591-987-1 (pbk. : alk. paper)
  1. Reading (Elementary)—United States. 2. Multicultural education—
United States. 3. Children—Books and reading—United States. 4. Language
arts (Elementary)—United States. I. Title.
  LB1573 .F95 2000
  371.41'2—dc21
                                                                        00-010017

Printed in the United States of America
0 9 8 7 6 5 4 3 2 1

Fulcrum Publishing
16100 Table Mountain Parkway, Suite 300
Golden, Colorado 80403
(800) 992-2908 • (303) 277-1623
www.fulcrum-resources.com

Contents

Contents

Acknowledgments

I have read that writing a book is a journey and that the writer must savor the process and the travels along the way. It's true that journeys often have some surprises in store for the traveler—and my journey was no exception. Writing this book would have been a long trek without the help and support of numerous people. Many thanks to my college students, who enthusiastically participated in a number of these lessons, tried them in their practicum placements, and gave me thoughtful feedback.

Heartfelt thanks to my husband for fixing countless dinners and tolerating my absences as I worked at the computer for hours on end. Finally, thanks to the following publishers who so willingly shared with me review copies of their children's books, a number of which found their way into the lessons in this book: Candlewick Press, Northland Publishers, Roberts Rinehart Publishers, William Morrow Children's Books, and Harcourt Brace.

Preface

....

Educators and parents alike maintain a strong belief in the power of literature to affect the hearts and minds of its readers, particularly when those readers are children and youth. Multicultural literature is one of the most powerful components of a multicultural education curriculum, the underlying purpose of which is to help make the society a more equitable one.

—Violet J. Harris, ed., *Teaching Multicultural Literature in Grades K–8* (Norwood, Mass.: Christopher-Gordon Publishers, 1993), 40

Plop! A pebble dropped onto the calm surface of a pond causes change—change that moves outward from the splash of impact. In ever-widening circles, the water ripples farther and farther away from the initial disturbance as calm is disrupted by movement. Compare a well-crafted multicultural picture book to that pebble. When it is introduced into the calm of a classroom where the teacher is aware of the continued need to focus on multicultural acceptance and of the values of cross-cultural understanding, positive educational changes can result. Ever-widening, mind-broadening ripples begin with one book, and then another. Over time, ripples of understanding will travel beyond the classroom and into life, transforming into a respect for other cultures.

This book demonstrates how appealing, well-written, authentic picture books can involve students in learning about other cultures while teaching reading strategies. Why begin with picture books? They quickly capture a reader's attention, are visually appealing, and can crack open the door to multicultural understanding with relative ease. The following pages demonstrate how judiciously selected titles can take readers through the reading curriculum and across other subjects on a journey of many discoveries. Research tells us that readers learn new strategies best when they are modeled and then applied, practiced within practical classroom activities, and then reinforced through additional practice. The lessons that follow are based upon such thinking. This is simply one of many possible ways to teach reading.

I want to acknowledge the fine work of every diligent teacher in classrooms around the world. Teaching is hard work. I know because I do it. The latest pressures on today's teachers seem to revolve around finding the one best way to teach reading. Those of us who work with children every day know, however, that there is no such thing. Wise teachers teach in the manner that works best for their students, mixing and matching numerous approaches depending on the needs of each child. Kudos to each of you!

It takes more than talk and heartfelt wishes to make today's society more equitable: It takes action. Perhaps that action can involve teachers willing to foster a multicultural community within the reading program. One by one, each culturally sensitive classroom can become a building block in the creation of an ever-growing, world-wise multicultural community. It is a challenge difficult to resist.

Introduction
A Guide to Using This Book

....

This book contains 42 lessons, each of which uses one book as its main focus. Each lesson is tailored to its focus book, and is divided into the following categories:

- The culture being focused on

- Necessary materials for teaching the lesson

- Motivators for the students

- Suggestions for teaching the lesson

- Evaluation questions and suggestions

- Possible extensions

- Recommended titles

The Essence of Reading

Reading is magical. It is a conduit to undiscovered worlds as well as to realms that exist only in the imagination. A book's magic lies in the connection between the author's words and the reader's imagination. Decoding those words, however, is a challenge that has little to do with magic. Much of the art of becoming a proficient reader must be taught. The journey to becoming an expert reader starts during the read-aloud years—for the lucky children, this journey will begin long before kindergarten. Exposure to books develops the roots needed to nourish a lifetime of reading. The read-aloud years quietly and irrevocably teach a child what a book is all about. Knowledge about how to hold a book, where it begins, and how the eye moves on the page becomes intrinsic.

Reading behaviors continue to develop in other ways. Young children soon learn to recognize print in their immediate environment.

The names on favorite boxes of cereal, labels on juice containers or cans of pop, and the stop sign on the corner are real and relevant reading materials. Strong connections between reading and writing are already being forged when toddlers pick up a bright, fat crayon or colorful marker and begin to scrawl. Their diligently formed squiggles emulate the writing of the adults around them. In time the scribbles take on the form of letters, albeit backwards, sideways, and upside down, before they straighten themselves out into some semblance of recognizable order.

Progress continues. Emergent readers begin to learn basic reading skills such as recognizing the names of letters and the sounds they make. Imagine a child's crow of delight when first writing his or her own name. These enthusiastic young learners are beginning to grasp the alphabetic principle. Through instruction and hours of reading, children eventually come to recognize a large number of words, learn practical strategies to unlock the meaning of a difficult sentence or paragraph, and develop other strategies to troubleshoot when comprehension falters. Along the way, skills and strategies modeled by the teacher can be practiced and then practiced again within the wondrous world of quality literature.

Although deciphering the written word involves an incredible number of skills and strategies, all of them can be taught in innovative and appealing ways. It has never been proven that skills can only be taught and acquired if they follow a specific skill and sequence chart, despite the fact that numerous popular basal reading series have long promoted this practice. The best-learned skills are taught and practiced in a real and lively context. A research-supported teaching sequence is one in which a new skill or strategy is carefully taught. Next, the skill or strategy is clearly modeled. Finally, students are provided opportunities to apply new knowledge in a variety of motivating ways involving quality literature. Budding readers will become more avid learners once they are moved beyond the drill and repetition long demanded on worksheets and are inspired by creative, well-prepared teachers who want to teach a different way.

Why Use Real Books?

A growing cadre of educators believe that actual books, rich with dynamic illustrations and finely honed stories, are the best medium with which to teach children to read. A number of learning theorists advocate teaching by reading the entire story first, stopping to focus on an essential skill or strategy, then returning to the whole story to put new learning into a real context. This approach facilitates readers' understanding of the relevance of what is being modeled by the teacher. Experiencing how a new reading tool works impels readers to make that skill their own as they tackle one appealing book after another.

Books of all kinds can be used to teach reading. Although picture books are as appropriate in the upper grades as they are in the lower grades to teach a lesson, older learners typically practice their reading abilities when wrapped up in an engrossing novel. *Teaching Reading with Multicultural Books Kids Love* uses picture books because they lend themselves so beautifully to illuminating a memorable lesson. Picture books offer teachers the opportunity to be inventive, to develop sound and unique lessons that reach specific learners in a particular classroom. This text does not offer any canned approaches, only suggestions for implementation. A colleague down the hall may take the same picture book and teach an entirely different lesson with resounding success.

Using books instead of basals to teach reading is a reinforcing step in the right direction for any teacher who has long relied on a basal series. Although the basal can still be consulted and used as a framework for the reading program, teaching with dynamic children's literature substantiates each teacher's own expertise, intuition, and child-generated wisdom about what works best when teaching reading. There are multiple ways of learning within a classroom, and diverse instructional techniques to match those ways of learning.

Beginning with an infusion of multicultural picture books is a proactive move to celebrate knowledgeable teachers as critical thinkers and all children as consumers of fine reading materials. This applies both in reading and when teaching across the curriculum to reinforce learning in other subjects.

A final argument for teaching via picture books is that today they are simply too beautifully crafted not to be an integral part of the classroom reading program. The fine artwork is an education in itself, providing an opportunity for students to learn about artistic styles and see how an artist can extend a story through the illustrations, and spurring learners to try some of the artistic media themselves. Picture books are catalysts, learning waiting to happen, and treasures to be savored again and again. They can pack within their pages unexpectedly potent lessons about life as well. Reading real books with real children—it can't get any better than that.

Multicultural Literature Explained

Multicultural literature typically relates stories about numerous cultural groups, clearly reflected by the faces of children in classrooms across the United States. These books offer tales about a broad range of humanity, including people of color, various religious groups who have been persecuted for their beliefs, and individuals with intellectual or physical disabilities. Other books address social class differences and broadening views of once firmly entrenched gender roles. Quality books authentically portray the unique lifestyles and heritages of all people who call themselves Americans today. As a rule, they center more specifically on characters representing non-Western cultures. Fictional titles depict main characters from cultures outside mainstream America, whereas nonfiction selections focus on real people from these parallel cultures.

Noted author Virginia Hamilton has coined the term *parallel culture* to replace the often used "minority group," a designation that is somewhat negative in tone. Not only does the use of *parallel culture* promote the image of people of all backgrounds living side by side on parallel planes, it also supports the idea that all cultures can interact positively with one another. Certainly this much-needed interaction can be reinforced—and even begin—within the nation's classrooms.

A Case for Multicultural Picture Books

Why the focus on multicultural picture books rather than picture books in general? The first reason is a powerful one for both beginning readers and those who are refining their skills. To make a strong connection with a book, to elicit that all-important affective response, every child should see his or her face reflected in some of the illustrations. His or her culture should be explored realistically within well-crafted stories. Real faces from different cultures are rapidly filling the nation's classrooms, but the books reflecting these cultures are not always awaiting them. Demographers estimate that 28 percent of the school-age population will be from cultures other than Caucasian by the year 2000. This figure is projected to increase to 47.5 percent by the year 2050. As a result of such classroom changes, one wonders whether these figures mean that multicultural literature may become *the* literature of use in the future rather than only a small portion of today's reading material. Whether or not such a change occurs, multicultural titles already have a much-deserved place on classroom bookshelves.

Regardless of the statistics, reality dictates that each learner deserves to be honored today as a growing number of diverse beliefs and traditional values increasingly become a part of the standard classroom curriculum. Both children and teachers must affirm and welcome every learner as a member of the classroom community. In this process, learning to read from appealing multicultural literature is one logical way to help every child develop a positive self-image while strengthening personal cultural pride. By using appropriate reading strategies carefully matched to superb literature that reflects all cultures, children can begin to learn what it means to respect diversity. In a small way, on a daily basis, young people will be able to practice the skills that will prepare them to meet the future challenges of living in our global society.

Multicultural literature also exposes learners to the actions of others in parallel cultures, enabling them to better understand the actions of others. Dipping into the growing body of well-written multicultural literature provides extensive opportunities for both teachers and students to develop respect for individuals in various cultural and ethnic groups. Learning together, they can compile a storehouse of more accurate and complete information. As they read book after book, students first glimpse the idea, and then grasp the concept, that people are connected to one another through the common threads of emotions, needs, and desires. Such potent understanding carries learning well beyond the reading classroom.

When they discuss the books at hand, students can become engaged in comparing and contrasting values, beliefs, and attitudes expressed by people from a variety of cultures. Such social interaction is an integral part of the reading comprehension process. Through talk and reflection students can examine how people are the same and how they are different, both within a culture and outside it, recognizing that different does not connote "less than." Here, too, is an opportunity to relish the fact that people from all backgrounds have achieved some incredible goals. Later, when older students read novels and delve into them at a more sophisticated level than picture books afford, they can expand their knowledge of peoples' histories and celebrate the contributions made by individuals from various cultures. Every culture has its heroes and heroines who have lessons to teach us all. Young children can begin with simple ideas and broaden their knowledge and understanding of people in other cultures year after year, aided by books that touch the heart as well as the mind.

The downside of using multicultural literature as a larger and larger part of the reading curriculum is the dearth of quality books available. Although more and more books reflect various cultures, progress is slow. Titles featuring the lives of real and fictitious African Americans seem to have shown the greatest growth during the 1990s. The number of such titles represented in this volume reflects that boom. In the early 1990s less than 1 percent of books published in the United States depicted Asian Americans, and the number is much the same for titles about Hispanic cultures. The outlook is somewhat better for books about Native Americans, almost 3 percent of the books published for young readers in the first five years of the 1990s. Altogether, only about 16 percent of the nearly 25,000 children's books published in the 1990s were devoted to African-American, Asian-American, Hispanic, and Native American cultures. Fortunately, many of those titles are of commendable quality.

Obviously, reading multicultural picture books and novels will not solve the divisions between races or immediately eradicate other problems created by cultural misunderstanding. Sadly, deeply rooted negative attitudes begin early in a child's life and are challenging to alter. Multicultural books provide a framework for change, however, and are inspiring vehicles with which to teach reading while broaching human understanding. To paraphrase American astronaut Neil Armstrong, this text's suggested approach to teaching reading skills and strategies immersed in multicultural literature could be one small step for man and, in time, one giant multicultural leap for mankind.

The Theory behind the Ideas

There is sound reading theory behind the activities suggested in the lessons included here. A teacher should have no fears about integrating any of the multicultural books, skills, or strategy-building activities into the current basal curriculum, or about using them as an integral part of a carefully balanced literature-based curriculum. For example, one important theory addressed through these lessons is the generative learning theory that evolved from work done by early cognitive researchers. The theory suggests that readers need to actively construct relationships between information in a book and their own background knowledge. Each lesson attempts to do just that by inviting readers into the lesson via motivators and/or thought-provoking questions.

A second theory that is used heavily in this book builds on earlier reading studies. Schema theory emerged from cognitive research done in the 1970s and 1980s. As does generative theory, schema theory helps to explain the comprehension process. It describes how people store information in their minds and how previously acquired knowledge can either help or hinder learning something new. A schema can be regarded as a package of knowledge made up of related concepts, events, emotions, and roles, all colored by life experiences. Each package is unique to a particular individual. During the learning process,

new knowledge is integrated into the old knowledge, all of which is continually reorganized to make a more comprehensive package. Thus, expanding one's comprehension can prove to be an intriguing, lifelong process.

Accessing what a student already has in his or her personal schema is addressed in each section of the upcoming lessons through activities that kindle prior knowledge. Employing this particular reading strategy is beneficial for teacher and student alike. First, in an effort to make the learning experience better for the child, this step gives the teacher an idea of where it might be important to supply additional information about a topic before beginning the book at hand. Second, by pulling past experiences into a new reading situation, the student often has a deeper comprehension of new materials. Third, the reader finds recognizing new words less challenging because they are couched in an understandable context. Altogether, this strategy creates an encounter with reading that is much more enjoyable than it might be otherwise. Underlying both theories and the lessons in this book is the fact that prior knowledge must be brought into play as much as possible at the beginning of each learning experience to promote the optimal integration of new knowledge with the old.

These lessons also address student engagement with learning. Educator and researcher Brian Cambourne initially explained engagement, and subsequent research underscores its importance. Simply stated, a crucial step in facilitating learning is for teachers to make learning safe and appealing as they promote interactions with classroom materials, with attempting something new, and among students in their classrooms. The classroom atmosphere must gently support all efforts toward learning in a safe environment, where students can take risks with reading, writing, and relationships. Students will then engage in reading and writing because they do not fear failure. They understand that they will eventually succeed in their efforts. Furthermore, these learners believe that what they are doing is useful. Above all, they are working in a learning environment with classmates and adults whom they like and trust. Obviously, setting the classroom tone for learning is important in ensuring that each student will succeed in becoming a proficient reader and writer.

Research supports the practice of reading itself as a means of improving reading expertise.

The more students engage in reading, the better they become. The area of vocabulary development is another example. Students greatly expand their acquisition of words through independent reading. When they meet an unfamiliar word, they may try to examine the context of a word to decipher its meaning. If sense isn't made at that point, other strategies can, of course, be applied. Continually making educated guesses and having those guesses confirmed by additional reading perpetuates the growth of usable vocabulary. The point to be emphasized here is that wide reading and vocabulary size are directly related. It is also interesting to note that once immersed in the world of print, students see reading and writing as interconnected, as natural as breathing, and as attainable as any other skill they want to make their own. Practice in reading is essential if proficiency is the goal.

Finally, the area of brain research deserves close scrutiny. This is a hotly debated topic, with some proponents eagerly making connections between emerging scientific knowledge about how the brain works and applying that knowledge to optimal classroom practice. Scientists themselves caution educators that it is far too soon to make such connections. While the debate rages, it behooves teachers to read both sides of the argument, to be prepared to discuss queries from parents who might not see the whole picture, and simply to be better informed about the activities of the brain. It is imperative that teachers understand this burgeoning and fascinating area of research as they strive to provide an optimal learning environment.

Obviously, learning what transpires in an organ made up of more than 100 billion cells is daunting, but the experts persist. The following suggestions are advocated by educators eager to make the connection to brain-based teaching practices in the classroom. They are firmly rooted in three decades of psychological research, and are good classroom practices no matter who advocates them.

1. Create lively, innovative classrooms to provide students with an optimal learning environment. A positive, challenging environment can affect the brain's wiring as much as a person's actual experiences, as demonstrated by our increasing understanding of the brain's plasticity and its amazing innate ability to grow in response to the environment.

2. Use enrichment programs for every learner, not just for students identified as talented and gifted, because experiences determine which synapses of the brain are retained and which are eventually discarded because of lack of use.

3. Maximize interactive feedback in the classroom between students, between student and teacher, and within the student through reflection. Feedback is most powerful when it is specific rather than general, and when it is as immediate as possible rather than delayed. Students can get personal feedback when they are asked to check their progress against individual goals they have set for themselves. Parents are another source of feedback. Computer programs designed to reinforce correct answers are another viable option.

4. Integrate physical activity into all curricular activities. Activity helps to keep the brain more highly involved in its cognitive functions. Vary the routine periodically and let the students move outside of a regimented daily pattern.

5. Integrate the arts across the curriculum. Emerging theory supports the fact that a strong foundation in art, music, and drama builds creativity and strengthens such skills as concentration, problem solving, self-efficacy, coordination, and self-discipline. It appears that the arts and reading are natural learning partners.

6. Provide a 5- to 10-minute break from the routine every hour and a half to keep students attentive. Allow students to stand and stretch, get a drink of water, sing a song with actions, or just chat quietly.

7. Give students time to process after learning a new concept.

This important part of learning might be equated to time for new ideas to "incubate" before they are assimilated into existing schema. Having occasional periods of quiet time for reflection or response journaling will facilitate knowledge processing following a learning activity.

8. Educate students and their parents about the value of eating well to enhance overall learning opportunities. Foods such as leafy green vegetables, salmon, nuts, lean meats, and fresh fruits facilitate the brain's ability to function optimally. Saturated fats, sugar, and simple carbohydrates impede learning when consumed frequently.

9. Allow students to keep a small bottle of water in their desks to facilitate learning and eliminate those incessant requests to go to the drinking fountain. Listless, inattentive students may simply need water— not juice or soft drinks—because the brain is made up of more water than any other organ in the body and dehydration will affect the students' level of alertness.

The Crucial Element of Response

Understanding the potential for multicultural picture books or novels to breach cultural differences lies in understanding reader response theory. Reading is not a passive process. Readers are busy decoding words, creating meaning as their personal experiences become intertwined with an author's words, and responding internally to what they have read. The perceptive teacher, aware of the myriad of readers' responses to both fiction and nonfiction titles, is adept at making some of those intrapersonal reactions public. One way to do so is by opening a class discussion with questions that are aimed at broadening readers' thinking as they listen to their peers' interpretations of a book. When different responses, perceptions, and impressions are encountered, students begin to weigh their own beliefs, altering them or confirming them in the process.

Such positive conversations, student interactions, and personal connections may foster cultural understanding.

Noted reading theorists, such as Jerome Harste and Judith Langer, have stated that each reader brings a personal accumulation of incidents, expectations, attitudes, and interests to the reading experience. This background will affect the way in which individuals interpret written text. Other theorists point to the author's efforts, including the arrangement of the written word upon the page, as the stimulus for a reader's particular response. Those words become the catalyst that ignites highly individual, vital interactions between reader and text. Response to the literature at hand will vary from reader to reader and situation to situation. Individual responses will be affected by a number of factors, including age, cognitive development, personality, life experiences, and the text itself.

More often than not, a response is internal, tucked inside the reader's mind as he or she visualizes a personal version of an unfolding narrative. Active involvement with the text elicits response. That response might include predicting what could happen next or connecting strongly to the emotional pull of the story. According to theorist Louise Rosenblatt, this is an aesthetic response to literature. It is personal and subjective. Activating the reader's feelings, memories, intellectual reactions, and reflections results in what Rosenblatt describes as a live current flowing between reader and the narrative text.

Rosenblatt explains that the stance changes when readers choose to read expository text, focusing on acquiring information. In this situation, they are in an "efferent" stance. Response has now moved from an aesthetic, private experience to a more public reaction, including activities such as generalizing, analyzing, manipulating, or theorizing about what has been read. Readers' particular purposes for engaging with text affect whether they are primarily in the aesthetic or the efferent stance as they read. In the end, adept readers learn to shift between these two stances, falling somewhere on a continuum depending on their reasons for reading.

When the situation warrants it, private, internal responses can become external through the direction of a creative and insightful teacher. For example, frequent discussions can elicit memorable learning as various ideas and reactions are shared in a small or large group. "How do you feel?" and "What do you think?" or "How do you know?" can be asked to strengthen the connections among a book, its reader, and people of different backgrounds. Written responses can be encouraged through personal response journal entries, a poem encapsulating the essence of a story, a letter to a main character, or a letter penned to the author. Illustrating a timeline or a favorite scene, singing a jingle to promote the book, and putting on a puppet show or reader's theater are attractive avenues through the arts. Shared responses will illuminate each reader's thinking, while private reflections can deepen the understanding of different multicultural issues or changing personal perspectives.

Being knowledgeable about reader response and the ways it can be taught or enhanced is important when linking multicultural literature to the process of strengthening cultural awareness. Through readers' reactions to books and ongoing discussion of those reactions, a judicious teacher can foster learning and thinking differently about various cultures while also being open to broadening his or her cultural consciousness.

How Do You Know It's Working?

Reading is the process of making meaning from print. Awareness about whether that is actually happening requires judicious efforts to monitor and measure how that meaning-making process is progressing. This happens through evaluation, an integral part of learning. Brain research supports the idea that learners need to know how they are progressing with the acquisition of useful skills and strategies just as teachers need to monitor that acquisition to inform their teaching. Overall quality assessment is more than the yearly standardized test or the periodic mastery test at the conclusion of a section in the basal reader. A test is but one piece of information needed to present a complete picture of an individual as a learner.

The suggestions for evaluation offered throughout this text often involve the process called "kidwatching." Noted reading authority Yetta Goodman popularized the term when she advocated evaluation efforts that support the development of literacy skills in a natural, less-invasive manner than standardized pencil-and-paper tests. Instead, she urged teachers to watch children. Goodman returned to all teachers the power of knowing their students as learners. Teachers jot down notes about students' interactions with print and with one another, day after day, as they are actively engaged in a rich learning environment. Information is gathered about a variety of misunderstandings, miscues when reading, and conceptual development as they play with and expand their use of language. Evaluation for each learner is an ongoing, yearlong process. The process is authentic because it measures what the student is doing in real learning situations in the classroom. Throughout the upcoming lessons, knowing what a learner has mastered and what he or she is still striving to grasp will fuel optimal instruction.

Kidwatchers use numerous evaluation tools. A teacher may periodically hold brief conferences with individual students. A teacher may also judge efforts on a story map, watch interactions with other learners in small groups, listen to a retelling of a story, or query a learner about what he or she does when trying to decipher a word during reading. Kidwatching evaluation may also include observations guided by a teacher-developed checklist, a completed reading inventory, or quick comments jotted on self-sticking notes to be attached to a sheet with the student's name on it. Another tactic is dating acquired skills on rating scales developed by a basal series, which lists various reading abilities. The overall picture of a student as a learner is pulled together from many pieces.

Of course, it is always wise to assess learners on individual progress rather than solely on a preestablished standard. Gather a variety of student work in portfolios that present a picture of student progress over time. Encourage students to set goals and self-assess. The students themselves are a critical part of the evaluation process. Compiling information from a number of sources gathered by both the learner and the teacher will take into account the diversity among a classroom of learners. In this manner, every student will be able to take pride in his or her strides in reading. Suggestions for different ways to monitor learning are presented in each of the lessons. Adapt and adjust them as needed.

Criteria for Evaluating Multicultural Literature

Evaluation is not directed merely at the student as a learner; it is applied to the materials brought into the classroom as well. It is exciting to think of the increasing level of creativity that will be generated in our nation's classrooms when teachers tackle reading via multicultural picture books, even if it is only done periodically for a change from the regular routine. The books used in each reading lesson must be selected with care, however. Just because the book is multicultural does not mean it is good literature. More and more superb books centered on different cultures are becoming available for teaching and for purely pleasurable reading. Before spending part of the classroom budget or personal funds on a title, examine it with the eyes of an informed critic. The following criteria are helpful in making wise selections:

- Does the book use quality language and illustrations? Do the words and illustrations work together to tell the story?

- Is there diversity and a wide range of representation in the portrayal of a parallel cultural group, including a broad spectrum of occupations, educational backgrounds, living conditions, and lifestyles?

- Is there a lack of stereotyping and an inclusion of more positive images of the culture?

- Do the illustrations show distinctive yet varied characteristics of a group?

- Is there an avoidance of derogatory terms for particular racial groups as well as an avoidance of inappropriate use of dialect? Are the characters and their behavior presented in a nonjudgmental manner?

- Does the book's perspective seem to truly reflect a particular culture's experiences?

- Are racial pride and positive self-image apparent in the story?

- Does the book include authentic, culturally specific values?

- Does the book help develop a reader's appreciation for our ever-changing, pluralistic society?

- Does the book present different perspectives and additional information about the depicted culture?

(Adapted from Charlotte S. Huck, Susan Hepler, and Janet Hickman, *Children's Literature in the Elementary School,* 5th ed. [San Diego, Calif.: Harcourt Brace, 1993], 568–569.)

A Look at the Lessons

In classrooms across the country, common elements contribute to successful reading programs. In general, exposure to literature of all kinds should include a wide variety of experiences with printed material. One experience of great importance is well-practiced, frequent reading aloud by teachers, parents, or other caregivers. There must also be opportunities to talk about those books that children hear or read independently. Finally, the reading experience should be extended through involvement in authentic, engaging activities that strengthen response to what is read. These threads are interwoven throughout the lessons in this book.

In addition, each of the lessons in this text focuses on one particular reading skill or strategy. In the process of teaching that skill, however, other reading skills naturally will be reinforced. For example, it is good teaching practice to focus students on the lesson ahead as an aid to comprehension. Each lesson does so. The skill of predicting what will come next and then listening carefully to confirm or revise that prediction is an additional strategy to build comprehension. These lessons frequently ask students to predict, but that skill is not singled out each time because it could become tedious to tease out or identify each specific skill or strategy in every lesson.

Reading is a highly active process. It is important to remember that readers apply a number of skills each time they attempt to make sense of the printed page. In reality, no skill is used in isolation, although it may need to be taught that way so that learners can add it to their repertoire of reading strategies. Eventually, learned skills will become so infused into the whole reading process that students will apply them automatically as needed. The goal of this book is to build those skills within the context of fabulous multicultural opportunities to read, knowing that readers will mix and match skills and strategies in their personal reading as needed. Researchers remind us that unless students have many chances to use reading strategies in authentic reading and writing, they may begin to doubt their usefulness and value. This text strives to reinforce that value.

Attuned to what works best to improve reading ability, each lesson concludes with suggestions for additional books that students might choose to read. An attempt has been made to provide variety, a key strategy in motivating students to read, while strengthening reading proficiency. Although some of the books may be earmarked for the additional practice of skills presented in the lesson, all are suggested as appealing adventures for students to read on their own. Some of the titles have been selected because they are personal favorites; others have been chosen from lists of award-winning titles.

Adapt each lesson to best fit your students. You are the expert. Quality teaching encourages the exploration of different ways of thinking about issues, recognizes multiple answers, and fosters creative insights in students. It is not built around a single "best" way to teach reading, but rather upon the flexibility to match individual learners with the most appropriate strategy. Augment your students' reading skills using these wonderful books and others that you will discover. Both you and your students will be much richer as a result. You are supported in your efforts by experts in the field of reading and children's literature, who concur with Rosenblatt:

> Prolonged contact with literature may result in increased social sensitivity. Through poems and stories and plays, the child becomes aware of the personalities of different kinds of people. He learns to imaginatively "put himself in the place of the other fellow." He becomes better able to foresee the possible repercussions of his own actions in the life of others.

—Louise M. Rosenblatt,
Literature as Exploration,
3d ed. (New York: Noble and
Noble, 1976)

Suggested Reading

The following materials provide more information about reading theory.

Anderson, R. C. "Research Foundations to Support Wide Reading." In *Promoting Reading: Views on Making Reading Materials Accessible to Increase Literacy Levels,* edited by V. Greaney, 55–77. Newark, Del.: International Reading Association, 1996.

Bruer, John T. "In Search of … Brain-Based Education." *Phi Delta Kappan* 80 (1999): 648–657.

Cambourne, B. "Toward an Educationally Relevant Theory of Literacy Learning: Twenty Years of Inquiry." *The Reading Teacher* 49 (1995): 182–190.

D'Arcangelo, M. "Learning about Learning to Read: A Conversation with Sally Shaywitz." *Educational Leadership* 57 (1999): 26–31.

Daniels, H., S. Zemelman, and M. Bizar. "Whole Language Works: Sixty Years of Research." *Educational Leadership* 57 (1999): 32–37.

Duffy, Gerald G., and James V. Hoffman. "In Pursuit of an Illusion: The Flawed Search for a Perfect Method." *The Reading Teacher* 53 (1999): 10–16.

Fitzgerald, Jill. "What Is This Thing Called 'Balance'?" *The Reading Teacher* 53 (1999): 100–107.

Fuhler, C. J. "Response Journals: Just One More Time with Feeling." *Journal of Reading* 37 (1994): 400–405.

Galda, L. "Readers, Texts, and Contexts: A Response-Based View of Literature in the Classroom." *The New Advocate* 1 (1988): 92–102.

Goodman, Y. "Kidwatching: Observing Children in the Classroom." In *Observing the Language Learner,* edited by A. Jaggar and M. T. Smith-Burke. Urbana, Ill.: National Council of Teachers of English; Newark, Del.: International Reading Association, 1985.

Guice, S., and R. Allington. "It's More Than Reading Real Books: Ten Ways to Enhance the Implementation of Literature-Based Instruction." In *Literature Update.* Albany, N.Y.: National Research Center on Literature Teaching and Learning, SUNY Albany, 1994.

Jensen, Eric. *Teaching with the Brain in Mind.* Alexandria, Va.: Association for Supervision and Curriculum Development, 1998.

Kiefer, B. "Picture Books as Contexts for Literary, Aesthetic, and Real World Understandings." *Language Arts* 65 (1988): 260–270.

McGee, L. M. "Focus on Research: Exploring the Literature-Based Reading Revolution." *Language Arts* 69 (1992): 529–537.

Rosenblatt, Louise M. *Literature as Exploration.* 3d ed. New York: Noble and Noble, 1976.

———. "Literature—S.O.S.!" *Language Arts* 68 (1991): 444–448.

Rumelhart, D. E. "Understanding Understanding." In *Understanding Reading Comprehension,* edited by J. Flood, 1–20. Newark, Del.: International Reading Association, 1984.

Strickland, D. S. "Reinventing Our Literacy Programs: Books, Basics, Balance." *The Reading Teacher* 48 (1995): 294–302.

Tunnell, M. O., and J. S. Jacobs. "Using 'Real' Books: Research Findings on Literature-Based Reading Instruction." *The Reading Teacher* 42 (1989): 470–477.

Turner, J., and S. G. Paris. "How Literacy Tasks Influence Children's Motivation for Literacy." *The Reading Teacher* 48 (1995): 662–671.

Teacher Resources

Bishop, Rudine S. *Kaleidoscope: A Multicultural Booklist for Grades K–8.* Urbana, Ill.: National Council of Teachers of English, 1991.

Day, Frances A. *Latina and Latino Voices in Literature for Children and Teenagers.* Portsmouth, N.H.: Heinemann, 1997.

———. *Multicultural Voices in Contemporary Literature: A Resource for Teachers.* Portsmouth, N.H.: Heinemann, 1994.

Gunning, Thomas G. *Best Books for Building Literacy for Elementary School Children.* Boston: Allyn and Bacon, 2000.

Harris, Violet J., ed. *Teaching Multicultural Literature in Grades K–8.* Norwood, Mass.: Christopher-Gordon Publishers, 1993.

Heller, M., and H. McLellan. "Dancing with the Wind: Understanding Narrative Text Structure through Response to Multicultural Children's Literature (with an Assist from HyperCard)." *Reading Psychology* 14 (1993): 285–310.

Jensen, Eric. *The Learning Brain.* Illustrated by Gary Johnson. San Diego, Calif.: Turning Point Publishing, 1995.

Sharp, V. F., M. G. Levine, and R. M. Sharp. *The Best Web Sites for Teachers.* Eugene, Oreg.: International Society for Technology in Education, 1996.

Siccone, Frank. *Celebrating Diversity: Building Self-Esteem in Today's Multicultural Classrooms.* Boston: Allyn and Bacon, 1995.

Zemelman, S., H. Daniels, and A. Hyde. *Best Practice: New Standards for Teaching and Learning in America's Schools.* Portsmouth, N.H.: Heinemann, 1998.

Section I

Celebrating Every Learner across the Grades

INTRODUCTORY LESSONS

....

These lessons are meant to be used as an introduction to the concept of celebrating all cultures. The following sections will focus on a specific kind of text.

Lesson 1

Setting the Tone for Celebrating Each Child and All Cultures

SKILL: Personalizing the Reading-Writing Connection

CULTURE OF FOCUS: All

Materials

The Important Book, by Margaret Wise Brown (HarperCollins, 1977)

Three different kinds of spoons and three different kinds of apples

Chart paper or chalkboard

Scratch paper

Pens or pencils

Selection of special paper for the final piece of writing

Art supplies for decorating the writing

Lesson Motivator

This activity motivates students to generate language, encourages creative thinking about common objects, and prepares students to look at the way language is used in *The Important Book.*

1. Pass the spoons around the room.

2. Invite students to brainstorm ways to use a spoon.

3. Record answers on the chalkboard or chart paper. Ask students to think about the similarities and the differences between the spoons. Jot down these responses on the chart as well.

4. Discuss the fact that despite the differences between the types of spoons, each is still a spoon.

5. Repeat the process with the apples. You might want to slice up several apples ahead of time and sprinkle them with lemon juice to keep them from browning. Encourage learners to look at the whole apples and taste samples, using their five senses to describe the characteristics and uses of an apple. The cut-up slices are a perfect opportunity to describe varying tastes and textures.

6. As you transition to the book, focus on the way the author uses language to help readers appreciate real items in the world around them.

Suggestions for Teaching the Lesson

- Prepare the students for listening. Read the title page, taking time to show how the book will be set up based on the example of the glass, which is opposite the title page.

- You might set the stage for reactions about the message in the book by pointing out the initial copyright date. Help the students figure out how old this particular story is. Ask the students to think about whether the message in the story is as important today as it was nearly 50 years ago.

- After reading about the spoon, stop briefly and have the students review their previously generated list about the uses of a spoon to find any similarities between their ideas and those of the author.

- Read through the remainder of the book, pausing briefly to let students think about each set of double pages.

- Upon completion of the book, invite student reactions. Do they think the book's message is still timely?

- Read through the book a second time, asking students to pay particular attention to the way the items are described.

- Demonstrate the reading-writing connection by involving the students in a writing activity patterned after an example from the book. Adjust the expectations for writing to the ability and grade level of the students.

- To model the writing assignment, use one of the pages from the book rewritten on the chalkboard or chart paper. To adapt the format of the book, have the students write about why they are important, beginning and ending with, "The important thing about me is … " Ask them to list four or more positive special characteristics, feelings, or traits they like about themselves between the opening and closing lines. This activity is a celebration of self. Be certain that you are writing right along with the students. Read your rough draft to the students to reinforce the fact that teachers are writers, too. Teacher modeling also confirms the importance of an activity because you are involved beyond merely assigning the task.

- Have the students revise and polish their writing, working through the established classroom writing process. When work is ready to be published, students can select some appealing, unusual paper, transfer their writing to it, and decorate the page appropriately.

- Invite students to share and celebrate themselves in class.

- Display completed work on a bulletin board or wall. Students could bring in small snapshots to be artistically arranged on or near their writing. If the classroom publishes a newsletter, several students could be highlighted in each issue.

Evaluation

- As individual students work, take time to focus on a particular skill or strategy they have mastered. Note how the students use language and spelling skills or, for example, how they problem solve if they get stuck on a word.

- How are students progressing as independent learners?

- What do you know about a learner that you didn't know before this activity?

- Did this activity help establish that everyone is important? Answers to questions like these can be jotted down on sticky notes or on one 5-x-8-inch index card per learner; be sure to note the date of your observations. Review progress, discuss your observations with each student, and make use of this information when reporting progress to parents at conference time.

Extensions

- Follow the same format to write about family members, including family pets, creating an "Important Book" about the whole family. Students might word-process the final product and scan appropriate pictures into it in the school's computer lab or using the classroom computer.

- Select one family member to celebrate, perhaps on Mother's Day, Father's Day, or Valentine's Day.

- Bring in nonperishable, interesting items to display in the classroom writing center. Encourage students to look at them in uncommon ways and continue their writing.

- Set the students' writing to music and let the children sing about their importance.

- Invite students to change their perspectives and view themselves on the back and front of a tablespoon. How does the image change from the bowl of the spoon to the back? Have them fold a piece of notebook paper in half and draw a sketch of themselves as reflected in the front of the spoon and the back to better examine both perspectives. Have one student look up the word *concave* and another look up *convex*. Share the information with the class. This is an unusual, memorable way to address perspective briefly and to integrate some science terms into the lesson.

- Send a "telegram" to someone in the class telling that person what you especially like about him or her. Draw names from a basket or box so that every student is included. This might be a monthly activity to lift spirits and to maintain a positive classroom climate throughout the year.

- Read other books by Margaret Wise Brown from the following list.

Suggested Titles for Independent Reading and Research

Brown, Margaret Wise. *The Golden Egg Book.* Illustrated by Leonard Weisgard. New York: Golden Press, 1976.

———. *Goodnight Moon.* Illustrated by Clement Hurd. 1947. Reprint, New York: HarperCollins, 1975.

———. *The Goodnight Moon Room.* Illustrated by Clement Hurd. New York: HarperCollins, 1984.

———. *The Little Scarecrow Boy.* Illustrated by David Diaz. New York: Joanna Cotler/HarperCollins, 1998.

———. *The Runaway Bunny.* Illustrated by Clement Hurd. 1942. Reprint, New York: HarperCollins, 1972.

Dillon, Leo, and Diane Dillon. *To Everything There Is a Season.* New York: Scholastic/Blue Sky, 1998.

Greenfield, Eloise. *For the Love of the Game: Michael Jordan and Me.* Illustrated by Jan Spivey Gilchrist. New York: HarperCollins, 1997.

Hoberman, Mary Ann. *My Song Is Beautiful: Poems and Pictures in Many Voices.* Illustrated by various artists. Boston: Little, Brown, 1994.

Lucado, Max. *You Are Special.* Illustrated by Sergio Martinez. Wheaton, Ill.: Crossway Books, 1997. (*Note:* This beautiful book has a religious theme that is certainly not overpowering, but you might want to preview it for appropriateness in your class.)

Paul, Ann Whitford. *All by Herself.* Illustrated by Michael Steirnagle. San Diego, Calif.: Browndeer/Harcourt Brace, 1999.

Weiss, George David, and Bob Thiele. *What a Wonderful World.* Illustrated by Ashley Bryan. New York: Simon & Schuster, 1995.

Lesson 2

Representing Cultures in the Classroom

SKILL: Creating a Classroom Multicultural ABC Book

CULTURE OF FOCUS: Japanese

Materials

A to Zen, by Ruth Wells (Simon & Schuster, 1992)
Large piece of butcher paper or chart paper
Markers and crayons
26 index cards, labeled with the letters of the alphabet (one letter per card)
Variety of art supplies with which to make a class book
Assortment of alphabet books (see list at end of lesson)

Lesson Motivator

1. Before students read the focus book, write the words *Hiroshima*, *origami*, and *sushi* on the chalkboard. Ask the class to take a few minutes to write their own definitions of each word.

2. Discuss their efforts and, if necessary, give the correct meanings before moving on.

3. Use the classroom map to locate the country of Japan and the city of Hiroshima. Explain that the book the class will be hearing is an alphabet book about Japan that will help them to better understand Japanese culture.

4. If possible, to broaden the knowledge base, bring in a well-crafted video about the country of Japan and enjoy it together before reading the book aloud.

Suggestions for Teaching the Lesson

- After having practiced reading the book on your own, gather the students around you so that they can see the book. Hold it up and show them the first few pages. Ask for a volunteer to explain what is unusual about the book. Someone will quickly note that the book is read backwards from the way we usually read a book; this, however, is the traditional way to read a Japanese book. Broaden understanding of the culture by reading the "About This Book" section before beginning the alphabet.

- Read the book to the students, stopping briefly to discuss each letter. Periodically, have the listeners think of a word from their culture that would fit with the letter you are presently discussing.

- Upon completion of the book, have students share what they found particularly unusual or interesting about the book and the alphabet. What things are similar between the Japanese culture and those cultures represented by the class? This time to talk is important because conversations about books are critical to the comprehension process, often helping learners to cement concepts and clear up misunderstandings.

- On the butcher or chart paper, write the letters of the English alphabet in columns, leaving room for words to be added by the class.

- Run through the alphabet once, asking students to brainstorm words on paper using objects in the classroom or other items that are familiar to them. Have students jot down three or four suggestions on their own per letter, then ask for a few contributions per letter and add them to the chart paper.

- Go through the alphabet again, asking students to contribute words that reflect their particular cultures. Give students a few suggestions to move this part of the activity along. Add several of these cultural contributions to the existing chart alphabet. Tell the students that this list might be of use later in the lesson.

- Briefly book-talk other alphabet books (collected previously), showing how the authors and illustrators presented different versions of the alphabet in creative and amazing ways. Invite class members to browse through the books, reading them individually or with a classmate. After students have had a day or two to examine a number of these books, noting how each one is unique, call the class together. Discuss what particularly appealed to them in some of the books. What worked and what didn't?

- Explain that the upcoming project involves creating a class alphabet book reflecting the different cultures in the class. Decide together how the class book will be created. Students may want to write a sentence containing alliteration, write a rhyme, or define their word modeled after *A to Zen*.

- After investigating the media used to create the artwork in the collection of books, ask students how they want to proceed with their illustrations. Maybe they would like to try collage, bring a photo of a cultural item from home, or use watercolors or chalk instead of crayons. Guide the class to a consensus, discuss the option of using mixed media, and let the work begin.

- Have each student choose a letter or pick from lettered index cards arranged upside down on a table or shuffled in a basket. Instruct students to consider their letter during the rest of the day and at home after school and come up with a word that represents their culture along with an idea for a sentence, definition, and illustration to coincide with the word. Students may want to ask their parents for help.

- In class the following day, provide sheets of paper, art supplies, and guidance for students to create a multicultural alphabet book that reflects the faces in the classroom. With the help of a parent volunteer or a classroom aide, check writing for errors before the text is finally put on the page for the book.

- Once each page has been completed, bind the class book. Invite each reader/artist/writer to read his or her page aloud. Place the book in a prominent place in the classroom reading center to be read and reread by the class.

Evaluation

- Set up a checklist of appropriate learning strategies so you can note each student's work habits.

- How did learners work together to decide how to make the class book? What reading behaviors did you note as students poured over other alphabet books in the room? Was interaction between classmates appropriate?

- Keep brief anecdotal notes on each student on self-sticking notes that you can later attach to individual sheets of paper, for use as a handy reference at parent conference time.

Extensions

- Students may opt to make their own individual alphabet books.

- Have the learning center director/ librarian gather a collection of Japanese folktales for a brief display in the classroom library.

- Bring in a book of simple origami designs to teach the ancient art of

paper folding one morning or afternoon. Use brightly colored origami paper or colorful print wrapping paper.

- Ask an adult who has traveled to Japan to come in to speak to the class and share any souvenirs he or she may have.

- Invite an aikido instructor to teach the class about this ancient form of martial arts.

- Invite a cook from a local sushi restaurant to come to class and talk about the meals served and the artistic arrangement of the food; possibly let the children taste some of the fare.

Suggested Titles for Independent Reading and Research

Ada, Alma Flor. *Gathering the Sun: An Alphabet in Spanish and English*. Illustrated by Simon Silva. New York: Lothrop, Lee & Shepard Books, 1994.

Agard, John. *The Calypso Alphabet*. Illustrated by Jennifer Bent. New York: Henry Holt, 1989.

Ajmera, Maya, and Anna Rhesa Versola. *Children from Australia to Zimbabwe: A Illustrated with Photographic Journey around the World*. Watertown, Mass.: Charlesbridge, 1997.

Base, Graeme. *Animalia*. New York: Abrams, 1987.

Bruchac, Joseph. *Many Nations: An Alphabet of Native America*. Illustrated by Robert F. Goetzl. Mahwah, N.J.: Bridgewater/Troll, 1997.

Chin-Lee, Cynthia. *A Is for Asia*. Illustrated by Yumi Heo. New York: Orchard, 1997.

Druker, Malka. *A Jewish Holiday A B C*. Illustrated by Rita Pocock. San Diego, Calif.: Gulliver/Harcourt Brace, 1992.

Ehlert, Lois. *Eating the Alphabet: Fruits and Vegetables from A to Z*. Illustrated by the author. San Diego, Calif.: Harcourt Brace Jovanovich, 1989.

Fain, Kathleen. *Handsigns: A Sign Language Alphabet*. New York: Chronicle, 1993.

Feelings, Muriel. *Jambo Means Hello: A Swahili Alphabet Book*. Illustrated by Tom Feelings. New York: Dial, 1974.

Hauseman, Gerald. *Turtle Island A B C*. Illustrated by Cara Moser and Barry Moser. New York: HarperCollins, 1994.

Johnston, Stephen T. *Alphabet City*. New York: Viking, 1995.

Judson, Wade, and Valerie Wesley. *Afro-Bets: Book of Black Heroes from A to Z*. Illustrated with photographs. Orange, N.J.: Just Us Books, 1988.

Musgrove, Margaret. *Ashanti to Zulu: African Traditions*. Illustrated by Leo Dillon and Diane Dillon. New York: Dial, 1976.

Provensen, Alice, and Martin Provensen. *A Peaceable Kingdom: The Shaker Abecedarius.* New York: Viking, 1978.

Rice, J. *Cajun Alphabet.* Gretna, La.: Pelican Publishing, 1991.

Shaw, Eve. *Grandmother's Alphabet.* Duluth, Minn.: Pfeifer-Hamilton, 1996.

Shelby, Anne. *Potluck.* Illustrated by Irene Trivas. New York: Orchard, 1991.

Stroud, Virginia. *The Path of the Quiet Elk: A Native American Alphabet Book.* New York: Dial, 1996.

Tapahonso, Luci, and Eleanor Schick. *Navajo A B C: A Dine Alphabet Book.* Illustrated by Eleanor Schick. New York: Simon & Schuster, 1995.

Van Allsburg, C. *The Z Was Zapped.* Boston: Houghton Mifflin, 1987.

Viorst, Judith. *The Alphabet from Z to A (with Much Confusion along the Way).* Illustrated by Richard Hull. New York: Atheneum, 1994.

Wilber, Richard. *The Disappearing Alphabet.* Illustrated by David Diaz. San Diego, Calif.: Harcourt Brace, 1998.

Lesson 3

It's More Than a Part of Speech

SKILL: Connecting Reading and Writing

CULTURE OF FOCUS: All

Materials

Thank You, Mr. Falker, by Patricia Polacco (Philomel, 1998)
Overhead projector or chalkboard
Pencils or pens
Paper

Lesson Motivator

1. Write the following words on the board or overhead: *reading, determination, respect,* and *courageous.*

2. Read each word aloud.

3. Ask students to think about each word and what it means to them for a few minutes.

4. Briefly review the roles of the parts of speech, including nouns, verbs, and adjectives.

5. Ask the students to use each of the words in a sentence of their own based upon their reflections. They should identify the part of speech of each word as it is used in their particular sentence and write a short definition of each word.

6. Invite several students to write their sentences and definitions on the chalkboard, including two or three offerings per word. Writers should circle the word and identify the part of speech.

7. Ask each learner to read his or her work. Discuss the similarities and differences in the examples and ask if the rest of the class was thinking about the words in a similar manner. Tell the students that these particular words are an integral part of the story to be read aloud.

Suggestions for Teaching the Lesson

• Read *Thank You, Mr. Falker* aloud to the class. Omit the final note at the end of the story until after you elicit class reactions. At the conclusion of the book, engage the class in a discussion, encouraging their reactions to the story and the experiences of the main character, Trisha. Do they think the story seems realistic? Have they ever endured similar situations?

• Read the touching endnote from the author. You might refer interested readers to other books by Patricia Polacco (see list at end of lesson).

• Invite thoughts on how the words on the chalkboard relate to the story.

• Divide the class into groups of three or four. Have one person in each group pick one of the following quotes out of a container. Each group should choose a recorder, who will jot down the ideas generated by the group in reaction to the quote. Connect reactions to real-life experiences when it is comfortably possible to do so.

> "To be different is the miracle of life. You see all of those little fireflies? Every one is different."
>
> "The honey is sweet, and so is knowledge, but knowledge is like the bee who made the honey, it has to be chased through the pages of a book!"
>
> "Are all of you so perfect that you can look at another person and find fault with her?"
>
> "You poor baby, he said. You think you're dumb, don't you? How awful for you to be so lonely and afraid."

- Before they report back to the entire class, ask students to tie their quotes to one of the words on the chalkboard. Groups should share their quotes and how they interpreted them in a large group discussion session.

Evaluation

- In an ongoing list of students' skills, note how a selected number of students are working in a small group situation. Which students are recorders? Do the same students volunteer for this kind of job on a routine basis? If so, make a note to volunteer different students for that job for a future project, enabling all students to develop a variety of skills.

- Is each student engaging in quality thinking in response to the quotes? For instance, which learners are interpreting the quotes at a more literal level and which thinkers delve a little deeper? Follow up the lesson with opportunities for engaging in higher-level thinking activities.

- In general, does the reading of this book enhance the level of respect directed at each learner by other students in your classroom?

Extensions

- Students could write a personal narrative describing themselves as a reader and relating individual challenges or successes. Alternatively, they could share a viewpoint on the values of reading.

- Switch the type of writing and suggest that students write an editorial about the importance of learning to read. Who do they think should help foster reading skills? Should more time or money be devoted to reading activities in their community? Polish and publish.

- Students may also choose to write about a teacher or another adult who helped them to learn a particular skill. Writers could extend this activity to include writing an appropriate thank-you note to that individual.

- Have students work with a partner to role-play a conversation they might have with Trisha, the main character, offering advice or support during one of the difficult times depicted in the story.

- As a class, make posters highlighting the joys of reading. Display the finished products in the library, the learning center, or school hallways. Could this activity be a part of boosting reading skills or time spent reading for students throughout the school?

- Each student can practice reading a favorite picture book. Go to kindergarten, first grade, and second grade classrooms and have the students read the book to a small group of children. Talk with the younger children about the excitement of being able to read.

- Have students become reading buddies and work with a struggling reader at a designated time each week. Just listening to another student read and giving him or her some undivided attention provides important practice time and moral support.

- Invite the school reading specialist to discuss common reading problems in a simple and understandable manner.

Suggested Titles for Independent Reading and Research

Bradby, Marie. *More Than Anything Else.* Illustrated by Chris K. Soentpiet. New York: Orchard, 1995.

Hest, Amy. *When Jessie Came across the Sea.* Illustrated by P. J. Lynch. Cambridge, Mass.: Candlewick Press, 1997.

Hopkins, Lee Bennett. *Good Books, Good Times!* Illustrated by Harvey Stevenson. New York: HarperCollins, 1990. (Poetry selections.)

Johnston, Tony. *Amber on the Mountain.* Illustrated by Robert Duncan. New York: Dial, 1994.

Kraus, Robert. *Leo the Late Bloomer.* Illustrated by Jose Aruego. New York: Windmill Press, 1971.

Lautre, Denzie. *Running the Road to ABC.* Illustrated by Reynold Ruffins. New York: Simon & Schuster, 1996.

Lyon, George Ella. *Book.* Illustrated by Peter Catalanotto. New York: DK Ink, 1998.

Marshall, Rita. *I Hate to Read!* Illustrated by Etienne Delessert. Mankato, Minn.: Creative Editions, 1992.

McGugan, Jim. *Josepha: A Prairie Boy.* Illustrated by Murray Kimber. New York: Chronicle, 1994.

McPhail, David. *Edward and the Pirates.* Boston: Little, Brown, 1997.

Miller, William. *Richard Wright and the Library Card.* Illustrated by Gregory Christie. New York: Lee & Low, 1997.

Mora, Pat. *Tomas and the Library Lady.* Illustrated by Raul Colon. New York: Alfred A. Knopf, 1997.

Polacco, Patricia. *Aunt Chip and the Great Triple Creek Dam Affair.* New York: Putnam, 1996.

———. *The Bee Tree.* New York: Putnam, 1993.

———. *Pink and Say.* New York: Philomel, 1994.

San Souci, Robert. *A Weave of Words.* Illustrated by Raul Colon. New York: Orchard, 1997.

Stewart, Sarah. *The Library.* Illustrated by David Small. New York: Farrar, Straus & Giroux, 1995.

Williams, Suzanne. *Library Lil.* Illustrated by Steven Kellogg. New York: Dial, 1997.

Winch, John. *The Old Woman Who Loved to Read.* New York: Scholastic, 1996.

Lesson 4

A Poetic Explanation of Me—Writing an Autobiographical Poem

SKILL: Following a Format to Create an Autobiographical Poem

CULTURE OF FOCUS: All

Materials

Whoever You Are, by Mem Fox (Harcourt Brace, 1997)
Copies of the "Autobiographical Poetry" instruction sheet (see end of lesson)
Chart paper, overhead projector, or chalkboard
Pens or pencils
Art supplies (for final copy)

Lesson Motivator

1. Hand each student three strips of paper (each approximately 3 x 8 ½ inches).

2. Ask students to write down something they like very much on one strip, something they fear or worry about on another, and a wish or a dream on the final one. The small size of the paper should ease the worries of students who do not like to write very much because there is not much room to do so on each strip.

3. When students have completed the task, invite volunteers to share, getting personal examples for each category.

4. Write the three categories on an overhead, chart paper, or the chalkboard. Record contributions in the appropriate categories.

5. Review each category with the class. Ask if other students wrote something similar. If so, discuss the fact that even though the classroom is filled with distinctive individuals from a variety of backgrounds, they share many of the same feelings, worries, and dreams.

6. Invite the students to look for themselves in the faces in *Whoever You Are*, a seemingly simple book with a powerful message.

Suggestions for Teaching the Lesson

- Ask the students to put their strips of paper aside to be used later and to direct their attention to the book. Read the book, allowing students time to study the unique artwork. When you are done, invite discussion. What are the similarities shared by people around the world? List the responses on the chalkboard or overhead. Do the students agree or disagree with the message in this book? If necessary, set the tone for a sharing environment by reminding the learners that they need to be sensitive to the feelings of others. It is essential to respect the ideas and opinions of others as they explore who they are through words and poetry.

- Hand out copies of the "Autobiographical Poetry" instruction sheet for students to use in writing poems about themselves. Explain that one easy way to begin to write poetry is to follow a prescribed format. Because they will be writing about themselves, they will be writing an autobiographical poem. For a future assignment, they may choose to adapt the poem, writing in social studies about a well-known person, or in reading describing the main character in a novel they have just completed. Tell the students that at that point they will be writing a biographical poem because it is about someone other than themselves.

- Have students go back to their strips of paper and see how their initial ideas can easily transfer to this poem. Read a poem that you have written as an example of what the completed version might be like. It is usually heartening for students to see the messy creative process that even teachers go through, so include several of your drafts for their scrutiny as well.

- If necessary, have the class create a poem together, writing about a person with whom they are all familiar. Of course, in this context, they are working on a biographical poem. A popular member of the community or a revered sports figure might be the subject of the group poem. Give students time to brainstorm ideas for each category before listing them on the chalkboard or overhead.

  Once all ideas have been shared, talk about which three would be the best for each area and write out a draft of the poem. Discuss and polish the work together. Write a final draft and then turn the creative process over to the students, letting them begin on their own autobiographical poems.

- Working from the draft stage, go through the writing process as practiced in the classroom until polished versions of the poetry are completed. Provide a variety of materials for students to use to publish their poems, from interesting paper to supplies for artistic embellishments.

- Students might sit in an "Author's Chair" at the front of the room as they read their poems or they may simply stand by their desks if it is less intimidating for them to read their work aloud that way.

- Display the poems attractively on a bulletin board so that they can be read and enjoyed by the entire class. This activity can be done at the beginning of the year as a memorable way for students to get to know one another.

Evaluation

- List the criteria for evaluation on a poster or on the chalkboard for students' use. Focus on spelling, punctuation, and neatness. Include criteria for reading the poems aloud. Students should evaluate their success in meeting these criteria and discuss their assessments with you.

Extensions

- As mentioned previously, this format can be adapted to highlighting a memorable historical figure in social studies. The artwork can extend the poem—for example, write the poem on a silhouette of the character, or depict key events in the person's life in small sketches around the border of the paper.

- To introduce a favorite character in a novel, students can write a biographical poem. This activity is one way to evaluate how critically a student read and thought about the main character and the changes that individual underwent as the story evolved. Have students illustrate appropriately.

- Have students celebrate a parent or grandparent following the format and present the polished product on Mother's Day, Father's Day, or Grandparents' Day.

- Move from this format to a student's choice of poetic form. Often an exercise such as this is an invitation to enter the world of poetry by overcoming the worry of having to rhyme, opening the doors to experimentation and resulting in some beautiful personal writing.

- Work in small groups to select and set short descriptive poems to music. Present an "Autobiographical Review" backed with music or a general "Poetry Review" highlighting a series of the short, descriptive poems.

- Post the poems on a website (such as one of the websites suggested in Appendix III), as an additional way of publishing.

Suggested Titles for Independent Reading and Research

Begay, Shonto. *Navajo: Visions and Voices across the Mesa.* New York: Scholastic, 1995.

Carlson, Lori M. *Sol a Sol: Bilingual Poems.* Illustrated by Emily Lisker. New York: Henry Holt, 1998.

———, ed. *Cool Salsa: Bilingual Poems on Growing Up Latino in the United States.* New York: Holt, 1994.

Cooper, Floyd. *Coming Home: From the Life of Langston Hughes.* New York: Philomel, 1994.

Giovanni, Nikki. *Grand Mothers: A Multicultural Anthology of Poems, Reminiscences, and Short Stories about the Keepers of Our Traditions.* New York: Holt, 1994.

———. *Spin a Soft Black Song.* New York: Farrar, Straus & Giroux, 1987.

Greenfield, Eloise. *For the Love of the Game: Michael Jordan and Me.* Illustrated by Jan Spivey Gilchrist. New York: HarperCollins, 1997.

Grimes, Nikki. *A Dime a Dozen.* Illustrated by Angelo. New York: Penguin/Putnam, 1998.

———. *Meet Danitra Brown.* Illustrated by Floyd Cooper. New York: Mulberry/ Lothrop, Lee & Shepard Books, 1994.

Hirshfelder, Arlene, and Beverly Singer, selectors. *Rising Voices: Writings of Young Native Americans.* New York: Scribners, 1992.

Hoberman, Mary Ann, selector. *My Song Is Beautiful: Poems and Pictures in Many Voices.* Boston: Little, Brown, 1994.

Janeczko, Paul B. *Looking for Your Name: A Collection of Contemporary Poems.* New York: Orchard/Jackson, 1993.

Navasky, Bruno, trans. *Festival of My Heart: Poems by Japanese Children.* New York: Abrams, 1993.

Nye, Naomi Shihab. *What Have You Lost?* Illustrated with photographs by Michael Nye. New York: Greenwillow, 1999.

Slier, Deborah. *Make a Joyful Sound: Poems for Children by African American Poets.* Illustrated by Cornelius Van Wright and Ying-Hwa Hu. New York: Scholastic, 1991.

Soto, Gary. *A Fire in My Hands.* Illustrated by James M. Cardillo. New York: Scholastic, 1991.

———. *Neighborhood Odes.* Illustrated by David Diaz. San Diego, Calif.: Harcourt Brace, 1992.

Steptoe, Javaka, ed. *In Daddy's Arms, I Am Tall: African Americans Celebrating Fathers.* Illustrated by Javaka Steptoe. New York: Lee & Low, 1997.

Strickland, Dorothy S., and Michael R. Strickland. *Families: Poems Celebrating the African American Experience.* Illustrated by John Ward. Honesdale, Pa.: Wordsong/Boyds Mills Press, 1994.

Thomas, Joyce Carol. *Brown Honey in Broomwheat Tea.* Illustrated by Floyd Cooper. New York: HarperTrophy, 1993.

Turcotte, Mark. *Songs of Our Ancestors: Poems about Native Americans.* Illustrated by Kathleen S. Presnell. Chicago: Children's Press, 1995.

Autobiographical Poetry

Follow the format below to create a unique poem about a very special person: yourself. Use the space below, write on the back, or write on scratch paper as you begin to create your poem. Work through your rough drafts until you have a polished poem. Then illustrate your finished poem and be ready to present it to the class.

Title: First and last name

_____

Line 1: First name

_____

Line 2: Four traits that describe you

_____

_____

_____

Line 3: Brother/sister of … (may substitute Son/daughter of …)

_____

Line 4: Lover of … (give names of three people or ideas)

_____

_____

_____

Line 5: Who feels … (give three feelings)

_____

_____

_____

Line 6: Who fears … (give three things)

_____

_____

_____

Line 7: Who would like to see … (give three things)

_____

_____

_____

Line 8: Resident of … (give city and state)

_____

Line 9: Last name

_____

Lesson 5

Sharing Troubles across Cultures: A Common Thread

SKILL: Activating Prior Knowledge: Making Personal Connections with a Book

CULTURE OF FOCUS: Native American (Papago Indians)

Materials

Big Moon Tortilla, by Joy Cowley (Boyds Mills Press, 1998)
Tagboard or sturdy, appealing paper
Art supplies
Pens and pencils
Scratch paper
A World of Words: An ABC of Quotations, by Tobi Tobias (Lothrop, Lee & Shepard Books, 1998) (optional)

Lesson Motivator

1. For a change of pace, involve some different senses to bring this story to life. Draw on taste and the sense of smell by bringing in tortillas from the grocery store to share with the class, warming them slightly before serving. Add butter and honey and savor a mouth-watering treat.

2. While students try them, have them jot down words to describe the taste, texture, and smell of tortillas.

3. Read Marta's description and see if students' reactions are similar. If possible, invite in several parents from the community who make tortillas as part of their daily family fare. They can bring in fresh tortillas to sample. If there is a willing and knowledgeable member of the community who could teach the class how to make this staple in many diets, students may enjoy a hands-on lesson in

tortilla-making. They will learn that the process requires a practiced touch and is not as easy as it looks.

4. Extend the learning by discussing the history of the tortilla, which in numerous cultures is a main ingredient in their daily meals. Investigate its nutritional value, then enjoy tortillas with various fillings.

5. Touch other cultures by inviting students to describe a staple in their family's meals that differs from tortillas. Rice, pasta, or other kinds of breads might fit this bill.

6. Explain that the Papago Indians, the particular culture depicted in the story, have lived a long time in a certain part of the United States. Show the cover and a few pages of the story and ask students to identify the possible geographic location of *Big Moon Tortilla.*

7. Once the location has been pinpointed, invite students who have traveled to the Southwest to briefly share their impressions and experiences.

8. As they listen to the read-aloud, ask students to be thinking of some kind of advice they have been given by a grandparent, parent, or other relative that has turned out to be as important to them as advice was to the main character in the book.

Suggestions for Teaching the Lesson

• Before beginning the story, have the listeners speculate about the title. What might this story be about? Do they have an idea of the possible problem? Read the story, stopping briefly to discuss the terrain and how it compares to where the students live, the clever use of words, or the catastrophes that befall Marta Enos. Check with students to see if their predictions were accurate. Are they adjusting them as the story unfolds? Remind them that to do so is an excellent reading strategy.

- Stop to savor the language or come back to it after reading the story. Point out how metaphors are used in this book and suggest that students try some on their own during writing time. For example, reread, "The wind huffed the papers high into the air. Then, with a little cough, it spread them over the village." Students might copy samples like this into their literature or writing journals as fine examples of using metaphors. In this way, they will have many tidbits of clever writing to try to emulate.

- Once the tale has been told, have the listeners share an experience like the one Marta had to deal with, when one thing after another went wrong, as a way to further connect with the story. Students may relate several mishaps aloud or you may suggest that they write them in their literature journals.

- Point out that Marta is being cared for by her grandmother. In many Native American cultures the grandparents spend a great deal of time with their grandchildren while the parents work. In the Navajo and Hopi cultures, children may live with their grandparents throughout the summer, helping them with general chores while learning about their culture. How is this the same as or different from the experiences of students in the class?

- Continue the general class discussion by asking the students who they turn to for comfort when problems seem insurmountable. Who gives them consolation from time to time or on a daily basis? What kinds of advice have they received in the past?

- Grandmother sings a lovely old healing song to Marta. Repeat it to the group. Then give students some quiet time to spend thinking about special advice that they have received that has made a big difference to them. Ask them to write down the situation (if they are comfortable sharing it) and the advice they received. If they have no specific memories of their own, students can continue working on this at home, asking parents, grandparents, or guardians for tidbits of important advice they want children to know.

- Once the advice has been written down and polished for spelling and grammar, students may pursue several avenues of publication. One form would be to make it part of a story, as in *Big Moon Tortilla*, to be illustrated and presented to the class. If several cultures are represented through these stories, be sure to point out what may or may not be obvious: Wise advice is shared across all cultures.

- Another way to publish the information is to make an attractive poster with the advice as the key feature, decorating it in an appealing manner. Arrange completed posters down the hallway outside the classroom so that other students can read and ponder the wisdom from various cultures.

- Finally, students may choose to make a class book, using *A World of Words* as a model. This volume contains quotes from famous people arranged in alphabetical order according to a key word in the quotation. A vivid illustration accompanies each quote. Students can adapt this idea by creating a book of their invaluable advice, which may or may not be arranged alphabetically. They might title it "A Multicultural World of Advice" and include two pages per student, one for the written advice and another celebrating the writer's culture in a wonderful illustration. You or a parent might write an appropriate foreword once the pages are completed. The book can be bound and shared in the classroom before being put on display in the school library.

Evaluation

- Focus on one particular skill across the class, making notes on it for each learner. Do students naturally access prior knowledge as they interact with a book during group discussions or in their literature journals?

- When writing as an extension activity, are students able to proofread their own work or go to others for appropriate help as needed? How do students work independently? Are they able to stay on task or are they too easily diverted? What kinds of measures would be handy to refocus those who are distracted?

Extensions

- Invite parents or grandparents to come in to tell a story about an event in their lives that resulted in receiving some valuable advice. Space the visits out so that they can be savored rather than having too many guests in one day.

- Teachers, the principal, and other staff in the school make wonderful guests as well. Do they have a story to tell? Invite them in!

- Videotape students who want to share their work. A student might be the moderator, moving from student to student with appropriate chatter and pleasant introductions for each student. Make several copies of the tape so that students can take the videotape home to share with family members.

- Students can read a number of the titles listed below for enjoyment. As they find other books on their own that discuss elders giving advice to the young, highlight foods common to a culture, or just celebrate family relationships common across cultures, they should bring them in and book-talk them so that other interested readers can enjoy them.

- Have the students work with partners to retell the story, changing the location or time in which it is set to reflect a different culture.

- Have students write a poem using metaphors, taking something common in their school or family lives and bringing it to life in a clever manner. Collect the poems throughout the year and put them into a personal poetry book for each student.

Suggested Titles for Independent Reading and Research

Belton, Sandra. *May'naise Sandwiches & Sunshine Tea.* Illustrated by Gail Gordon Carter. New York: Four Winds Press, 1994.

Dengler, Marianna. *The Worry Stone.* Illustrated by Sibyl Graber Gerig. Flagstaff, Ariz.: Northland Publishing, 1996.

Dorros, Arthur. *Abuela.* Illustrated by Elisa Kleven. New York: Dutton, 1991.

Farris, Pamela J. *Young Mouse and Elephant: An East African Folktale.* Illustrated by Valeri Gorbachev. Boston: Houghton Mifflin, 1996.

Flournoy, Valerie. *Tanya's Reunion.* Illustrated by Jerry Pinkney. New York: Dial, 1995.

Guback, Georgia. *Luka's Quilt.* Illustrated by Caroline Birch. New York: Greenwillow, 1994.

Heide, Florence Parry, and Roxanne Heide Pierce. *Tio Armando.* Illustrated by Ann Grifalconi. New York: Lothrop, Lee & Shepard Books, 1998.

Howard, Elizabeth Fitzgerald. *Aunt Flossie's Hats (and Crab Cakes Later).* Illustrated by James Ransome. New York: Clarion, 1991.

Hunes, Susan Miho. *The Last Dragon.* Illustrated by Chris Soentpiet. New York: Clarion, 1995.

James, Betsy. *Blow Away Soon.* Illustrated by Anna Vojtech. New York: Putnam, 1995.

Joose, Barbara M. *Mama, Do You Love Me?* Illustrated by Barbara Lavallee. San Francisco, Calif.: Chronicle Books, 1991.

Kusugak, Michael Arvaarluk. *Northern Lights: The Soccer Trails.* Illustrated by Vladyanna Krykorka. New York: Annick Press, 1995.

Lacapa, Michael, and Kathleen Lacapa. *Less Than Half, More Than Whole.* Flagstaff, Ariz.: Northland Publishing, 1994.

Luenn, Nancy. *A Gift for Abuelita: Celebrating the Day of the Dead.* Illustrated by Robert Chapman. Flagstaff, Ariz.: Rising Moon/Northland Press, 1998.

Miles, Miska. *Annie and the Old One.* Illustrated by Peter Parnall. Boston: Little, Brown, 1971.

Nez, Redwing T. *Forbidden Talent.* Flagstaff, Ariz.: Northland Publishing, 1995.

Paulsen, Gary. *Tortilla Factory.* Illustrated by Ruth Paulsen. San Francisco, Calif.: Harcourt Brace, 1995.

Polacco, Patricia. *Thunder Cake.* New York: Philomel, 1990.

Reiser, Lynn. *Tortillas and Lullabies.* Illustrated by Corazones Valientes. New York: Greenwillow, 1998.

Soto, Gary. *Too Many Tamales.* Illustrated by Ed Martinez. New York: Putnam, 1993.

Section II

Comprehension Strategies in Fiction

COMPREHENSION: AN OVERVIEW

Reduced to a simple definition, reading comprehension is the process of determining meaning from the written word. It is the fundamental goal of reading instruction in classrooms across the country. Although this definition may be simple, the process itself is quite complex.

Few would dispute the fact that teaching the fundamentals of reading comprehension is actually the heart and soul of reading. Comprehension involves the process of constructing meaning from text beyond the mere recognition of letter sounds, knowing basic phonetic principles, and recognizing simple words. In addition to those basics, children must know that when words are added to other words on a page, they are relating information that is supposed to make sense. For reading comprehension to occur, there must be three key ingredients: the readers with their unique background knowledge, the print, and the environment in which reading actually takes place. All three are imperative to this interactive process in which comprehension becomes the act of making a connection between what the reader already knows and what is not known but will be gleaned from the text.

Although it seems simplistic to mention this, it is important to emphasize that reading comprehension is much more than being able to answer the questions at the end of a basal story or a particular social studies lesson. According to Dolores Durkin, a noted authority in the field of reading research, comprehension instruction involves the teacher actively assisting, defining, modeling, explaining, and guiding students' efforts to construct meaning from the text. Facilitating reading comprehension is actually giving readers the appropriate tools to use as they dig for meaning within an author's words. In the mix of modeling how the various tools work is a demonstration of when to use them. Facilitating the comprehension process includes teaching students to develop metacognitive awareness. That awareness alerts them when understanding is faltering and it's time to select the appropriate tools to apply to remedy the situation.

The following lessons contain a number of strategies and skills that teachers can demonstrate for classroom readers. They are, in effect, some of the tools that students can reach for as they build and fine-tune their comprehension abilities. Don't just tell students about these strategies. Research suggests that students learn new skills best when they are actively taught, modeled, and practiced under guidance. These lessons are just a few creative ways in which knowledgeable teachers can communicate how to touch the heart and soul of reading—the process of comprehension—to every learner in the classroom.

Lesson 6

Modeling the Shared Reading Process

SKILL: Learning Strategies to Facilitate Making Meaning from Text

CULTURE OF FOCUS: African American

Materials

Mufaro's Beautiful Daughters: A West African Tale (Big Book presentation), by John Steptoe (Lothrop, 1987)
Art supplies
Other versions of the Cinderella tale reflecting different cultures (see list at end of lesson)

Lesson Motivator

1. Ask your students to recount the story of Cinderella. Have several students quickly relate the story, one picking up where the other left off so that more than one person has an opportunity to practice verbal skills.

2. Ask the class if the version just retold is the one with which they are familiar.

3. Explain that there are hundreds of versions of this popular tale. The story they are about to read with you is a variant from Zimbabwe, West Africa.

4. Locate the country on a classroom map, perhaps discussing how many miles away it is or how long it would take to travel there by airplane. This might be a project for investigation via the Internet.

5. Read the foreword, writing the words from the Shona language on the chalkboard for the class to practice.

6. Shared reading is an excellent lesson to do at all grade levels to model how efficient readers process text.

It is suitable for a review lesson and is especially helpful for struggling readers or ESL (English as a second language) students. During this shared reading lesson, think out loud, modeling for the class how you make meaning from the text.

Tell the class that your purpose is to demonstrate what effective readers do before, during, and after reading a book, but that you are only going to focus on a few specific reading skills or strategies in this particular lesson.

As you model how you personally compose meaning from the author's words, you are highlighting how active the process of reading is, even though that action ordinarily occurs inside one's head.

7. Using a Big Book should allow all your students to see the print clearly. If that is impossible, make overhead transparencies of the pages so that they can be read from a large screen at the front of the room. Note that this lesson can be changed repeatedly depending on the strategies to be reviewed. This is such an effective way to teach the reading process that it ought to be used a number of times during the year.

Suggestions for Teaching the Lesson

- Begin the lesson by demonstrating how you preview a book to get a sense of what it is about. Look at the title page and examine a few of the illustrations, talking about what you think the book might be about. Make a few predictions, then confirm or correct them aloud as you proceed through the story.

- Demonstrate self-questioning, showing how you try to make sense of the story. There is no set way to do this, of course, so practice what you want the students to hear ahead of time so that you can model your questioning process smoothly. Suggestions: "I wonder what … "; "Why would he or she … ?"; "Who could that be?"; "What could happen next?"; "Does he or she mean … ?"; "What would happen if … ?"

- Spend some time during the lesson revealing how you make sense of words. Model how you might try to sound out the word or try to get the meaning from the context of the sentence. At some point, illustrate how you can still enjoy the book without being able to pronounce every word perfectly when reading silently.

- After reading the book, continue your self-talk, including your reactions to the story, a character, or thoughts about what you might like to do to extend your learning.

- Once your shared reading lesson is completed, ask students for questions. Is there a strategy needing clarification that you could demonstrate again? Then revisit *Mufaro's Beautiful Daughters* and ask for responses to the story and illustrations.

- Rereading: Have the students read the text aloud again. This time, instead of you doing the reading, have them try a page as pairs or trios as well as independently. In this way even the more able readers will enjoy the novelty of reading a Big Book.

- Encourage learners to browse through the previously collected versions of Cinderella available in the classroom. After choosing one, they should read it and reflect on how they apply their own reading skills.

Evaluation

- Ask students to record in a journal entry (or as a separate assignment) the processes they use as they read

a variant of the Cinderella story. Meet with students individually to discuss their observations and troubleshoot as necessary. Urge students to monitor their reading actions because this process builds useful metacognitive skills.

Extensions

- After reading a number of the variants of the Cinderella tale, students can compare and contrast them. What do they like best in each version? Which one is their favorite? Ask students to present their favorite version to the class, explaining why they like it.

- Have students work in pairs to rewrite this particular tale from the young king's point of view.

- Have student pairs role-play a conversation between two characters in the story.

- Book-talk the version of *Cinderella* retold by Amy Ehrlich and illustrated by Susan Jeffers (see list below). This illustrator uses the crosshatching technique, as John Steptoe does. If the art teacher is familiar with this process, a mini-lesson on crosshatching might be enjoyable.

- Discuss the Caldecott Award, the award given to the best illustrated book for a particular year. The gold seal indicates the winner for the year; a silver seal denotes a runner-up or Honor Book. Encourage readers to look for the Caldecott-winner seal on the cover of picture books in the library or in bookstores. Add selections of Caldecott winners to the classroom library for students to study and enjoy.

- Make a wall chart listing the variants read and highlighting the truths or cultural values depicted by each tale.

- Present a storytelling festival, with volunteers retelling their favorite version of the Cinderella tale.

- Have students write a job advertisement for the queen's job from two different perspectives. One might be under the heading "Position Wanted" as the prospective queen looks for a job; another might be from the perspective of the king: "Vacancy … Queen Wanted."

- Have students create a reader's theater script for the story and perform it for the class and for students in other classrooms.

Suggested Titles for Independent Reading and Research

Climo, Shirley. *The Egyptian Cinderella*. Illustrated by Ruth Heller. New York: Crowell, 1989.

———. *The Korean Cinderella*. Illustrated by Ruth Heller. New York: HarperCollins, 1993.

Compton, Joanne. *Ashpet: An Appalachian Tale*. Illustrated by Ken Compton. New York: Holiday House, 1994.

Ehrlich, Amy. *Cinderella*. Illustrated by Susan Jeffers. New York: Dial, 1985.

Garner, Alan. "Mossycoat." In *Alan Garner's Book of British Fairy Tales*. Illustrated by Derek Collard. New York: Delacorte, 1984.

Greaves, Margaret. *Tattercoats*. Illustrated by Margaret Chamberlain. New York: Clarkson N. Potter, 1990.

Hamilton, Virginia, collector and reteller. "Catskinella." In *Her Stories: African American Folktales, Fairy Tales, and True Tales*. Illustrated by Leo Dillon and Diane Dillon. New York: Scholastic, 1995.

———. "Good Blanche, Bad Rose, and the Talking Eggs." In *Her Stories: African American Folktales, Fairy Tales, and True Tales*. Illustrated by Leo Dillon and Diane Dillon. New York: Scholastic, 1995.

Haviland, Virginia. "The Indian Cinderella." In *North American Legends*. Illustrated by Ann Strugnell. New York: HarperCollins, 1979.

Hickox, Rebecca. *The Golden Sandal: A Middle Eastern Cinderella Story*. Illustrated by Will Hillenbrand. New York: Holiday House, 1998.

Hooks, William. *Moss Gown*. Illustrated by Donald Carrick. New York: Clarion, 1987.

Huck, Charlotte. *Princess Furball*. Illustrated by Anita Lobel. New York: Greenwillow, 1989.

Jackson, Ellen. *Cinder Edna*. Illustrated by Kevin O'Malley. New York: Lothrop, Lee & Shepard Books, 1994.

Jacobs, Joseph, collector and ed. *Tattercoats*. Illustrated by Margot Tomes. New York: Putnam, 1989.

Louie, Ai-Ling. *Yeh-Shen: A Cinderella Story from China*. Illustrated by Ed Young. New York: Philomel, 1982.

Lum, Darrell, reteller. *The Golden Slipper: A Vietnamese Legend*. Illustrated by Makiko Nagano. New York: Troll, 1994.

Martin, Rafe. *The Rough-Face Girl*. Illustrated by David Shannon. New York: Putnam, 1992.

Minter, Frances. *Cinder-Elly*. Illustrated by G. Brian Karas. New York: Viking, 1994.

Perrault, Charles. *Cinderella*. Illustrated by Marcia Brown. New York: Scribner, 1954.

———. *Cinderella, or The Little Glass Slipper*. Illustrated by Errol Le Cain. New York: Bradbury, 1973.

Pollock, Penny. *The Turkey Girl: A Zuni Cinderella Story*. Illustrated by Ed Young. Boston: Little, Brown, 1996.

San Souci, Robert D., and Daniel R. San Souci. *Cendrillon: A Caribbean Cinderella*. Illustrated by Jerry Pinkney. New York: Simon & Schuster, 1998.

———. *Sootface: An Ojibwa Cinderella Story*. Illustrated by Daniel San Souci. New York: Doubleday, 1994.

———. *The Talking Eggs*. Illustrated by Jerry Pinkney. New York: Dial, 1989.

Schroeder, Alan. *Smokey Mountain Rose*. New York: Dial, 1997.

Wilson, Barbara Ker. *Wishbones*. New York: Bradbury, 1993.

Winthrop, Elizabeth. *Vasilissa the Beautiful*. Illustrated by Alexander Koshkin. New York: HarperCollins, 1991.

Lesson 7

Comprehension and a Literary Road Map

SKILL: Examining the Literary Elements through Story Mapping

CULTURE OF FOCUS: Mexican American

Materials

Alejandro's Gift, by Richard E. Albert (Chronicle Books, 1994)
Copies of the "Story Map" worksheet (see end of lesson)
Overhead projector or chalkboard
Sheets of butcher paper
Newspaper for stuffing the animals
Markers or crayons
Staplers
5-x-8-inch index cards
Yarn

Lesson Motivator

1. Explain to the students that they are going to take an imaginary trip before reading a book together. Tell them they will use their imaginations and their memories on this trip.

2. Ask them to take a deep breath and then close their eyes, turn on their imaginations, and travel quickly to the desert, where they are going to spend the next few minutes.

3. Guide their visual imagery with questions such as: "What do you see in your part of the desert?"; "What do you hear?"; "What can you smell?"; "If you bend over to touch something, what is it and how does it feel?"

4. Give the listeners about five minutes to visualize their trip and then bring them back to the classroom by telling them to remember as much as they can and be ready to share.

5. Invite individual children to relate what they saw, heard, felt, and smelled. List responses on the chalkboard or overhead.

6. Hold up *Alejandro's Gift,* showing the lovely cover and scenic endpapers.

7. Ask students if they saw some of these scenes on their imaginary trip. If students have vacationed in desert areas or once lived in the Southwest, they may have additional information to relate.

Suggestions for Teaching the Lesson

- Write the five key literary elements on the chalkboard or overhead:

plot: a series of events in the story involving a conflict or a problem and how it is resolved

setting: the time and place in which the story takes place

characters/characterization: the way the story teaches the reader about the characters, including personality, behavior, goals, and physical and emotional traits

theme: the author's purpose for writing the story (Remember: A single story can have more than one theme. It is important to remind readers that there is not just one right answer for theme.)

conflict: the opposition of persons or forces that gives rise to the dramatic action

- Tell the class that these elements are important pieces that belong in every fictional story they read. Recognizing the literary elements and how they help with the comprehension of a story is important knowledge to apply to personal reading. Explain that you are first going to discuss each of the elements, then read the story together, and then go back and fill in each part on a special kind of literary map called a story map.

- Read the story. Take some time to discuss it when you are done, letting the listeners share their responses to Alejandro and what he did. Pass out copies of the "Story Map" worksheet. Explain that a story map is a visual way to examine the various parts of a story. Knowing these five basic elements can help readers better understand and appreciate any story. Write the title and author on the chalkboard so that students can copy the information onto their maps.

- Begin with setting, going back through the beginning of the story and having the listeners describe the setting. Write responses on the chalkboard. Select the most appropriate descriptors and have students fill in that section of their story maps.

- Continue with characters and what Alejandro was like, giving the class time to complete that section of their maps. What was the problem Alejandro had to solve in this story?

- Ask the students to retell the story, putting events in the proper sequence. Aid them in the retelling by showing the illustrations to the story as they relate the events. List responses on the chalkboard, ordering them correctly so that learners can copy the plot onto their maps.

- Discuss the word *resolution,* explaining that it refers to how a main character solves his or her problem by the end of a story. What did Alejandro do to solve his particular problem?

- Finally, as a group, talk about the theme. What do the students think the author was trying to say in this story? Write down all suggestions. Use this as a "teachable moment" by telling the students that stories can have more than one meaning or theme. They can pick the one they like the best and write it on their story maps.

- To encourage personal response to literature, ask the students to turn their maps over and write a reaction to *Alejandro's Gift.* They might write about what they liked or what they learned as they listened to this book.

- Have readers select another book focusing on the Hispanic culture (see list below) to read on their own. When they are done, have them complete a fresh story map, applying the skills and knowledge you have just reviewed in class.

Evaluation

- Meet with each student briefly to review the newly completed story map. When reviewing each map, evaluate how well each reader grasped the elements. Chat about any reactions to the particular story. Reteach or review the five literary elements as needed. Use the maps again in several months to keep the skills fresh. Add additional literary elements at that time if desired.

Extensions

The end of the book is filled with the fascinating, distinctive animals that visited Alejandro. A little bit of information is included about each desert dweller.

- Have students work in pairs, select an animal of interest, and make a large, puffy version of the animal from butcher paper. They should draw a life-size shape of each animal and cut out two copies. Each member of the pair can color or paint one piece appropriately. Have them staple the pieces together at close intervals nearly all the way around, leaving an opening large enough to stuff crumpled newspaper through to give the animal a puffy dimension. After the animal has been stuffed, the opening should be stapled shut. Students may decorate their animals using markers or crayons.

- When the animals are completed, have students fill in 5-x-8-inch index cards with the information from *Alejandro's Gift* plus three other interesting facts located from a nonfiction resource. Pairs can present their animals and additional information to the class. To display, suspend the desert dwellers by colorful yarn from the ceiling.

- Number each animal, including a corresponding number on its information card. Store the cards for easy access in a folder in the reading room. If a student is curious about a particular animal, he or she can review the matching card. This visual display of desert life will delight classmates as they look up and remember both their imaginary journey and the beautiful book.

- As a writing extension, have students write an acrostic poem using the name *Alejandro* or the word *loneliness.*

- Have students write a prequel to the story. Ask the writers to imagine what Alejandro's life might have been like when he was a young man or a child. How did he end up in such an isolated place?

- Invite a knowledgeable speaker to talk about desert plants and animals.

- Take a field trip to a natural history museum, if there is one in the immediate vicinity, to learn more about desert habitats.

- Purchase several small cacti to add a bit of desert life to a sunny corner of the classroom.

Suggested Titles for Independent Reading and Research

Aardema, Verna. *Borreguita and the Coyote.* Illustrated by Petra Mathers. New York: Alfred A. Knopf, 1991.

Ada, Alma Flor. *The Lizard and the Sun/La Lagartija y el Sol.* Illustrated by Felipe Davalos. New York: Doubleday, 1997.

Altman, Linda Jacobs. *Amelia's Road.* Illustrated by Enrique O. Sanchez. New York: Lee & Low, 1993.

Bunting, Eve. *A Day's Work.* Illustrated by Ronald Himler. New York: Clarion, 1994.

———. *Going Home.* Illustrated by David Diaz. New York: HarperCollins, 1996.

———. *Smoky Night.* Illustrated by David Diaz. San Diego, Calif.: Harcourt Brace, 1994.

Cruz Martinez, Alejandro. *The Woman Who Outshone the Sun: The Legend of Lucia Zenteno.* Illustrated by Fernando Olivera. San Francisco, Calif.: Children's Book Press.

Ets, Marie Hall. *Gilberto and the Wind.* New York: Puffin, 1978.

Garay, Luis. *Pedrito's Day.* New York: Orchard, 1997.

Garza, Carmen Lomas. *In My Family/En Mi Familia.* San Francisco, Calif.: Children's Book Press, 1996.

Gollub, Matthew. *Uncle Snake.* Illustrated by Leovigildo Martinez. New York: Tambourine, 1996.

Gonzalez, Lucia M. *The Bossy Gallito/El Gallo de Bodas.* Illustrated by Lulu Delacre. New York: Scholastic, 1994.

Johnston, Tony. *The Tale of Rabbit and Coyote.* Illustrated by Tomie dePaola. New York: Putnam, 1994.

Lowell, Susan. *The Three Little Javelinas.* Illustrated by Jim Harris. Flagstaff, Ariz.: Northland Publishing, 1992.

———. *The Tortoise and the Jackrabbit.* Illustrated by Jim Harris. Flagstaff, Ariz.: Northland Publishing, 1994.

Soto, Gary. *Too Many Tamales.* Illustrated by Ed Martinez. New York: Putnam, 1993.

Stevens, Jan Romero. *Carlos and the Cornfield/Carlos y la Milpa de Maiz.* Illustrated by Jeanne Arnold. Flagstaff, Ariz.: Northland Publishing, 1995.

———. *Carlos and the Skunk/Carlos y el Zorrillo.* Illustrated by Jeanne Arnold. Flagstaff, Ariz.: Northland Publishing, 1997.

———. *Carlos and the Squash Plant/Carlos y la Planta de Calabaza.* Illustrated by Jeanne Arnold. Flagstaff, Ariz.: Northland Publishing, 1993.

Story Map

Title: _____

Author: _____

Setting:

Characters:

Conflict (problem to be solved):

Plot (list major events in the story):

Theme:

Lesson 8

Setting and Sequencing Using Sentence Strips

SKILL: Understanding the Setting of a Story

CULTURE OF FOCUS: Australian

Materials

The Old Woman Who Loved to Read, by John Winch (Scholastic, 1996)
Sentence strips, either purchased or teacher-made, containing one sentence or beginning phrase from the story; black marker for writing the sentences
Music from Australia
Notebook paper
Pencils
Other books about life in Australia (see list at end of lesson)

Lesson Motivator

1. Play a selection of music from Australia that includes the unusual sounds of the didgeridoo.

2. Tell the students that the music is a clue to the location of the story they will be listening to.

3. Hand out sheets of white paper and make sure students have a pen or pencil.

4. Tell them that they will be playing a guessing game as you read this book aloud to them. As book detectives, they are to sketch anything from the story that gives them a clue to where this story might take place.

Suggestions for Teaching the Lesson

- Be certain that the students are able to see the delightful pictures in this book, because they will be using them to look for clues to the setting of the story.

- Write the word *setting* on the chalkboard. For listeners who do not know this term, explain that the setting of a story is where it takes place. As detectives they are to study the illustrations carefully, looking for clues to this story's setting. Rather than writing any words, they can quickly sketch any clues that they find.

- Read the title and author on the cover and give the students a few minutes to study the appealing illustration. Are there clues here?

- Read the story, giving the class time to study each illustration. You might talk a little about the first few double-page illustrations to see what kind of details they are picking out. The animals are certainly good clues, but you may have to identify some of them, without pointing out where they live. Those with especially sharp eyes or experience with Australia might pick out Ayers Rock in the third double-page illustration, although most students probably won't be knowledgeable about this unique formation in Australia. Take time to talk about it once you have read the book aloud.

- Upon completion of the story, ask your detectives to share their clues. Write their guesses about the location on the chalkboard. This would be a good time to show a nonfiction book to back up some of the clues discovered.

- Students might enjoy a little more detecting as they try to discover the names of the animals in the illustrations. Some of the Australian animals are a dingo (wild dog), a prickly echidna, a koala, a platypus, an emu, rosellas (parrotlike birds), kangaroos, a lizard-like goanna wrapped around the tree in the flood scene, a black swan, and a black-and-white magpie.

- If it hasn't been detected, explain that the setting is Australia. A brief discussion of how some of the scenes in the story are similar to where the students live and how other scenes are different may follow naturally at this point. This could become a "teachable moment" as you review the terms *same* and *different* or *compare* and *contrast.*

- Depending on the age level and ability levels of the students, you might choose to reread the story again so that students can enjoy it with no activity attached. If you feel that the listeners understand the story line, put them to work on the sequencing activity. Even older readers enjoy the opportunity to solve a puzzle.

- Hand out sentence strips containing sentences from the story to various students in the class. Be certain the sentences are out of order compared to the story. Have students line up randomly at the front of the classroom. Each can read his or her strip, or the remainder of the class can read them aloud.

- Appoint another reader to be the "Arranger." The class should begin to put the story in order, one person and sentence strip at a time. The Arranger's job is to help position each student according to the directions from classmates. He or she will also have the book in hand to ascertain whether the sequencing is accurate once the class thinks they are done.

- When the story is in the proper sequence, invite the class members who are still seated to read it aloud together. Discuss the kinds of clues students used to determine sentence order. Did they look at capital letters and punctuation? This can certainly help with sequencing. Were there words that aided in putting the story in order, such as the seasons mentioned?

- Staple the sentence strips to the bulletin board to make the story readily accessible to independent reading by students. Invite those who are interested to illustrate their favorite parts.

- On the same bulletin board, place a chart with handy words and phrases to use in sequencing. These can be referred to when students are doing their own writing and want to be certain that one thing logically follows another. Useful words and phrases include:

finally	now	in the first place
then	next	to begin with
last	later	before
after	following	soon
previously	at last	meanwhile
immediately	in the end	therefore
although	but	as you can see
still	first, second (etc.)	

- Show the other books in the reading center that are also set in Australia. Book-talk each briefly, explaining that each title will reveal a little more about the culture there.

- At this point, readers can select a title for independent reading.

- In a large group discussion session, have students tell the rest of the class what they have learned while investigating this fascinating culture and country on their own. Ask students to zero in on how the lives of people in Australia are similar to or different from the lives of people in the United States.

Evaluation

- Work with learners independently to check their understanding of the setting and the sequence of a story. Each student can reread a favorite book on life in Australia and then retell the story to you, briefly explaining what the setting is. During the retelling, you will be monitoring the ability to put events in the story in the proper sequence.

- Jot down and date notes on each reader's understanding on a sheet of paper with his or her name on it, on a large file card, or on a sheet of reading skills. Add skills to the sheet as they are taught so that you will have an ongoing record of each reader's progress and acquisition of skills throughout the year.

Extensions

- Show a video of life in Australia, such as *Australia, the Southeast Experience,* available from Teacher's Discovery (800-543-4180). Continue the discussion of how life is the same or different for children in various locations in the country as compared to where your readers live.

- Invite a guest speaker who is from Australia or who has traveled there extensively. If the visitor is a native, the class will certainly enjoy listening to him or her speak because the Australian accent is delightful. The guest can further explain life in the country, customs, traditions, the schooling, typical vacations, and so forth. Facilitate the discussion by compiling a list of questions that the learners would like answered before the visit.

- If possible, take a field trip to a zoo that has some of Australia's wildlife to follow up on the unusual animals depicted in some of the books about this country.

- Use the tape or CD of music that you started the lesson with, including the unusual sound of a didgeridoo. If possible, invite a musician from the area who plays this unique instrument. Under the direction of a musician, students can make a simple didgeridoo

from empty paper-towel roles, decorating them with aboriginal art, and learn to mimic the sound of this instrument.

- Rewrite the story, changing the main character slightly, altering the focus, and selecting a different setting. "The Little Old Man Who Loved to _____" or "The Little Boy/Girl Who Loved to _____" will be the story starters. Students can add four or five incidents before coming to a satisfying conclusion. Have students peer-edit and polish the stories before making them into a book that can be read to the entire class and stored for independent reading in the reading center.

- Ask students to design a tool, a shortcut, or a machine for the Little Old Woman to help her complete her chores more quickly so that she will have more time to read. Have them draw a picture of the invention or actually create a model of it, then share it with the class.

Suggested Titles for Independent Reading and Research

Breeden, Stan. *Growing Up at Uluru, Australia.* Illustrated with photographs by the author. Queensland, Australia: Steve Parish Publishing, 1995.

Breeden, Stan, and Belina Wright. *Growing Up in Kakadu, Australia.* Illustrated with photographs by the authors. Queensland, Australia: Steve Parish Publishing, 1995.

Cobb, Vicki. *This Place Is Lonely: The Australian Outback.* Illustrated by Barbara Lavallee. New York: Walker, 1991.

Fox, Mem. *Koala Lou.* Illustrated by Pamela Lofts. New York: Harcourt Brace, 1988.

———. *Possum Magic.* Illustrated by Julie Vivas. New York: Harcourt Brace, 1993.

Hathorn, Libby. *The Tram to Bondi Beach.* Illustrated by Julie Vivas. Sydney, Australia: Angus & Robertson; New York: HarperCollins, 1996.

Kids Discover Magazine. Australia. Vol. 6, no. 1. New York: Kids Discover, 1996.

Mattingley, Christobel. *The Race.* Illustrated by Anne Spudvilas. Sydney, Australia: Scholastic Australia, 1995.

Morin, Paul. *Animal Dreaming: An Aboriginal Dreamtime Story.* San Diego, Calif.: Silver Whistle/Harcourt Brace, 1998.

Oliver, Narelle. *The Best Beak in Boonaroo Bay.* Illustrated by the author. Golden, Colo.: Fulcrum Publishing, 1995.

Parish, Steve. *ABC of Australian Animals.* Illustrated with photographs by the author. Queensland, Australia: Steve Parish Publishing, 1994.

Paterson, A. B. *Waltzing Matilda.* Illustrated by Desmond Digby. Pymble, Australia: Angus & Robertson; New York: HarperCollins, 1996.

Vaughan, Marcia K. *Wombat Stew.* Illustrated by Pamela Lofts. Englewood Cliffs, N.J.: Silver Burdett, 1984.

Wheatley, Nadia. *My Place.* Illustrated by Donna Rawlins. Brooklyn, N.Y.: Kane/Miller Publishers, 1994.

Lesson 9

Using a Story Wheel

SKILL: Understanding Sequencing in Narratives

CULTURE OF FOCUS: Jewish

Materials

The Always Prayer Shawl, by Sheldon Oberman (Boyds Mills Press, 1994)
Several shawls
Copies of a list of personal names and their meanings
Overhead projector or chart paper
Copies of the "Story Wheel" worksheet (see end of lesson)
Pens and pencils
World map to help establish the setting
Guest speaker

Lesson Motivator

1. Hold up the shawls and ask students what they are, what they might be used for, and who might use them. Are shawls used for anything special in their families?

2. Explain that a shawl is an important part of the book you are going to be sharing together. In this case, it is a special prayer shawl that students will learn more about throughout the story.

3. Ask the students if they know why they were named as they were. If they don't know, give them an investigative homework assignment to ask their parents or grandparents why they were named as they were.

4. Pass out copies of a list of common and unusual names and their meanings, which can be found in naming-a-baby books (often available at grocery story checkout counters) or in parenting books.

5. Let students browse to try to find out what their names mean. Spend a little time sharing and enjoying their reactions.

6. Give the class some background on why you were named as you were and what your name means. They'll love it. You might comment on whether you think the meaning is fitting personally and if you have always liked your name.

7. If possible, invite in a guest—a parent or a rabbi—to give a brief introduction to the Jewish culture so that classmates have a foundation of understanding before the story is read.

Suggestions for Teaching the Lesson

- Tell the students that understanding the sequence of events, the order in which things happen in a story, helps them to better comprehend the story line. Note that although this lesson uses a story wheel to teach and review sequencing, there are several other ways to accomplish this, such as using sentence strips (see Lesson 8).

- Delineate a large sample story wheel on the overhead or on a large sheet of chart paper. Tell the students to listen carefully to *The Always Prayer Shawl,* because once the book is completed, you will go back through the story as a group, retelling it in the sequence that it happened based on key events in the story.

- Read the first three double pages to the class and stop. Ask volunteers to quickly compare and contrast their lives to what they know at this point about Adam's life. Then tell the students to listen to the changes that are a part of Adam's life and continue reading the story.

- Upon completion of the book, go back and review the pictures, asking students why they think there is a shift from black and white to color. Discuss some of the changes that Adam experienced, recording three or four in order on the sample story wheel. Point out the word *resolution* at the bottom of the sample. Remind or teach the class that the resolution of a story refers to how the problems are finally solved to end the story satisfactorily.

- Hand out copies of the "Story Wheel" worksheet to students. Have them fill in the information from the class wheel and then complete the worksheet on their own, based on their own opinions of which events were especially important.

- Circle the room, monitoring students' work and providing support as needed. After a designated period of time, invite students to share their wheels. One student at a time can add his or her idea to the class wheel. After discussing the value of sequencing and reviewing what has been learned to this point, give students the opportunity to select another title and create a story wheel of their own.

Evaluation

- Practice retelling the story each student read by using the story wheel. The student will probably notice if an important part has been left off the wheel and can correct the sequencing as the story unfolds.

- Note the understanding of the skill on a chart or anecdotal record sheet or reteach as warranted. Individual students may need more practice. Working with them in a small group briefly may be enough to cement their understanding.

Extensions

- Ask students to write poetry reflecting the phrase from the story: "Some things change, and some things don't."

- Have students talk with a grandparent and write down what his or her life was like as a child. They should gather a photo or two and prepare a poster report on that grandparent. Do they have items in their family that were passed down to them from grandparents? Ask them to share that information too.

- Have students write about moving and personal changes that occur as a result of this change. Prepare a bulletin board to display pictures, stories, or poetry reflecting those changes. Discuss whether students felt the changes were good or bad. If they were bad, was there still something good that came out of the event or experience?

- Ask students to research the time period in which this story might have taken place. It probably was during World War II, when many Jewish people had to relocate because of Hitler's program to eliminate them. This book talks about Adam's family coming to the United States, but other countries also offered homes to the Jewish people. Groups of students can study several different countries, discussing what they learned within their group. They should present what they learned as a panel, with one or two members per group on the panel.

Suggested Titles for Independent Reading and Research

Adler, David A. *Chanukah in Chelm.* Illustrated by Kevin O'Malley. New York: Lothrop, Lee & Shepard Books, 1997.

———. *One Yellow Daffodil: A Hanukkah Story.* Illustrated by Lloyd Bloom. San Diego, Calif.: Harcourt Brace, 1995.

Druker, Malka. *Grandma's Latkes.* Illustrated by Eve Chwast. San Diego, Calif.: Gulliver/Harcourt Brace, 1992.

Feder, Paula Kurzband. *The Feather-Bed Journey.* Illustrated by Stacey Schuett. Morton Grove, Ill.: Whitman, 1995.

Fishman, Cathy Goldberg. *On Hanukkah.* Illustrated by Melanie W. Hall. New York: Atheneum, 1998.

Gilman, Phoebe. *Something from Nothing.* New York: Scholastic, 1992.

Goldin, Barbara Diamond. *Night Lights: A Sukkot Story.* Illustrated by Louise August. San Diego, Calif.: Gulliver/Harcourt Brace, 1995.

Hoestlandt, Jo. *Star of Fear, Star of Hope.* Translated by Mark Polizzoti. Illustrated by Johanna Kang. New York: Walker, 1995.

Innocenti, Roberto, and Christophe Gallaz. *Rose Blanche.* Mankato, Minn.: Creative Education, 1985.

Jaffe, Nina. *The Way Meat Loves Salt: A Cinderella Tale from the Jewish Tradition.* New York: Holt, 1998.

Kimmel, Eric. *Hershel and the Hanukkah Goblins.* Illustrated by Trina Schart Hyman. New York: Holiday House, 1989.

Levine, Arthur A. *All the Lights in the Night.* Illustrated by James E. Ransome. New York: Morrow, 1991.

Manushkin, Fran. *Starlight and Candles: The Joys of the Sabbath.* Illustrated by Jacqueline Chwast. New York: Simon & Schuster, 1995.

Mochizuki, Ken. *Passage to Freedom: The Sugihara Story.* Illustrated by Dom Lee. New York: Lee & Low, 1997.

Nerlove, Miriam. *Flowers on the Wall.* New York: McElderry, 1996.

Polacco, Patricia. *Mrs. Katz and Tush.* New York: Dell, 1992.

———. *Thundercake.* New York: Philomel, 1990.

Rosen, Michael J. *Elijah's Angel: A Story for Chanukah and Christmas.* Illustrated by Aminah Brenda Lynn Robinson. San Diego, Calif.: Harcourt Brace, 1992.

Rothenberg, Joan. *Inside-Out Grandma.* New York: Hyperion, 1995.

Schnur, Steven. *The Tie Man's Miracle: A Chanukah Tale.* Illustrated by Stephen T. Johnson. New York: Morrow, 1995.

Schram, Peninnah. *Ten Classic Jewish Children's Stories.* Illustrated by Jeffrey Allon. New York: Jerusalem, 1998.

Schur, Maxine Rose. *Day of Delight: A Jewish Sabbath in Ethiopia.* Illustrated by Brian Pinkney. New York: Dial, 1994.

Schwartz, Howard, and Barbara Rush. *The Sabbath Lion: A Jewish Folktale from Algeria.* Illustrated by Stephen Fieser. New York: Harper, 1992.

Wolkstein, Diane. *Esther's Story.* Illustrated by Joan Wijngaard. New York: Morrow, 1996.

Story Wheel

Using each line as a spoke on the wheel, write a brief phrase to explain how events follow each other, one after the other, in the following story: _____

_____

_____

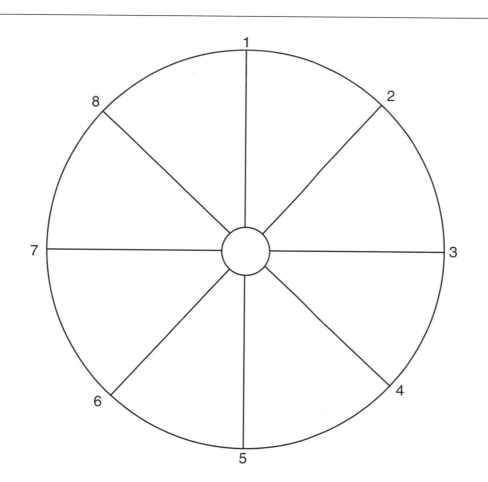

Resolution:

_____

_____

_____

_____

_____

_____

Lesson 10

Differentiating between Reality and Fantasy

SKILL: Charting Examples of Realistic and Imaginative Incidents

CULTURE OF FOCUS: Native American (Ute)

Materials

Beardream, by Will Hobbs (Atheneum, 1997)
Large piece of butcher paper or chart paper
Markers
Native American music
Copies of the "Guided Learning Chart" worksheet (see end of lesson)
Pens or pencils

Lesson Motivator

1. As students prepare for the lesson, have a tape or CD of Native American music playing quietly in the background. Let the music play softly during the introduction to the lesson and the reading of the story so that it sets the tone and becomes a part of the background without disturbing the learners.

2. Ask the students to briefly share a tradition they have in their family to celebrate a special event.

3. After everyone who wants to share has done so, explain that *Beardream* is a Native American tale that tells how the Ute Beardance began. Tell the listeners that stories have long been used by Native American elders to teach lessons to young children.

4. As the students listen to this particular tale, have them think about a lesson being taught. They will share their ideas at the end of the book as classmates are responding to the story.

Suggestions for Teaching the Lesson

- Continue to activate prior knowledge by asking students if they are familiar with any particular Native American traditions or ceremonies. If there are general questions about Native Americans that students would like answered or some misconceptions that need clarification, write them down on the chalkboard at this point. They can be researched later. If questions arise about some of the ceremonies, write them down also. Students can choose different areas to investigate after the lesson is completed.

- Write the words *reality* and *fantasy* on the butcher or chart paper. Begin with *reality*, asking students to define the word and give examples. Do the same thing with *fantasy*. You are striving for definitions of *reality* that include "true-to-life," "actual rather than imagined," "authentic or genuine," or "something that actually exists." *Fantasy* might be defined as "a stretch of the imagination," "unreal," or "a creation of the mind." Once you are certain that students understand the differences between these terms, read *Beardream*, including the dedication, publisher, and copyright date.

- As in all quality picture books, the illustrations are critical to this story. Stop periodically to discuss them. For example, on the second double-page spread, the bear is dreaming of a lovely green hillside. Ask the students how the illustrator shows the reader that the bear is dreaming. Their response should be that part of the mountain in the background is shaped like a sleeping bear. Have them watch for another instance when the illustrator does something similar. Then, to pull them further into the story, invite listeners to discuss what they might hear if they were a part of the picture.

- At the conclusion of the book, ask for student reactions, giving listeners time to respond verbally to the story. Take a few minutes to chat about the lesson that might be taught via the book. Then return to reviewing the concepts of reality and fantasy.

- Explain to the students that you are going to read the story once more, stopping after each set of double pages to ask them to tell whether what has just happened is real or is part of Short Tail's dream, and thus fantasy. Record reactions under the appropriate term on the butcher paper. Under *reality*, for example, students might note that bears do hibernate, coming out of their dens in the spring. Under *fantasy*, they might say that bears probably don't dream about catching trout, sliding down grassy hills, or eating wildflowers.

- Upon conclusion of the activity, invite students to speculate about why the author switched between reality and fantasy to tell his story. In their opinion, is this a good writing strategy?

- Finally, it is time to apply newly learned skills. Have students work independently or in pairs to read another book selected from titles gathered ahead of time. Using the "Guided Learning Chart" worksheets, have them differentiate between reality and fantasy once again.

Evaluation

- Evaluate learning by discussing the completed worksheets with each student or pair of students. Collect the worksheets in a student-designed folder that might be titled "Lessons about Reality and Fantasy." Keep this folder in the classroom reading center for students' future reference. Students may want to read different titles already critiqued by their classmates, reviewing the accompanying "Guided Learning Chart" worksheet to see if they concur.

Extensions

- If possible, invite several Native Americans from different tribes to speak to the class. A local museum might have a list of speakers. Ask each guest to discuss a special tradition or ceremony that is important to his or her tribe.

- Provide nonfiction titles for students to read, particularly on the Utes. Ask the school learning center director for other titles students might like to read and assemble them for easy access in the classroom.

- Do an author study on Will Hobbs and present some of his novels to the students for future reading.

- Have students write to Will Hobbs (in care of his publisher) about his books.

- For a future writing assignment, encourage students to try patterning a piece of their own writing after this book.

- With proper instruction, engage students in learning to do the Bear-dance.

Suggested Titles for Independent Reading and Research

Alexander, Lloyd. *The Fortune-Tellers.* Illustrated by Trina Schart Hyman. New York: Dutton, 1992.

Brett, Jan. *The Mitten.* New York: Putnam, 1989.

Brown, Anthony. *The Tunnel.* New York: Knopf, 1989.

Cohen, Caron L. *The Mud Pony.* Illustrated by Shonto Begay. New York: Scholastic, 1988.

Compton, Patricia. *The Terrible Eek.* Illustrated by Sheila Hamanaka. New York: Simon & Schuster, 1991.

Goble, Paul. *The Girl Who Loved Wild Horses.* New York: Bradbury, 1985.

Hillman, Elizabeth. *Min-Yo and the Moon Dragon.* Illustrated by John Wallner. San Diego, Calif.: Harcourt Brace, 1992.

Kipling, Rudyard. *Rikki-Tikki-Tavi.* Illustrated by Jerry Pinkney. New York: Morrow Junior Books, 1997.

Lawson, Julie. *The Dragon's Pearl.* Illustrated by Paul Morin. New York: Clarion, 1993.

Lester, Julius. *John Henry.* Illustrated by Jerry Pinkney. New York: Dial, 1994.

Mayer, Mercer. *Shibumi and the Kitemaker.* New York: Marshall Cavendish, 1999.

Mendez, Phil. *The Black Snowman.* Illustrated by Carole Byard. New York: Scholastic, 1989.

Mollel, Tololwa M. *Orphan Boy.* Illustrated by Paul Morin. New York: Clarion, 1991.

Nelson, S. D. *Gift Horse: A Lakota Story.* New York: Harry N. Abrams, 1999.

Van Allsburg, Chris. *The Wretched Stone.* Boston: Houghton Mifflin, 1991.

Yolen, Jane. *Greyling.* Illustrated by David Ray. New York: Philomel, 1991.

Guided Learning Chart

Title of book: _____

Author: _____

Summary:

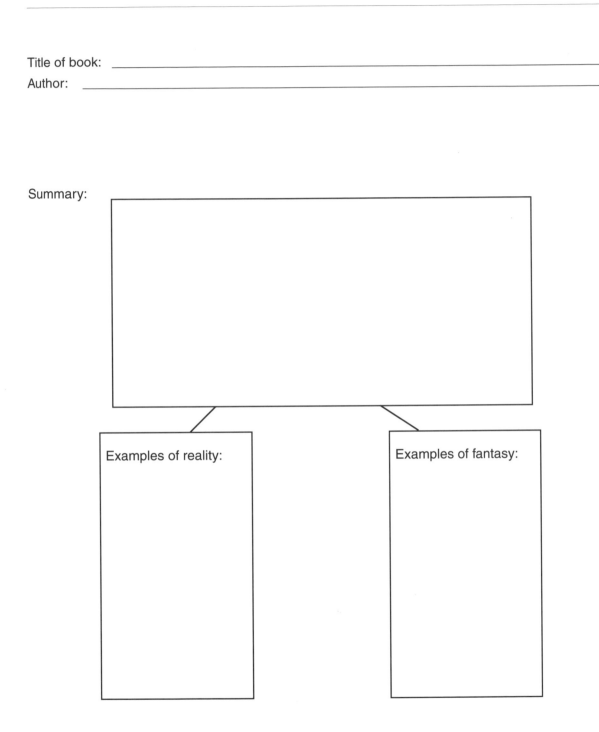

Examples of reality:

Examples of fantasy:

Lesson 11

A Lesson in Inferences

SKILL: Inferring Character Traits

CULTURE OF FOCUS: African American

Materials

My Name Is York, by Elizabeth Van Steenwyk (Rising Moon/Northland Publishing, 1997)
Copies of the "Characterization Wheel" worksheet (see end of lesson)
Pens or pencils
Wall map of the United States
Video: *Lewis and Clark* (PBS Home Video, 800-645-4727, item A2761, $29.98) (optional)

Lesson Motivator

1. Take the class back in time to the early 1800s by reading the foreword of the book and/or by showing a short clip from the video *Lewis and Clark.*

2. Trace the journey of Lewis and Clark on the classroom map, using the endpapers of the book as a guide. Overhead transparencies of the endpapers would give the whole class access to the trek to find a water passageway to the Pacific Ocean.

3. Invite the students to discuss the terrain, speculate about the means of transportation at the time, guess what foods could be taken along and what foods were available in the wild, and estimate the duration of such an expedition. Students may have had some camping or backpacking experiences that they can relate to help others grasp what life in the wilderness might be like.

4. Ask students to do some imaginative writing in their personal journals.

Tell them to imagine that they have just been hired by Lewis and Clark to join their exciting expedition to chart unfamiliar lands. They will be away from their families for many months, not really knowing what the journey holds. Give students at least 15 minutes to settle themselves into that time period and write about their feelings and their dreams for the success of the expedition.

5. Ask students to address pertinent personal characteristics that will enable them to withstand the hardships or deal daily with the unknown. Once the writing is completed, invite several students to read their entries to the rest of the class.

6. As you return to the picture book, focus the students' attention on York, who is relating this story. Can students infer what kind of a man he is from the words and the pictures?

Suggestions for Teaching the Lesson

- As you read, stop periodically to discuss an incident or elicit comments on the journey from the class. Once you have completed the book, discuss the story together. Involve students in relating their thoughts about being involved in such a journey.

- Break into small discussion groups, each one talking about a different issue that arose in the story. Some suggestions are living as a slave, the desire for personal freedom, facing the unknown, and interacting with Native Americans whose ways were unfamiliar.

- Delineate a sample "Characterization Wheel" on a transparency. Explain that readers can learn something about York from the story but much of that understanding must be inferred, a reading skill that involves "reading between the lines."

Work together as a group to fill in the traits that students either discovered or inferred about York. Suggestions may include that York was a slave who could not read. He was also a dreamer in the best sense, longing for freedom. He was physically strong, which can be inferred because he prevailed in battling the elements of the wilderness. He accepted others who appeared to be different, enjoyed music and dancing, appreciated the beauty of nature, and was a survivor. Finally, he was brave, as evidenced by his jumping into the river to save Captain Clark. As a listener suggests a character trait, have him or her write it on the transparency and then explain why it was chosen.

- Tell the students that this process of learning about characters transfers easily to the novels they may be reading and is a tool to help them understand those characters better.

- Provide a selection of multicultural picture books for use in practicing and let the students complete a "Characterization Wheel" worksheet on their own. Sharing their knowledge by discussing the completed wheels in groups of three or four might be the final step in practicing inference as related to fleshing out characters.

Evaluation

- Collect students' wheels and check them for understanding. As students work on their practice wheels, move about the room, observing their skills in using inference.

- Listen to discussions in the small groups, assessing whether students have mastered the ability to infer characteristics of a main character.

- Have the students use the same procedure in a novel in a future review lesson. Are they still comfortable using this skill? Is any reteaching needed?

Extensions

- Show clips from the PBS version of the Lewis and Clark expedition.

- Set up a display of nonfiction books about the expedition for interested students.

- After additional research, students can create a travel brochure to entice people to travel through the lands explored by Lewis and Clark.

- Have students write a letter to a family member or additional journal entries from an imaginary person on the expedition.

- Have students work in pairs to research the expedition and then conduct an interview, one being interviewed by the other, about highlights of their experiences while on the expedition.

- Have students research what daily life was like in the early 1800s in this country, then present their findings in several interesting dioramas. Another group can research the Nez Perce or the Mandan tribe to learn about their traditions and beliefs.

- Have students present a thumbnail sketch of Sacajawea after reading several biographies about her.

Suggested Titles for Independent Reading and Research

Bartone, Elisa. *American, Too.* Illustrated by Ted Lewin. New York: Lothrop, Lee & Shepard Books, 1996.

Covault, Ruth M. *Pablo and Pimienta.* Illustrated by Francisco Mora. Flagstaff, Ariz.: Northland Publishing, 1994.

Dengler, Marianna. *The Worry Stone.* Illustrated by Sibyl Graber Gerig. Flagstaff, Ariz.: Northland Publishing, 1996.

Fraden, Dennis. *Sacajawea: The Journey to the West.* Illustrated by Nora Koeber. New York: Silver Press/Simon & Schuster, 1997.

Gleiter, Jan, and Kathleen Thompson. *Sacagawea.* Illustrated by Yoshi Miyake. Milwaukee, Wis.: Raintree/Steck-Vaughn, 1995.

Hest, Amy. *When Jessie Came across the Sea.* Illustrated by P. J. Lynch. Cambridge, Mass.: Candlewick Press, 1997.

Johnston, Tony. *The Wagon.* Illustrated by James E. Ransome. New York: Tambourine, 1996.

Kidama, Tatsuharu. *Shin's Tricycle.* Illustrated by Noriyuki Ando. New York: Walker, 1995.

Kroll, Steven. *Lewis and Clark: Explorers of the American West.* Illustrated by Richard Williams. New York: Holiday House, 1994.

Pinkney, Andrea D. *Bill Pickett, Rodeo-Ridin' Cowboy.* Illustrated by Brian Pinkney. San Diego, Calif.: Gulliver Books/Harcourt Brace, 1996.

Polacco, Patricia. *Pink and Say.* New York: Philomel, 1994.

Ringgold, Faith. *If a Bus Could Talk: The Story of Rosa Parks.* New York: Simon & Schuster, 1999.

Roop, Peter, and Connie Roop, eds. *Off the Map: The Journals of Lewis and Clark.* Illustrated by Tim Tanner. New York: Walker, 1993.

Rowland, Della. *The Story of Sacajawea, Guide to Lewis and Clark.* Illustrated by Richard Leonard. New York: Dell/Yearling, 1989.

Schanzer, Rosalyn. *How We Crossed the West: The Adventures of Lewis and Clark.* Washington, D.C.: National Geographic Society, 1997.

Shea, Pegi Deitz. *The Whispering Cloth.* Illustrated by Anita Riggio. Stitched by You Yang. Honesdale, Pa.: Boyds Mills Press, 1995.

Towle, Wendy. *The Real McCoy: The Life of an African-American Inventor.* Illustrated by Wil Clay. New York: Scholastic, 1993.

Yolen, Jane. *Encounter.* Illustrated by David Shannon. San Diego, Calif.: Harcourt Brace, 1992.

Characterization Wheel

Write the name of the character you are reading about at the center of this wheel. Put characteristics that describe your character in each of the outer segments to show what your character is like.

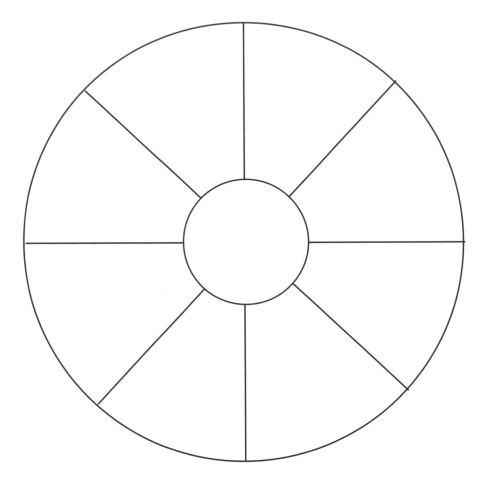

Write a "word picture" of the character you have chosen. Justify why you have selected particular characteristics that have helped you to know this individual better.

Lesson 12

Working with Comparison and Contrast in Narrative

SKILL: Comparing and Contrasting Variations of a Folktale

CULTURE OF FOCUS: Hispanic

Materials

The Three Little Pigs (Los Tres Cerdos): Nacho, Tito, and Miguel, by Bobbi Salinas (Piñata Publications, 1998)

Overhead projector or chalkboard

Sheets of chart paper or copies of the "Folktale Variants" worksheet (see end of lesson) for individual student charts

Markers

Large chart for recording the findings of each group

Paper, pens, and pencils for writing personal observations about what is learned as students compare and contrast variants of The Three Little Pigs

Lesson Motivator

1. Write the following statement by Les Brown on the chalkboard: "Shoot for the moon. Even if you miss it, you will land among the stars." Beside it write the Spanish translation: *"Trata de alcanzar la luna. Si no llegas a ella, jestaras entre las estrellas!"* Ask for volunteers to read each one.

2. Spend about 10 minutes letting students write in their journals what the quote means to them personally. Invite them to share their thoughts if desired.

3. Display a selection of books that retell the story of *The Three Little Pigs* (see list of suggested titles below) in a place where students

can browse through them at the beginning of class.

4. Ask students to quickly retell the story, taking turns to highlight the parts they remember.

5. Explain that many fairy tales and folktales come with variations and that you are going to share one with the class and then investigate some of the other variants in small groups.

Suggestions for Teaching the Lesson

- Introduce a particularly clever version of this story, *The Three Little Pigs (Los Tres Cerdos): Nacho, Tito, and Miguel,* by Bobbi Salinas. If you do not speak Spanish, enlist the aid of someone who does so that this story can be read in both English and Spanish, as it is written.

- As you read the story, ask the students to listen and look for what has been done to the version they may be familiar with to make this book unique.

- Point out interesting items in the wonderful illustrations.

- Once the book has been completed, go back through it as students discuss it, pointing out items that make this Spanish version quite authentic. Even the paper on which the text is printed looks like adobe walls. Discuss items listed at the end of the book that are an integral part of the Spanish culture, including artists, illustrators, foods, plants, and the setting itself.

- List the following literary elements in chart form on the chalkboard or overhead: *setting, plot, main characters, conclusion, theme, style,* and *point of view.* Review each with the class.

- Go through the elements one by one based on the reading of *The Three Little Pigs,* filling in the chart with information generated by the class. Write the title and author first. Individual students can take turns recording the information on the chart.

- Hand out the "Folktale Variants" worksheets or large sheets of chart paper for students to create their own charts. Have students break into pairs, triads, or foursomes depending on how many versions of *The Three Little Pigs* you are able to acquire.

- Have each group read its choice, record the information as modeled in the class demonstration, and discuss their book. To encourage some literary analysis, invite each group to talk about what they particularly liked or disliked in their version.

- Group by group, share the books and record the information on a large classroom chart that may fill the bulletin board or be stretched across the chalkboard.

- Review the work on the chart by asking students to note similarities and differences in the various versions of *The Three Little Pigs*. Have them write down their reactions, beginning with rough drafts of observations and editing them to a polished state.

- Engage the class in a conversation after the pieces are written. Post writing around the class chart on the bulletin board. Artists and nonartists alike can decorate the borders of the bulletin board with characters, items, or distinctive scenes from their books.

Evaluation

- Assess whether students have mastered the meaning of the literary elements based on their group work, by listening to them during classroom discussions, and by checking over their written work.

- Evaluate the quality of each student's written work based on a specific rubric developed for this assignment or on established writing criteria for the class. The focus of this particular assign-

ment might be to include a main idea and three or four supporting details in each paragraph.

- Tell students that each sentence must begin with a capital letter and end with the proper punctuation. Sometimes it is more successful to have students zero in on just a few specifics as they edit their own writing. In this way they are not overwhelmed by the editing process and specific skills can be fine-tuned.

Extensions

- Act out one of the books with simple costumes inspired by suggestions at the end of the focus book.

- Have the students write a version of this tale reflecting their culture.

- Create a diorama or quadrama of favorite scenes from one of the versions.

- Have students pick another favorite fairy tale or folktale and read three different versions, presenting the books, along with their similarities and differences, on a colorful poster.

- Have students build models of the homes of the three pigs using materials described in the book.

- Create a board game that follows a version of the story. Include clearly written directions, a colorful board, and clever playing pieces. Keep the game in a reading center to be used during quiet time or teach it to a younger group of students and let them enjoy it in their classroom reading center.

Suggested Titles for Independent Reading and Research

Claverie, Jean, reteller. *The Three Little Pigs*. New York: North-South Books, 1989.

Floury, Marie-France, adapter. *The Three Little Pigs: A Tale by Perrault*. Illustrated by Agnes Mathieu. New York: Abbeville Press, 1998. (France)

Galdone, Paul. *The Three Little Pigs*. New York: Clarion, 1979. (England)

Harris, Marian. *The Three Little Pigs*. Illustrated by Jim Harris. Denver, Colo.: Accord, 1995.

Hooks, William H., reteller. *The Three Little Pigs and the Fox.* Illustrated by S. D. Schindler. New York: Macmillan, 1989. (Appalachia)

Kellogg, Steven. *The Three Little Pigs.* New York: Morrow, 1999.

Liard, Donivee M. *The Three Little Pigs and the Magic Shark.* Illustrated by Carol Jossem. Portsmouth, N.H.: Barnaby, 1981.

Lowell, Susan. *The Three Little Javelinas.* Illustrated by Jim Harris. Flagstaff, Ariz.: Northland Publishing, 1993. (American Southwest)

Reinl, Edda. *The Three Little Pigs.* Saxonville, Mass.: Picture Book Studio, 1983.

Rounds, Glen. *Three Little Pigs and the Big Bad Wolf.* New York: Holiday House, 1992.

Scieszka, Jon. *The True Story of the Three Little Pigs.* Illustrated by Lane Smith. New York: Viking, 1989. (America)

Trivizas, Eugene. *The Three Little Wolves & the Big Bad Pig.* Illustrated by Helen Oxenbury. New York: McElderry, 1993.

Zemoch, Margot, reteller. *The Three Little Pigs: An Old Story.* New York: Farrar, Straus & Giroux, 1997.

Folktale Variants

Title of folktale:_____

Author/reteller: _____

Setting:_____

_____

_____

Plot overview:_____

_____

_____

_____

Main characters:_____

Conclusion: _____

_____

_____

Theme:_____

Point of view: _____

_____

Style: _____

Personal reactions: _____

_____

_____

_____

Lesson 13

Using a Herringbone Graphic Organizer as a Comprehension Tool

SKILL: Recalling and Organizing Information

CULTURE OF FOCUS: African American

Materials

Richard Wright and the Library Card, by
  William Miller (Lee & Low, 1997)
Copies of the "Herringbone Graphic
  Organizer" worksheet (see end of
  lesson)
Overhead projector or chalkboard
Pens or pencils
Notebook paper

Lesson Motivator

1. Invite two students to present a
   mock interview debating the values of owning a library card from
   the local public library. One student must try to convince a reluctant reader to visit the library and
   learn about its possibilities. At the
   conclusion of their interactions,
   ask how many class members
   have their own cards. Reinforce
   the advantages of owning a library card. Explain how easy the
   process is and how to go about
   getting a card.

2. Focus the students on the upcoming
   read-aloud by explaining that this
   story is about a young man who
   does not have a library card. Tell
   students to listen for why that
   situation is particularly distress-
   ful to the main character, Richard
   Wright.

Suggestions for Teaching the Lesson

- Introduce the book by reading the
  title, author, dedication, and date
  of publication. Read the story
  through, stopping periodically to
  discuss segments or illustrations
  that might be of particular interest to the class. The illustration of
  the imposing, distrustful librarian
  is bound to elicit a few comments.

- Upon completion of the story, encourage the students to respond
  by sharing their reactions. Then
  read the author's note at the end
  of the book so that students know
  that Richard Wright was a real
  person who was an extremely
  successful writer as an adult. You
  might discuss the effect that reading had on this writer's life
  and/or on their own lives as possible writers.

- Hand out the "Herringbone Graphic
  Organizer" worksheets. Explain
  that a graphic organizer like this
  is a particularly useful aid in the
  comprehension of expository or
  nonfiction materials. Six important comprehension questions are
  addressed in the Who? What?
  Where? When? Why? and How?
  segments. Give the students some
  time to recall information from
  the read-aloud to fill in the worksheet. Circulate around the room,
  assessing how much the students
  have absorbed at this point.

- Reread the story again, encouraging
  students to fill in the sections they
  didn't recall.

- As a class, fill in a large graphic organizer sketched on the chalkboard or use a transparency on
  the overhead to complete the activity. Ask for volunteers to fill in
  each segment. In this way you are
  helping students to double-check
  their comprehension and illustrating what kind of information
  fits each question.

• Spend a short time reflecting as a group about this book. Briefly recap what kind of a person Richard appeared to be based on this segment of his life. What qualities did he have that made him successful? Are those qualities important to everyone who seeks success? How do the students view reading and its importance in their lives?

• Let the students practice their skills using a fresh graphic organizer and a selection from the classroom library. This time, the final reflection will be in writing. Based on the information in their graphic organizers, they should write a paragraph on what they learned about an individual from their independent reading. The polished paragraph must meet established criteria for classroom writing.

• Invite student writers to sit in the "Author's Chair" if this is a common practice in your classroom. Give them an opportunity to read their paragraphs to the class and answer questions about the main character in the books they read.

Evaluation

• When reviewing the second graphic organizer and the paragraph of reflection, it should be easy to assess whether the students have gained an understanding of how to use a herringbone graphic organizer to facilitate their comprehension of informational or expository materials.

• Set criteria for an acceptable paragraph before the writing begins and match the polished paragraph to those specifications. Ask students to evaluate their writing using a short written evaluation form or during a short one-on-one conference. Take time to chart your observations about each student.

Extensions

• Take a field trip to the library and have a tour conducted by an enthusiastic and knowledgeable librarian. After checking with parents ahead of time, invite students who do not have library cards of their own to sign up for them.

• Have each student present a book and its main character to the class by dressing as the character in a simple costume. Students could do a "chalk talk" on the board using different colors of chalk to highlight each of the six comprehension questions.

• Have children draw cameralike snapshots of events in the life of the person they have learned about, mounting them on a large piece of tagboard. They should use this visual aid to teach the class about their book and character.

Suggested Titles for Independent Reading and Research

Adler, David. *A Picture Book of Anne Frank.* Illustrated by Karen Ritz. New York: Holiday House, 1993.

Ancona, George. *Earth Daughter: Alicia of Acoma Pueblo.* Illustrated with photographs by the author. New York: Simon & Schuster, 1995.

———. *Pablo Remembers: The Fiesta of the Day of the Dead.* Illustrated with photographs by the author. New York: Lothrop, Lee & Shepard Books, 1993.

Bradby, Marie. *More Than Anything Else.* Illustrated by Chris K. Soentpiet. New York: Orchard Books, 1995.

Bruchac, Joseph. *A Boy Called Slow: The True Story of Sitting Bull.* Illustrated by Rocco Baviera. New York: Philomel, 1994.

———. *Crazy Horse's Vision.* Illustrated by S. D. Nelson. New York: Lee & Low Books, 2000.

Catalanotto, Peter. *The Painter.* New York: Orchard Books, 1995.

Cha, Dia. *Dia's Story Cloth: The Hmong People's Journey of Freedom.* Stitched by Chue and Nhia Thao Cha. Published in Cooperation with Denver Museum of Natural History. New York: Lee & Low Books, 1996.

Christian, Mary Blount. *Who'd Believe John Colter?* Illustrated by Laszlo Kubinyi. New York: Macmillan, 1993.

Coles, Robert. *The Story of Ruby Bridges.* Illustrated by George Ford. New York: Scholastic, 1995.

Ekoomiak, Normee. *Arctic Memories.* New York: Holt, 1990.

Hoyt-Goldsmith, Diane. *Arctic Hunter.* Illustrated with photographs by Lawrence Migdale. New York: Holiday House, 1992.

Medina, Juan. *A Migrant Family.* Illustrated with photographs by Larry Dane Brimner. Minneapolis, Minn.: Lerner, 1992.

Mora, Pat. *Tomas and the Library Lady.* Illustrated by Raul Colon. New York: Alfred A. Knopf, 1997.

Nez, Redwing, T. *Forbidden Talent.* Flagstaff, Ariz.: Northland Publishing, 1995.

Oppenheim, Shulamith Levey. *The Lily Cupboard.* Illustrated by Ronald Himler. New York: HarperCollins, 1992.

Pinkney, Andrea D. *Bill Pickett, Rodeo-Ridin' Cowboy.* Illustrated by Brian Pinkney. New York: Gulliver Books/Harcourt Brace, 1996.

———. *Duke Ellington.* Illustrated by Brian Pinkney. New York: Scholastic, 1998.

Rappaport, Doreen. *The Journey of Meng.* Illustrated by Yang Ming-Yi. New York: Dial, 1991.

Ringgold, Faith. *If a Bus Could Talk: The Story of Rosa Parks.* New York: Simon & Schuster, 1999.

Say, Allen. *Grandfather's Journey.* New York: Houghton Mifflin, 1993.

———. *Tea with Milk.* New York: Houghton Mifflin, 1999.

Schroeder, Alan. *Satchmo's Blues.* Illustrated by Floyd Cooper. New York: Doubleday, 1996.

Stewart, Sarah. *The Library.* Illustrated by David Small. New York: Farrar, Straus & Giroux, 1995.

Towle, Wendy. *The Real McCoy: The Life of an African-American Inventor.* Illustrated by Wil Clay. New York: Scholastic, 1993.

Turner, Ann. *Nettie's Trip South.* Illustrated by Ronald Himler. New York: Macmillan, 1987.

Van Steenwyk, Elizabeth. *My Name Is York.* Illustrated by Bill Farnsworth. Flagstaff, Ariz.: Rising Moon/Northland Publishing, 1997.

Herringbone Graphic Organizer

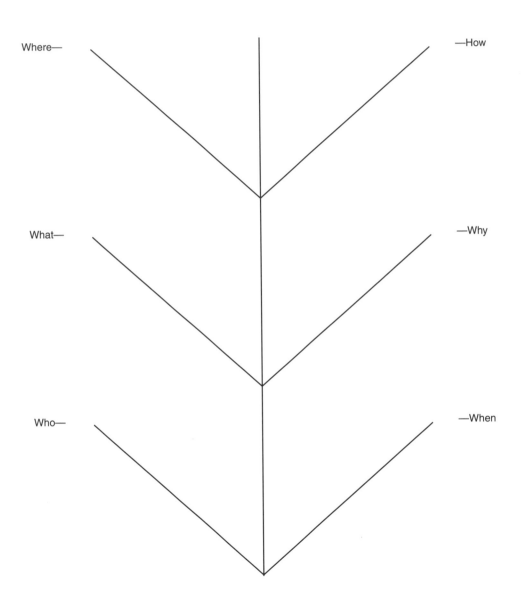

Where—

—How

What—

—Why

Who—

—When

Lesson 14

Reader's Theater

SKILL: Strengthening Comprehension

CULTURE OF FOCUS: African American and Native American

Materials

Knots on a Counting Rope, illustrated by Bill Martin Jr. and John Archambault (Henry Holt, 1990) (two copies)

The Best Beak in Boonaroo Bay, by Narelle Oliver (Fulcrum, 1995)

Copies of reader's theater scripts for *The Best Beak in Boonaroo Bay* (see end of lesson)

"Spider Flies to the Feast" in *Why Leopard Has Spots,* by Won Ldy Paye and M.H. Lippert (Fulcrum, 1998)

Copies of reader's theater scripts for "Spider Flies to the Feast" (see end of lesson)

Paper and pens or pencils to create reader's theater scripts

Lesson Motivator

1. Invite the school principal, secretary, or another teacher to present a reader's theater version of *Knots on a Counting Rope* as your partner. If you have two copies of the book, the entire script can be read straight from the book. Otherwise, prepare two scripts, taking the dialogue directly from each page. There are only two characters, Grandfather and Boy (the grandson).

2. The text is a conversation between the characters. Be sure to practice together several times so that the story flows smoothly and appropriate expression can be used to bring the words to life. You may use a hat and a headband, but no props are really needed. Introduce the book by giving the title and author and briefly explaining the setting.

3. Explain to the class that reader's theater is an opportunity to adapt a story from a picture book or part of a novel and present it to the class by reading the parts instead of memorizing them first. Although simple props can be used, these presentations can be done without them.

4. Demonstrate how reader's theater works by reading your parts directly from the script.

5. After the story has been performed, invite reactions from the class. Ask how hearing a story this way helped listeners to visualize it more clearly or to understand it better than if they had just heard it read aloud by the teacher alone or read it independently.

Suggestions for Teaching the Lesson

- Because this is a demonstration lesson, you should choose seven students who are likely to settle into this task quickly and competently. They are to present a reader's theater production of *The Best Beak in Boonaroo Bay,* by Narelle Oliver, using the script at the end of this lesson.

- Another group can try a different tale, "Spider Flies to the Feast," by Won Ldy Paye and M. H. Lippert, using the script at the end of this lesson. The presentations will be the model other students will eventually follow when they have created scripts. These students should to go out into the hall to practice. Suggestions for their preparation:
  —Have students read through the script silently before selecting parts.
  —Then have them read through the script orally, trying out their parts.

—With the third reading, students should try to put expression into their voices to best interpret their characters.

—Depending on the group, one more practice may be enough; then it's "curtain time."

- While those students are preparing, explain to the remainder of the class how additional scripts will be written. The following steps can be written on a chart for easy reference. Everyone is going to get the opportunity to present a reader's theater production:

  —Show examples of a script and how it differs from the text in a book. Students will be modeling their scripts after the samples.

  —Students will work in groups, choosing a book from a selection of titles gathered for classroom use. They will read their book, develop the story into a reader's theater format, and perform it.

  —The students will decide on the number of parts, including a narrator or two depending on the length of the book.

  —They will take dialogue for each character directly from the story.

  —The narrator's part should include the title and author, enough of an introduction to set the scene, and any descriptive parts that will fit smoothly between the characters' parts.

  —Students will write out parts in a script form that you will check before the presentation.

  —Students will decide on basic dress and any simple props and get them ready for the day of the presentation. One idea is to have everyone in the group wear a turtleneck. Dress is not critical to the presentation, however. Have student performers stand in front of the class or sit on stools as they do their own theater reading. To add interest a collection of stools of varying heights can be used. Besides being fun, this is an excellent opportunity to practice oral reading skills and interpretive reading. In addition, it is a motivational way to enhance deep comprehension of a story.

  —Practice and present and shine!

- After the performances, have the entire class work on developing scripts for a reader's theater production. Assure students that you will circulate among the groups as they work, helping as needed. It will benefit each group if they can have a copy of *The Best Beak in Boonaroo Bay* or "Spider Flies to the Feast" scripts and access to the books to see how the script evolved from the story.

- Again, remind the class that all drafts of a script will be presented to you to be checked for clarity before practices begin. The final scripts should be typed or word-processed for easier reading. Competent class typists, volunteer parents, or a classroom aide can help with this task. Scripts can be stapled into matching colored folders or construction-paper covers for uniformity.

- On the day of the presentations, suggest that students dress in similar colors or simple T-shirts for a more professional appearance.

Extensions

- Present the productions to other classrooms. Readers young and old will appreciate the diversion from the regular class routine and will be getting an opportunity to practice their listening skills at the same time.

- Adapt other picture books or narrative poems to reader's theater productions. Then adapt segments of novels to this format. Presenting them to the class would be a good way to entice other students to read the books, a memorable variation on a book talk.

- Invite students from the high school or a nearby college department to put on a skit and give pointers to the younger, novice students about performing.

- Put on several productions at a parents' night program, a cultural celebration, or as part of end-of-the-year festivities. In addition, your class could visit a local nursing home and entertain the residents.

Evaluation

- Give each group continuous feedback as they prepare their scripts and discuss the simple presentation. Note how students work together as a group and support those who have difficulty in doing so.

- Videotape each performance and ask the students to comment on their overall performance and on individual performances. Give support or advice as needed to improve future performances.

Suggested Titles for Reader's Theater Scripts

Note: Choose books that have action, plenty of dialogue, and description that can be rewritten if necessary to keep the story moving.

Aardema, Verna, reteller. *Borreguita and the Coyote.* Illustrated by Petra Mathers. New York: Alfred A. Knopf, 1991.

Begay, Shonto. *Ma'ii and Cousin Horned Toad: A Traditional Navajo Story.* New York: Scholastic, 1992.

Bruchac, Joseph. *Gluskabe and the Four Wishes.* Illustrated by Christine Nyburg Shrader. New York: Cobblehill Books/Dutton, 1995.

Farris, Pamela J. *Young Mouse and Elephant: An East African Folktale.* Illustrated by Valeri Gorbachev. Boston: Houghton Mifflin, 1996.

Flournoy, Valerie. *The Patchwork Quilt.* Illustrated by Jerry Pinkney. New York: Dial Books, 1985.

Keams, Geri. *Grandmother Spider Brings the Sun.* Illustrated by James Bernardin. Flagstaff, Ariz.: Northland Publishing, 1995.

Kimmel, Eric A. *Anansi and the Moss-Covered Rock.* Illustrated by Janet Stevens. New York: Holiday House, 1995.

Lottridge, Celia Barker. *The Name of the Tree.* Illustrated by Ian Wallace. New York: McElderry, 1989.

Martin, Rafe. *The Rough-Face Girl.* Illustrated by David Shannon. New York: Putnam, 1992.

Myers, Walter Dean. *Harlem.* Illustrated by Christopher Myers. New York: Scholastic, 1997. (This is a poem that can be read by three or four persons.)

Polacco, Patricia. *Chicken Sunday.* New York: Putnam & Grosset, 1992.

———. *Pink and Say.* New York: Philomel, 1994.

Salinas, Bobbi. *The Three Little Pigs (Los Tres Cerdos): Nacho, Tito, and Miguel.* Alameda, Calif.: Piñata Publications, 1998.

Schroeder, Alan. *Carolina Shout!* Illustrated by Bernie Fuchs. New York: Dial Books, 1995.

Reader's Theater

Adapted from *The Best Beak in Boonaroo Bay*, by Narelle Oliver, (Fulcrum 1995)

Characters:

Narrator	Spoonbill
Darter	Cormorant
Curlew	Oyster-catcher
Pelican	

Narrator: Today's story is set in a coastal mangrove swamp in Queensland, Australia. Join us in Boonaroo Bay, where life is calm and quiet. It has not always been this way, however. There was a time when the birds began to bicker among themselves about what they considered to be a most serious topic: Who had the best beak in the bay?

Spoonbill: My beak has the most exquisite shape!

Darter (scoffingly): Exquisite? I can't imagine how you catch anything with that monstrosity.

Cormorant: Of course, nothing is quite so handsome and useful as a hook.

Curlew (spluttering): A hook! A hook is no match for my slender curved beak.

Oyster-catcher: The best kind of beak is a strong, sharp wedge … just like mine!

Narrator: The argument went on and on until it was interrupted by a wise old pelican.

Pelican: If you must decide who has the best beak in Boonaroo Bay, a contest is the answer.

Narrator: The birds quite liked this idea and began to plan carefully. They devised a contest of skill open to all those who had beaks in the bay. The judge's decision was to be final.

Pelican: There are five events. The bird who wins the most events will have, without a feather of a doubt, the best beak in Boonaroo Bay.

Spoonbill: Easy!

Pelican: Let's begin. To win the first event, you must collect shrimp from the shallow mud near the mangroves.

Narrator: The royal spoonbill swished his beak from side to side, sieving quickly through the mud to gather the shrimp. He was clearly the winner.

Spoonbill: I knew my beak was the best!

Pelican: The contest is not finished yet. To win the next event, the contestant must spear a fish.

Narrator: The darter quickly accomplished this task.

Pelican: Superbly spiked! However, remember that the contest is still not over. To win the next event, you must extract a clam from its rock-hard shell.

Narrator: All of the birds began to hammer and prod at the shells. Carefully, the oyster-catcher forced her chisel beak between the two parts of the shell and snapped it open.

Pelican: Expertly opened! Two events remain. The winner of the next event must find a worm deep down in the sand.

Narrator: This time only the curlew was successful and was commended by the pelican.

Pelican: For the last event, you must catch a slippery, slithery eel.

Spoonbill: Impossible!

Narrator: The cormorant did not hear him because she was expertly hooking the prize. The contest was now over.

Pelican: Congratulations to you all.

Spoonbill: This can't be!

Darter: I'm afraid so. It seems incredible but it appears that we are all winners. There simply is no very best beak in Boonaroo Bay.

Narrator: As you can see, there is no longer a need for any more bickering in Boonaroo Bay. Except for a splash here and a snap there, as each beak hunts in its own best way, the quiet and peace in the mangrove swamp is rarely disturbed.

Reader's Theater

"Spider Flies to the Feast" Adapted from *Why Leopard Has Spots: Dan Stories from Liberia,* by Won-Ldy Paye and Margaret H. Lippert, Illustrated by Ashley Bryan (Fulcrum, 1998)

Characters:

Narrator 1	Great Spirit
Spider	Quail
Dog	Parrot
Narrator 2	Hummingbird
Eagle	

Narrator 1: Our story is set far away near a small village on the west coast of Africa. Spider and Dog were good friends. Spider floated downriver to visit Dog so that they could spend time together every day. Unfortunately, he had to walk all the way home after each visit, because no one could swim upstream against the swift current. Now, Spider was a trickster and loved playing tricks on his friend.

Listen to the following story to see the kinds of tricks Spider played.

Spider: I have a new trick. I can go home without walking on the ground. Can you do that?

Dog: No. And neither can you.

Spider: Yes, I can. I can walk in space.

Dog (laughing): Nobody can walk in space.

Spider: Nobody except me.

Dog: Prove it.

Narrator 1: Spider climbed to the top of Dog's house. He released a silky thread so thin that Dog couldn't see it. Then he waved one leg.

Dog: Let go. You aren't walking through space. Anybody can wave a leg out in space.

Narrator 1: Spider waved another leg and then another. What he was really doing was waiting for the wind to blow a little.

Dog: Let go with all of your legs.

Narrator 1: The wind came up. It blew the end of the thread toward Spider's house where it caught on the roof. Spider stepped out onto the thread and began to walk home. Dog followed Spider all the way home.

Dog: How do you do that? I never saw anybody walk in space before.

Spider (grinning): Did you like my trick?

Dog: You were lucky, Spider. You could have crashed and hurt yourself. Tricks can really get you in trouble. So from now on, no more tricks.

Narrator 1: Dog wagged his tail good-bye, jumped into the river, and floated home. The next day, Spider visited his friend again.

Spider: I have a better trick. I can get home without walking on the ground or walking in space.

Dog: How?

Spider: On the river.

Dog (scratching behind his left ear and shaking his head): The current is too fast. No one can go upriver.

Spider: I can.

Dog: Prove it.

Narrator 1: Spider took a deep breath and plunged into the river. He sank below the surface. Then his head bobbed up as Dog watched.

Spider: Watch carefully.

Narrator 1: Spider began moving all eight legs at once, very fast, skating on the surface of the water. Gradually he worked his way upstream.

Dog (amazed): How did you do that? I never saw anybody walk on water before. That's dangerous, Spider. You could have drowned. I told you that tricks can really get you into trouble. So no more tricks.

Narrator 1: Dog jumped into the river and floated home.

Spider (waving a dripping leg): Tomorrow I will come visit you without walking on the ground, without walking in space, and without skating on the river.

Narrator 1: Dog arrived home, shook himself dry, and wondered what Spider would do next. Early the next morning, Spider cooked a huge pumpkin, cut off the lid and scooped out the seeds. He climbed inside to hide from Dog. He knew Dog would carry the delicious pumpkin back to his house when he became tired of waiting for Spider.

Dog waited and worried when his friend did not arrive. Thinking he may have been hurt, he went up the path looking for his friend. As he neared the house he smelled the delicious pumpkin. It would make a delicious lunch for the two friends.

Dog: Spider, where are you?

Narrator 1: From his hiding place, Spider had to cover his mouth with three legs to keep from laughing out loud.

Dog: Hmm. I guess I missed Spider. I'll just take a taste out of this pumpkin to be sure it's ready.

Narrator 1: He sank his teeth into the pumpkin and accidentally bit Spider's leg.

Spider: Ouch!

Dog (thinking): Oh, dear. Spider must be hurt. I'd better go look for him, but I'll just take one more bite of this delicious pumpkin before I go.

Narrator 1: Dog took a big bite and almost bit off Spider's leg. Spider crawled out of the pumpkin, rubbing his leg.

Spider: Stop biting me!

Dog: What were you doing in there?

Spider: Waiting for you to carry me to your house.

Dog: THAT was your trick?

Spider (sadly): Yes.

Dog: That was not very smart. I could have eaten you up by accident. I told you that tricks can really get you into trouble.

Spider: All right, Dog. From now on, no more tricks.

Narrator 2: Spider remembered what he said to Dog for many months even though he kept thinking of great tricks to play. He swung lazily from a thread during the dry season, trying to catch a breeze. Because this was so long ago, his legs were long and straight. As he dangled, Spider watched Eagle soaring high above him.

Eagle (calling to the other birds): It's cool here. Come on up.

Narrator 2: The Great Spirit watched the soaring birds from her home high above the clouds. She loved watching them zoom and glide.

Great Spirit (calling to the birds): I would like to reward you for entertaining me. Come to my house tomorrow for a feast.

Narrator 2: Spider wanted to join the party too. He felt that it was unfair because he was surely better than the birds with his eight legs. After all, those birds only had two legs.

Spider: I know! I'll make my own wings and fly to the feast myself. Quail, do you have some extra feathers around?

Quail: You can have the ones over there in the grass.

Spider: Thank you. Eagle, could I borrow some feathers?

Eagle: Take the ones on the ground below my nest.

Narrator 2: Spider asked many other birds, including Vulture, Woodpecker, and Blue Heron. He had feathers of all sizes and all colors of the rainbow. He arranged them on the ground in the shape of a coat with wings. Using a sharp rock, he scraped the bark of a rubber tree to get sticky white gum, which he spread on the feathers. Once the glue was dry, he put on his feather coat and practiced flying. After a bumpy start, he began to soar smoothly.

Spider: I'm flying! Wait till the other birds see this!

Narrator 2: Spider overslept the next day. The other birds were up early and on their way to the feast when Spider awoke.

Spider: Hey, wait for me. Here I come.

Narrator 2: Spider flew all morning. He arrived tired and hungry as the Great Spirit was talking.

Great Spirit: Welcome. I hope you all enjoy this feast. This is the first time all of you have been together, so before we eat, I would like you to introduce yourselves to one another.

Eagle (preening): My name is Eagle.

Parrot (squawking): My name is Parrot.

Hummingbird: I am Hummingbird.

Narrator 2: The Great Spirit smiled and held out her hand. Hummingbird alighted there and folded her wings. After all of the birds had introduced themselves, the Great Spirit pointed at Spider.

Great Spirit: I see that we have a guest. What is your name?

Spider (surprised at being singled out): My name is All of You.

Great Spirit (nodding): Now that the introductions are finished, it is time to eat.

Spider: Wait! Great Spirit, who is this feast for?

Great Spirit: The feast is for all of you.

Spider: Wow! This feast is just for me, because my name is All of You. You can't eat any of my food.

Narrator 2: Spider snatched the food away from Hummingbird, Parrot, and Pepper Bird. Despite the anger of the other birds, Spider was fast. He ate every bit of food himself. The Great Spirit knew that Spider was going to be sorry for what he had done. When it was time to leave, the other guests all had something to say.

Eagle (to Hummingbird): Those little tail feathers on All of You look a lot like yours.

Hummingbird: Yes, they are mine. And those long feathers on his wings look a lot like yours. All of You must really be Spider.

Spider: Whoops. I think I heard my name. I'd better go now.

Narrator 2: Spider took off for home. As he flew, Eagle joined him.

Eagle: Spider, you tricked us. I want my feathers back.

Spider: Oh, sure. I have plenty more.

Narrator 2: Spider broke off Eagle's feathers and gave them to her. All of the other birds took back their feathers, too. Before long when Spider tried to flap his legs, he could longer fly. Instead he was falling.

Spider: What am I going to do now? Help me, little Hummingbird. Hurry down to earth and tell my family to cover the ground under me with soft leaves.

Narrator 2: Hummingbird remembered what Spider had done to all of the birds. She sped down to earth with a message.

Hummingbird: Spider has a new trick he wants to show you! Bring thorny branches and stick them in the ground with the points up. Spider will stop just above them.

Narrator 2: Spider's family was used to his tricks. They did as they were told.

Spider's family: Hey, Spider! Come on, Spider! Show us your new trick!

Spider: What's wrong with you? Where are the soft leaves? Why are there sharp bran—

Narrator 2: Of course, Spider could not stop just above the branches. He lay on the thorns barely able to move. Fortunately, the hard glue from the feathers had saved his life. Unfortunately, all of his legs were broken, which is why Spider's legs are crooked today. Spider learned a lesson from his latest trick. From then on, he only tried to fly using his silken thread on a windy day. What lessons did Spider teach you?

Lesson 15

Identifying the Theme

SKILL: Interpreting an Author's Message

CULTURE OF FOCUS: Native American

Materials

The Ledgerbook of Thomas Blue Eagle, by Gaty Matthaei and Jewel Grutman (Thomasson-Grant, 1994)

Posterboard definitions of the words in the glossary of the book

Art supplies and ledger paper so that students can write their own short stories and illustrate them in ledgerbook style

Overhead transparency or chalkboard

Lesson Motivator

1. Make a posterboard or butcher paper chart ahead of time that tells a story using simple pictographs or picture writing. The book tells us that these pictograph stories usually read from right to left.

2. Display the finished story and ask the students if they can decipher it, giving them the clue that it "reads" from right to left.

3. Have students quietly write their versions on scratch paper. When time is up, invite volunteers to read the story. Explain that this is the way the Plains Indians, including the Dakota Sioux, wrote their stories.

4. Tell students that this carefully researched book you will be reading together includes both pictures and story in unique ledgerbook format, inspired by lovely ledger paintings done by the Plains Indians in the late 1800s.

Suggestions for Teaching the Lesson

- Explain that this lesson focuses on the theme of a book. Write the definition of *theme* on the chalkboard or overhead. The theme is the main idea or the central meaning of a book. It may be implicitly tucked into the words of the story or be stated directly at some point. It is an idea that ties the story together.

- Remind students that there is often more than one theme in a story and that personal interpretation should be honored in discussions about the theme of any book. There is no such thing as only one right answer, which leaves plenty of room for creative thinking.

- Read the title, authors, dedication, and information about *Thomas Blue Eagle*. Set the tone for listening to this story by telling the students about the Carlisle Indian School, basing your description on the information provided in the book.

- Pass out the vocabulary words, which should be written and defined on good-sized pieces of posterboard or tagboard. When a word is used in the story, the student who has it can stand up, read the word and definition, and line it up on the chalk rail beneath the chalkboard. In this way, students can refer back to any terms that are unfamiliar to them.

- Read the book through, asking students to listen for the main idea or theme of the story. They will be listening for the most important idea or the idea that they want to take away from the book.

- List student responses on the board after discussing the book. Have students choose the idea they support and write it on a piece of notebook paper. Read the book through again. As the students listen, have them jot down incidents or details from either the text or the illustrations to support their theme choices.

- Break the class into groups of four or five. Have each student read his or her theme or main idea and give the supporting details. Ask the group for reactions and to decide if their ideas are similar or quite different. After small group discussions, reconvene the class and talk about the students' different impressions of the story and the process of deciding what the theme is.

- Is there a common thread in the thinking? Are themes relatively similar or quite diverse? Review the definition of *theme* before giving students a chance to read another book and decide its theme. Multiple copies of some of the titles will give students the opportunity to compare thoughts and discuss their themes once again.

Evaluation

- Sit with individual groups and monitor their discussion of the book they are enjoying. Note how students ponder the message the author might be trying to convey.

- Encourage students to do their own thinking, reminding them that often one reader will take a different message away from a book than another. The question to answer is whether each student can ferret out a sensible meaning from an encounter with a book. Note accomplishments in the anecdotal records you are maintaining for each learner.

Extensions

- Have some students research the Carlisle Indian School and present the information to the class.

- Have other students pick one of the Plains Indians tribes to research and present the information in a nonfiction book format.

- Assign the students to work in pairs to write and illustrate a ledger-book story that reflects a particular culture.

- Hold a panel discussion on the practice of taking children from their homes and putting them into boarding schools, looking at the advantages and disadvantages in the 1800s and today.

- Locate a Native American speaker who may have had experience with boarding schools and can elaborate on attending school away from home, as many Native American children had to do and still do today.

- Have the class write a poem based on the feelings generated by reading this book or others listed for independent reading below.

Suggested Titles for Independent Reading and Research

Baker, Olaf. *Where the Buffaloes Begin.* Illustrated by Stephen Gammell. New York: Puffin Books, 1981.

Casler, Leigh. *The Boy Who Dreamed of an Acorn.* Illustrated by Shonto Begay. New York: Philomel, 1994.

Cohen, Caron Lee, reteller. *The Mud Pony.* Illustrated by Shonto Begay. New York: Scholastic, 1988.

dePaola, Tomie, reteller. *The Legend of the Indian Paintbrush.* New York: Putnam, 1988.

Goble, Paul. *The Gift of the Sacred Dog.* New York: Aladdin, 1980.

———. *Love Flute.* New York: Bradbury, 1992.

———. *The Return of the Buffaloes: A Plains Indian Story about Famine and Renewal of the Earth.* Washington, D.C.: National, 1996.

Goble, Paul, and Betsy James. *The Mud Family.* Illustrated by Paul Morin. New York: Putnam, 1994.

Keams, Geri. *Snail Girl Brings Water: A Navajo Story.* Illustrated by Richard Ziehler-Martin. Flagstaff, Ariz.: Rising Moon, 1998.

Luenn, Nancy. *Nessa's Story.* Illustrated by Neil Waldman. New York: Atheneum, 1994.

MacGill-Callahan, Sheila. *And Still the Turtle Watched.* Illustrated by Barry Moser. New York: Dial, 1991.

Martin, Rafe. *The Boy Who Lived with the Seals.* Illustrated by David Shannon. New York: Putnam, 1993.

———. *The Rough-Face Girl.* Illustrated by David Shannon. New York: Putnam, 1992.

McLerran, Alice. *The Ghost Dance.* Illustrated by Paul Morin. New York: Clarion, 1995.

Nez, Redwing. *Forbidden Talent.* Flagstaff, Ariz.: Northland Publishing, 1995.

Roop, Peter. *The Buffalo Jump.* Illustrated by Bill Farnsworth. Flagstaff, Ariz.: Northland Publishing, 1996.

Savageau, Cheryl. *Muskrat Will Be Swimming.* Illustrated by Robert Hynes. Flagstaff, Ariz.: Northland Publishing, 1996.

Sheldon, Dyan. *Under the Moon.* Illustrated by Gary Blythe. New York: Dial, 1994.

Wisniewski, David. *The Wave of the Sea-Wolf.* New York: Clarion, 1994.

Wood, Audrey. *The Rainbow Bridge.* Illustrated by Robert Florczak. San Diego, Calif.: Harcourt Brace, 1995.

Lesson 16

Scaffolding Students' Comprehension

SKILL: Investigating Plot

CULTURE OF FOCUS: All

Materials

Mama Provi and the Pot of Rice, by Sylvia Rosa-Casanova (Atheneum, 1997)
Wooden building blocks
Scratch paper
"Connection words," written individually on tagboard (see below)
Chart paper
Pens and pencils
Overhead projector or chalkboard

Lesson Motivator

1. Pile an assortment of building blocks on a table at the front of the classroom. Tell the class that you are going to use them as tools to teach a concept and that they will get their turn to create with blocks before the lesson is over.

2. Write the words *plot, chronological,* and *flashback* on the chalkboard or overhead (see definitions below). Ask students to look at each word and write a quick definition of it. Assess their understanding of these words by inviting volunteers to relate their definitions and give an illustrative example. Clarify understanding as needed.

Plot: The sequence of incidents that make up a story and move that story to a logical conclusion. The majority of plots unfold in chronological order, with tension building as one chapter follows another, drawing the reader further and further into the story. A second type of plot is episodic. In this case, each chapter is a distinct event that is not necessarily linked to the previous chapter. An especially interesting variation on plot is found in books written with alternating plots. Although they are not the focus of this lesson, examples of episodic and alternating plots in novel form will be included at the end of the lesson.

Chronological: The events in a story are told in the order in which they happen, one following right after the other.

Flashback: Used to hook a reader's attention. Flashbacks allow a glimpse into a character's past or provide information about earlier events that might have led to the creation of the problem the character currently faces or that might have triggered a current event. Because it requires a higher level of thinking to be able to understand the switching from past to present, the use of flashbacks occurs more frequently in fiction for older readers.

3. Hand out the "connection words," which should be written on tagboard. Some commonly used connectors are:

first	now
at last	later
second	before
in the end	following
third	afterward
as you can see	meanwhile
fourth	finally
to begin with	soon

Words should be large enough that they are legible to students all over the room. Ask individuals to hold up their particular words and read them aloud one at a time.

4. When they are done, ask the students to speculate about how these words and the definitions that were just reviewed might interact. The point to be made is that these particular words help to put pieces of a plot in the right order. In fact, they are clues to aid readers in conveying the chronological flow of events when they retell or review a story. Connection words are used at the beginning of the sentence to indicate how the event described by the rest of the sentence fits into the overall chain of events.

5. Tell the class that they will see these words again soon. Set the words aside and ask the class to settle back to listen to a story. The unfolding plot will be the key to integrating those building blocks that they are probably still wondering about, putting the vocabulary to work, and using the connection words.

Suggestions for Teaching the Lesson

- Introduce *Mama Provi and the Pot of Rice*, a delightful Reading Rainbow selection, by quickly building a tall apartment building out of the blocks. Tell the class that Mama Provi, the main character in the upcoming story, lives on the first floor of an apartment. Her granddaughter, Lucy, lives on the eighth floor of the same building. In this book Lucy comes downstairs to visit her grandmother and to spend the night twice a month. But something happens to prevent one visit. Ask for a few quick speculations about what might interfere

with the regular visit and then read the story.

- After the students learn that Lucy has the chicken pox and that Mama Provi has decided to make her feel better by making her favorite dish, encourage the class to listen to the sequence of events that follows.

- Challenge listeners to remember what occurs in chronological order when the story is over.

- When the story is finished, invite the students to chat about it. Relate the book to their lives by asking how many of them live close enough to grandparents or other relatives to enjoy visiting, spending the night, and having meals together. Invite them to talk about the different foods from the story that they have had or are a regular part of their lives. You could even ask them to think about a favorite dish that they would enjoy if they were ill.

- Hand out the "connection words" to various students. Work together to use the words to help put the story into chronological order. Use chart paper to quickly recapture the events, cut those events into sections, and hand the appropriate section to the student with a connector that would work, based on the class's decisions. There is bound to be discussion and disagreement before this activity all comes together, but the interactive learning is well worth the increased noise level.

- Finally, have students, with their corresponding words and story pieces in hand, stand in chronological order at the front of the room so that the remainder of the class can reread the story aloud from their "living book." After that, settle the class down for the remainder of the lesson.

- Return to the blocks and demonstrate how they can be used to show the way in which the plot of a story moves along. Using the sequence of events related by the students, build a plot line showing how action builds. Even though this story is not fraught with conflict, Mama Provi is problem solving as she is getting higher in the building, stopping to trade foods that transform her original meal. One block can be used for the first event, two blocks piled on top of each other will depict the second event, three blocks are used for the third event, and so forth, as the diagram "Example of a Plot/Block Wall" indicates (see end of lesson).

- The same process would be used to identify growing conflict in another kind of book. This block wall becomes a visual representation for readers of how action in a plot rises to a peak, the climax of the story, and then usually resolves itself to a lower level, often referred to as the resolution of the conflict.

- Discuss how some books have more tension or conflict than *Mama Provi and the Pot of Rice* does. The next task is to read just such a book. Divide readers into small groups, have each take a book from titles gathered ahead of time for independent practice, and have them collect a pile of blocks. They will try their hands at looking at plot by reflecting it via a wall of building blocks.

- When they are done with the book, learners should work together using scratch paper to quickly review the events and then build their wall accordingly, noting the satisfying ending or resolution in the process. Each group will retell their story to the rest of the class, based on their investigation of the plot, their notes, and their plot wall.

- To extend learning, involve the readers in some critical thinking. Have them create a wall illustrating a book whose plot moves along quietly with no apparent conflict.

In this instance, they should come up with a straight wall. How would their wall look if the tale built with suspense, but didn't come to a satisfying resolution? Sometimes an author will leave readers hanging, letting them surmise a probable conclusion. That wall would go uphill and simply stop, wouldn't it? Urge readers to watch for these different kinds of plot action in the novels they read in the future.

- After the practice with chronological plot, give the students several examples of how flashbacks work. Read several picture books, such as those listed below, to illustrate how authors use flashbacks. Ask for student reactions about their effectiveness. Have they read novels that used flashbacks effectively?

- Have the students read, for example, *The Worry Stone,* by Marianna Dengler (Northland Publishing, 1996). When they meet on a park bench, a lonely elderly woman befriends Jason, a lonely young boy. The flashback takes readers back to a time when the woman was very young. She spends time with Grandfather, who tells her marvelous stories and teaches her the Chumash tale about the origins of the worry stone. The worry stone she finds at that time is treasured by her over the years. Moving back into the present, the elderly woman begins to tell those childhood stories to Jason after passing her worry stone on to him.

- Another book to read is *The Black Snowman,* by Phil Mendez (Scholastic, 1989). This story also begins with a flashback. In this instance an elderly storyteller wraps a brightly colored kente cloth about himself before beginning his tales. There is a magical quality about the kente cloth that is carried with it when it appears again many, many years later in contemporary times. Present-day Jacob is angry about being a black American and about being poor.

He and his younger brother, Peewee, go outside to play and end up making a snowman. Unfortunately, because of the grime in the area, they create a black snowman, which does not make Jacob happy. Peewee finds the ancient kente cloth along with other items in the trash and uses it to decorate the snowman. The magic isn't gone from the tattered cloth, and the snowman comes to life. He has lessons to teach Jacob, including another flashback to highlight the glory of his ancestors. Then the snowman melts away while saving the boys from a burning building.

- Another book to use is Riki Levinson's *Watch the Stars Come Out* (Dutton, 1985). A young child hears a bedtime story told by her grandma, who describes the little girl's great-grandma's journey to America as an immigrant child.

- Although they are not the focus of this lesson, interested readers can find examples of episodic and alternating plots in the following books, among others:

   Novels that present a story through episodic plots: Beverly Cleary's popular books about Henry Huggins, Kenneth Graham's classic *Wind in the Willows*, and Arnold Lobel's enduring Frog and Toad series. An appropriate picture book is by Demi: *The Dragon's Tale and Other Animal Fables of the Chinese Zodiac* (Henry Holt, 1996).

   Novels that present a story through alternating plots: In stories such as the following, chapters alternate between main characters. Their stories are intertwined, but you get their points of view as conflicts are presented and resolved: E. L. Konigsburg, *View from Saturday* (Atheneum, 1996); Kathryn Lasky, *True North: A Novel of the Underground Railroad* (Blue Sky Press, 1996); and Gary Paulsen, *Canyons* (Delacorte, 1990).

Evaluation

- Make anecdotal notes on the students' performance as they read and discuss a tale in small groups. How are they grasping the concept of chronological plots? In the following weeks, after appropriate instruction, are they able to identify the different kinds of action within a plot? Query each learner over the next few weeks on how his or her understanding of plots is improving and how the work is helping comprehension of what he or she reads.

- Watch for skills in retelling, cooperation within a group, willingness to practice this new knowledge in other books, and so forth. Add the information gleaned from student observation and individual conferences to the growing picture of each student as a competent reader. Information about growing abilities can be added to portfolios and discussed with parents at parent conferences, preferably by the learner as he or she recounts an overview of reading abilities.

Extensions

- Have students apply their knowledge by becoming "Plot Critics." As they review a book in light of its plot, they should consider the following questions:

   —Is the plot developed using chronological order? Are flashbacks included? Do you feel that they are used successfully?
   —Is the plot inventive? Is it believable?
   —What audience do you think would find this book appealing? Explain.
   —Does the development of the plot fit the world of the book as created by the author?

—Does the plot line develop in a logical manner? Does it move along at an engaging pace?

—Is the ending or resolution sensible and/or satisfying?

—On a scale from 1 to 10 (10 being the highest rating), how would you rate this book?

- Books that have been critiqued can be displayed in the classroom reading corner, along classroom bookshelves, or in a classroom library to catch the eye of other potential readers and "Plot Critics." Some schools have their own television studios that present morning announcements to the classrooms. Periodic appearances by the "Plot Critic" might be an exciting way to present a book to potential readers.

- Have a meal just like Mama Provi and Lucy enjoyed. Invite parents to prepare different authentic recipes corresponding with the foods in the book. Encourage them to partake of the meal and make it a celebration of cultures, generations, and reading.

- Take a field trip to different ethnic restaurants; this would be great fun and a memorable experience.

- Have the class write to the author, discussing the book and why they particularly like it.

- Have students retell a favorite story by altering the location and nationality involved.

- Using a feltboard, have students create the characters and retell the story to a younger class of students.

- Make a puppet theater out of a refrigerator box or wardrobe box from a moving company. Have students design simple sock puppets and put on a puppet show retelling an action-packed tale.

Suggested Titles for Independent Reading and Research

Bodkin, Odds. *The Crane Wife*. Illustrated by Gennady Spirin. New York: Gulliver, 1998.

Bruchac, Joseph. *Gluskabe and the Four Wishes*. Illustrated by Christine Nyburg Shrader. New York: Cobblehill, 1995.

Bunting, Eve. *So Far from the Sea*. Illustrated by Chris K. Soentpiet. New York: Clarion, 1998.

Chambers, Veronica. *Amistad Rising: A Story of Freedom*. Illustrated by Paul Lee. San Diego, Calif.: Harcourt Brace, 1998.

Chanin, Michael. *The Chief's Blanket*. Illustrated by Kim Howard. Tiburon, Calif.: H. J. Kramer/Starseed, 1998.

Echewa, T. Obinkaram. *The Magic Tree: A Folktale from Nigeria*. Illustrated by E. B. Lewis. New York: Morrow, 1999.

Gollub, Matthew. *Uncle Snake*. Illustrated by Leovigildo Martinez. New York: Tambourine Books, 1996.

Hobbs, Will. *Beardream*. Illustrated by Jill Kastner. New York: Atheneum, 1997.

Keams, Gerri. *Snail Girl Brings Water: A Navajo Story*. Illustrated by Richard Ziehler-Martin. Flagstaff, Ariz.: Rising Moon, 1998.

Kherdian, David. *The Golden Bracelet*. Illustrated by Nonny Hogrogrian. New York: Holiday House, 1998.

Kimmel, Eric. *Ten Suns: A Chinese Legend*. Illustrated by YongSheng Zuan. New York: Holiday House, 1998.

MacDonald, Margaret Read. *The Girl Who Wore Too Much: A Folktale from Thailand*. Illustrated by Yvonne Lebrum Davis. Little Rock, Ark.: August House LittleFolk, 1998.

Martin, Rafe. *The Rough-Face Girl*. Illustrated by David Shannon. New York: Putnam, 1992.

Morse, Hamilton. *Belching Hill*. Illustrated by Forest Rogers. New York: Greenwillow, 1997.

Polacco, Patricia. *Thank You, Mister Falker*. New York: Philomel, 1998.

Roop, Peter. *Buffalo Jump*. Illustrated by Bill Farnsworth. Flagstaff, Ariz.: Northland Publishing, 1996.

San Souci, Robert D. *The Talking Eggs*. Illustrated by Jerry Pinkney. New York: Dial, 1989.

Tarbescu, Edith. *Annushka's Voyage*. Illustrated by Lydia Dabocvich. New York: Clarion, 1998.

Thomassie, Tynia. *Feleciana Meets D'Loup Garou: A Cajun Tall Tale*. Illustrated by Cat Bowman Smith. Boston: Little, Brown, 1998.

Tseng, Grace. *White Tiger, Blue Serpent*. Illustrated by Jean Tseng and Mou-sien Tseng. New York: Lothrop, Lee & Shepard Books, 1999.

Vagin, Vladimir. *The Enormous Carrot*. New York: Scholastic, 1998.

Waite, Michael P. *Jojofu*. Illustrated by Yoriko Ito. New York: Lothrop, Lee & Shepard Books, 1996.

Wolfson, Margaret Olivia. *Marriage of the Rain Goddess*. Illustrated by Clifford Alexander Parms. New York: Barefoot Books, 1999.

Yep, Laurence. *The Dragon Prince: A Chinese Beauty and the Beast Tale*. Illustrated by Kam Mak. New York: HarperCollins, 1997.

Example of a Plot/Block Wall

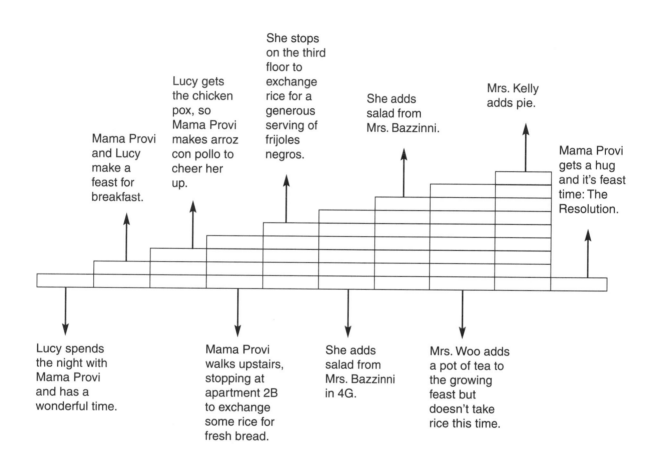

Example of a plot/block wall using *Mama Provi and the Pot of Rice.*

Lesson 17

Using Autobiographical Art

SKILL: Reinforcing Speaking and Listening Skills

CULTURE OF FOCUS: Greek

Materials

Marianthe's Story: One—Painted Words; Two—Spoken Memories, by Aliki (Greenwillow, 1998)

Personal pictures depicting interesting events in your life

Art materials for students to use to paint or draw pictures of events in their lives

Chart paper

Pens or pencils

Scratch paper for practice sketches and drafts of commentary to accompany the pictures for "Life Story Time" (see below)

Lesson Motivator

1. Mine the depths of personal memories within scrapbooks and photo albums of your life for major events and illuminating pictures that you would like to share with the students. Your goal is to bring a selection of pictures to class to relate events of your life as Marianthe does through her drawings.

2. Arrange the originals or photocopies of the originals in an artful collage to be displayed and closely examined at some point by students.

3. As you recount your story to the class, a good way to bring photographs and students into close proximity is to have each photograph enlarged and developed into a transparency, so everyone in the class can see them clearly. A local copy service can often do this for you relatively inexpensively.

Perhaps the best approach, though, is to draw those selected events from your life, because that will be the upcoming assignment for the class. There is much more credibility in what a teacher asks of his or her students if the teacher completes the assignment as well. This effort on the teacher's part sends a clear message about just how important the ensuing lesson is.

4. If you quail at the thought of drawing because you worry about the quality of your artwork, share those feelings with the class. Other hesitant artists will take heart and give it their best try if they know the teacher did so with misgivings as well. Make a point that the artwork is not what will be judged, but that genuine effort will earn kudos.

5. After conveying pertinent personal events of your life, introduce *Marianthe's Story: One—Painted Words*. Ask the students to listen to the story and think about what you have shown them and what Marianthe has to say about her life. Tell them that they will be depicting memorable events in their lives in the same way and to tuck that thought away as they listen. In this way you are setting the stage for the upcoming assignment, a part of "Life Story Time."

Suggestions for Teaching the Lesson

- Read *Marianthe's Story: One—Painted Words*. Spend some time chatting about Marianthe's experiences. Ask students if they can relate to anything in this story. What, in particular, stood out in the story for them? What words might they come up with to describe this main character? List the words on the board. Look over the words and put them into categories. Do those words describe characteristics of a person?

Do they describe emotions? Just what is the relationship between pictures and words? Leave the words on the board to be reviewed later and then read *Book Two—Spoken Memories.*

- Before reading, take a minute to discuss the interesting way in which this book has been created, with the stories back to back, one right-side up and the other upside down. Ask students if they see any advantages to marketing a book in this manner. This is one way to turn a critical eye on the world of book publishing.

- After reading about Marianthe's memories, begin a discussion of the kinds of events one remembers in one's life, based on what you recently related and the read-aloud. In those cases, were happy or sad memories more distinct than those involving common, daily events? Review the words on the board. Are there others to add now? What is the relationship between those words and one's memories? Students may come to the conclusion that emotions and memories seem to be closely related.

- Again, tie the book to students' lives. Ask listeners to reflect for a few minutes. What memories capture their attention as they look back at the past year? Several years ago? Take time for additional discussion. Were those personal events particularly happy or sad?

- Explain the upcoming assignment. Remind students that like Marianthe, everyone has a story to tell. In preparation for "Life Story Time," have students create a presentation for the class depicting a selected number of key events in their lives by capturing those times in pictures. The pictures, done using their own selection of art materials, will be supported by notes as a simplified form of spoken memories. The assignment will enable them to work with art to tell a story, give them practice in speaking in front of the class, and provide ample opportunity to fine-tune listening skills as they enjoy the visual and spoken stories of one another's lives. In fact, in the process of preparing for the work ahead and then presenting the final project, they are reinforcing all the closely related literacy skills. Remember, reading, writing, speaking, listening, and thinking are enhanced through authentic, engaging, creative work.

- Using a classroom collection of appropriate titles, briefly introduce other books about general or specific events remembered by a variety of characters. Then break into threes or fours to read a group-selected book together. The task at hand is to reflect on Marianthe's story and the additional title. First, have students brainstorm the kinds of occurrences that made up memories in the books. After that they can quickly record personal memories triggered by their reading, adding them to their brainstorming list.

- After an appropriate length of time, return to a large group session to pool ideas. Use chart paper to jot down key phrases or ideas for students to review later when they begin their personal reflections and generate memories to illustrate. Chat briefly about any events that need clarification, but don't dwell on contributions. Some of these may grow into a part of a classmate's story. This collective thinking process eases the stress for those students who simply cannot think of anything to draw because it presents a fertile planning ground from which everyone in the class can borrow at least one idea. Thus, no one is having to start with that ever-intimidating blank page.

- Send students to their desks to continue to work on their own.

Circulate through the room, providing guidance and support as needed. Monitor the progress of students from day to day as you set the stage for an upcoming celebration of self.

- Encourage the class to take their preliminary efforts home to discuss with parents or guardians. In this way initial ideas can be clarified and additional memories sparked, and the family is provided with an opportunity to be a part of this generative process.

- Post a schedule to be followed for various stages of the project to help students stay on task and on target for completion of their work. For example, a rough draft of six to eight events might be due first, preliminary sketches would follow, a draft of notes to accompany the pictures would be turned in for teacher-student discussion, and then all work would be polished for presentation in the form of the "Life Story."

Evaluation

- One useful way to take anecdotal notes on student work during a project such as this is by using 5-x-8-inch lined index cards and a standard clipboard. Use one card per student and arrange the cards in alphabetical order. Begin at the bottom of the clipboard, working backward through the alphabet, attaching the last name in the class to the clipboard with a 2- or 3-inch piece of clear tape. Line up the bottom of the board and the bottom of the index card.

- The next index card goes on top of the last one. You will need to gauge the appropriate space to get all the cards onto one clipboard. If class numbers are high, adjust the process and use two clipboards. Tape the second card at the top of the card to secure it to the clipboard. The remainder of the cards go on the same way, continuing in reverse alphabetical order.

- When the process is done, the first student in class will be the top card. You can quickly flip through the cards as you take notes on a student's progress. All the cards are handily arranged on a clipboard right at your fingertips. In addition, set up 5- to 10-minute conferences with each student to continue to monitor individual progress. That personal talk time is supportive for the students and informative for you. Focus on only one or two issues per conference so that the student leaves with a strong sense of direction.

Extensions

- Students may choose to write their stories out in more detail than they used when presenting the highlights of their lives during "Life Story Time." They can combine pictures and narratives in the same format as Aliki uses in this wonderful book. Completed books can be displayed in the classroom learning center for other students' enjoyment.

- Each author/illustrator can tape record his or her story so that other students can "reread" it along with the pictures in the reading center, another reinforcement of listening skills.

- Invite parents and guardians to tell snippets of stories of their lives.

- Send students to the library or the Internet to learn more about Aliki and what she has written. Have them share that information with the class.

Suggested Titles for Independent Reading and Research

Altman, Linda Jacobs. *Amelia's Road.* Illustrated by Enrique O. Sanchez. New York: Lee & Low, 1993.

Bartone, Elisa. *American Too.* Illustrated by Ted Lewin. New York: Lothrop, Lee & Shepard Books, 1996.

Belton, Sandra. *May'naise Sandwiches & Sunshine Tea.* Illustrated by Gail Gordon Carter. New York: Four Winds Press, 1994.

Bruchac, Joseph. *Fox Song.* Illustrated by Paul Morin. New York: Philomel, 1993.

Bunting, Eve. *Going Home.* Illustrated by David Diaz. New York: HarperCollins, 1996.

Calhoun, Mary. *Tonio's Cat.* Illustrated by Edward Martinez. New York: Morrow, 1996.

Cohen, Barbara. *Molly's Pilgrim.* Illustrated by Daniel Mark Duffy. New York: Lothrop, Lee & Shepard Books, 1983 (text), 1998 (illustrations).

Fox, Mem. *Whoever You Are.* Illustrated by Leslie Staub. San Diego, Calif.: Harcourt Brace, 1997.

Herron, Carolivia. *Nappy Hair.* Illustrated by Joe Cepeda. New York: Alfred A. Knopf, 1997.

Howard, Elizabeth Fitzgerald. *Aunt Flossie's Hats (and Crab Cakes Later).* Illustrated by James Ransome. New York: Clarion, 1991.

Knight, Margy Burns. *Who Belongs Here? An American Story.* Illustrated by Anne Sibley O'Brien. Gardiner, Maine: Tilbury House, 1993.

Larrabee, Lisa. *Grandmother Five Baskets.* Illustrated by Lori Sawyer. Tucson, Ariz.: Harbinger House, 1993.

London, Jonathan. *Ali, Child of the Desert.* Illustrated by Ted Lewin. New York: Lothrop, Lee & Shepard Books, 1997.

McCully, Emily Arnold. *Beautiful Warrior: The Legend of the Nun's Kung Fu.* New York: Scholastic, 1998.

Merrill, Jean. *The Girl Who Loved Caterpillars.* Illustrated by Floyd Cooper. New York: Philomel, 1992.

Mora, Pat. *Tomas and the Library Lady.* Illustrated by Raul Colon. New York: Alfred A. Knopf, 1997.

Nolen, Jerdine. *In My Momma's Kitchen.* Illustrated by Colin Bootman. New York: Lothrop, Lee & Shepard Books, 1999.

Pinkney, Andrea Davis. *Duke Ellington.* Illustrated by Brian Pinkney. New York: Scholastic, 1998.

Polacco, Patricia. *The Keeping Quilt.* New York: Simon & Schuster, 1988.

Say, Allen. *Tea with Milk.* Boston: Houghton Mifflin, 1999.

Schick, Eleanor. *My Navajo Sister.* New York: Simon & Schuster, 1996.

Shaik, Fatima. *The Jazz of Our Street.* Illustrated by E. B. Lewis. New York: Dial, 1998.

Steptoe, John. *Creativity.* Illustrated by E. B. Lewis. New York: Clarion, 1997.

Surat, Michele Maria. *Angel Child, Dragon Child.* Illustrated by Vo-Dinh Mai. New York: Scholastic, 1983.

Lesson 18

Using Multicultural Folktales

SKILL: Learning the Art of Retelling

CULTURE OF FOCUS: Asian/Japanese

Materials

The Funny Little Woman, retold by Arlene Mosel (Dutton/Penguin, 1972)

Belching Hill, by Morse Hamilton (Greenwillow, 1997)

Collection of folktales for guided practice and independent reading (see list at end of lesson)

Copies of prompts for retellings if desired (see below)

Chart paper or chalkboard

Tell Me a Tale: A Book about Storytelling, by Joseph Bruchac (Harcourt Brace, 1997) (teachers may draw ideas to share with their students from this valuable title)

Lesson Motivator

1. Teachers reach far back into the past when they pull this skill out of their teaching repertoire. Storytellers in one culture after another have practiced the art of retelling as they mesmerized listeners of all ages with tale after tale around blazing fires, both indoors and out. In the guise of a comprehension technique, retelling has been proven effective in improving comprehension when students review the story, providing them with an increased sense of text structure as they draw on information about setting, plot, and characters, and in further developing language skills. Finally, retellings direct students' attention to relevant information in fiction or nonfiction, a practical way to focus selective attention.

2. If possible, invite a storyteller into the classroom. You may find a local professional who is willing to donate his or her time, or enlist the services of another teacher who has practiced this art. A new face at the front of the classroom is often a motivator in itself. The storyteller could share with the class what kinds of preparations are made before telling a story and perhaps the origins of the story or stories to be told.

3. After this exciting visit, model the process of retelling a story using the Caldecott-winning focus book, *The Funny Little Woman*. Next, read a different version of the same tale, such as *Belching Hill*, explaining to the listeners that stories often change a little in the retelling. Ask them to watch

for similarities and differences between the two versions of the
same tale.

Suggestions for Teaching the Lesson

- Briefly discuss the two versions of
  this Japanese folktale. Encourage
  critical thinking by asking students which one they liked best
  and why. Then ask them if the
  basic story changed much in the
  retelling. Choose one version and
  proceed with the lesson.

- Explain the process of retelling to the
  students, discussing how it can be
  an aid to comprehension. Tell the
  students that it involves the
  process of retelling a story by hit-
  ting key points in a tale that one
  has read or heard. It is often used
  personally by a reader to monitor
  the understanding of a story just
  read or by a teacher who wishes
  to gain insight into a student's
  reading process.

- List the main points of the story on
  the board. Only these are used in
  a retelling. If the story is fictional,
  then the story problem, key plot
  episodes, resolution of the problem, and the ending are told. If
  the text is nonfiction, then the
  statement of main idea, details,
  sequential presentation, and brief
  description are included.

- Model the process by reading the
  focus book to the class so that they
  understand the story. Then close
  the book and retell the story yourself. Write your retelling next to the
  appropriate points on the board as
  a learning aid for the listeners.

- Give students individual copies of
  useful prompts to help them
  when they try retellings with a
  partner or small group. Fiction
  prompts include:

  1. When and where does the story
     take place? (setting)

  2. Who are the main characters?
     (characters)

  3. What action starts the story? (plot)

4. What happens next? (plot)

5. How does the story end? (plot)

Nonfiction prompts include:

1. What is the main point or main
   idea that the author is trying
   to convey?

2. What key details, facts, happen-
   ings, or examples are used to
   explain the main idea?

- Pick another title and read it to the
  class. On chart paper or the chalkboard, follow the prompts for a
  fictional selection and let the class
  retell the story. Ask students to
  volunteer for each section; the rest
  of the class can react to each con-
  tribution. This additional practice
  will make the students feel more
  confident when they attempt
  retellings on their own.

- Have students work in pairs and select a folktale from the preassembled collection reflecting a
  number of different cultures, read
  it together, and then take turns
  retelling the tale. This process requires one of the students to be an
  active listener, another important
  skill. Students can switch roles
  with the same tale or select another one for practice. Perhaps
  one student will choose a fictional
  retelling while another tries his or
  her hand with nonfiction.

- At any point during the retelling, if a
  student begins to have difficulty,
  the listening partner can ask a pertinent question. Questioning is a
  key way to draw out information
  that the student knows but may
  not have at his or her fingertips.

Evaluation

- Move about the room as students
  work in pairs, jotting down notes
  about each learner's progress toward the acquisition of this skill.

- Spend some time with each student
  in the class, having each retell a
  major portion of a tale he or she
  has read to monitor the ability to

apply this skill. To facilitate this process when working with the whole class, ask for major ideas or look at the story grammar components. Again, use questioning to assess whether the student actually has the information and has just forgotten, or whether it has been completely missed during the reading of the story. The latter case might indicate a need to spend some time modeling and reteaching an aspect of comprehension that the student has not grasped. It could also mean that the student is not comprehending the story for some other reason and a closer evaluation is needed.

- Students may tape the retelling process with a classmate or during the teacher assessment and keep this sample as part of their portfolios.

Extensions

- Develop a storytelling troupe and have students entertain in classrooms throughout the building or move outside the realm of the school and make periodic visits to retirement communities.

- After reading a folktale in a small group setting, have each student pick a scene to illustrate and use the illustrations as props when retelling the story to the class. Each student should take part in the retelling as well as the illustrating.

- While a narrator retells the story, have a small group of students act it out using pantomime.

- Students can work with their parents or grandparents to learn a tale that reflects their culture. After recording the story, a student should practice storytelling skills and share the story with the class.

- Have students research elements that are important to their particular culture and write an original folktale complete with illustrations.

- Have students work with a partner or a small group to illustrate

favorite parts of a story. They can accompany the artwork with a practiced rereading on an audiotape, to be presented to a lower-grade classroom for use in their reading center.

Suggested Titles for Independent Reading and Research

Aardema, Verna, reteller. *Borreguita and the Coyote.* Illustrated by Petra Mathers. New York: Alfred A. Knopf, 1991.

———. *Why Mosquitoes Buzz in People's Ears: A West African Tale.* Illustrated by Leo Dillon and Diane Dillon. New York: Dial, 1975.

Climo, Shirley. *The Korean Cinderella.* Illustrated by Ruth Heller. New York: Harper, 1993.

Cohen, Caron Lee, reteller. *The Mud Pony.* Illustrated by Shonto Begay. New York: Scholastic, 1988.

dePaola, Tomie, reteller. *The Legend of the Indian Paintbrush.* New York: Putnam, 1988.

Hoffman, Mary, reteller. *Clever Katya: A Fairy Tale from Old Russia.* Illustrated by Marie Cameron. New York: Barefoot Books, 1998.

Jaffe, Nina. *The Golden Flower: A Taino Myth from Puerto Rico.* Illustrated by Enrique O. Sanchez. New York: Simon & Schuster, 1996.

———, reteller. *The Way Meat Loves Salt: A Cinderella Tale from the Jewish Tradition.* Illustrated by Louise August. New York: Henry Holt, 1998.

Jones, Jennifer Berry, reteller. *Heetunka's Harvest: A Tale of the Plains Indians.* Illustrated by Shannon Keegan. Niwot, Colo.: Roberts Rinehart Publishers, 1998.

Kimmel, Eric A., reteller. *Anansi and the Moss-Covered Rock.* Illustrated by Janet Stevens. New York: Holiday House, 1988.

———. *Anansi Goes Fishing.* Illustrated by Janet Stevens. New York: Holiday House, 1992.

Lottridge, Celia Barker. *The Name of the Tree: A Bantu Folktale.* Illustrated by Ian Wallace. New York: McElderry, 1989.

Martin, Rafe. *The Boy Who Lived with the Seals.* Illustrated by David Shannon. New York: Putnam, 1993.

Melmed, Laura Krauss. *Little Oh.* Illustrated by Jim Lamarche. New York: Lothrop, Lee & Shepard/Morrow, 1997.

Oughton, Jerrie. *How the Stars Fell into the Sky.* Illustrated by Lisa Desimini. Boston: Houghton Mifflin, 1992.

Soto, Gary. *The Old Man and His Door.* Illustrated by Joe Cepeda. New York: Putnam, 1996.

Waite, Michael P. *Jojofu.* Illustrated by Yoriko Ito. New York: Lothrop, Lee & Shepard Books, 1996.

Wisniewski, David. *The Warrior and the Wise Man.* New York: Mulberry, 1998.

Wolkstein, Diane. *White Wave.* Illustrated by Ed Young. San Diego, Calif.: Harcourt Brace, 1996.

Yep, Laurence. *The Dragon Prince: A Chinese Beauty and the Beast Tale.* Illustrated by Kam Mak. New York: HarperCollins, 1997.

Lesson 19

Using the Story Cube

SKILL: Facilitating Personal Response

CULTURE OF FOCUS: Japanese

Materials

Tea with Milk, by Allèn Say (Houghton Mifflin, 1999)
Tagboard for patterns
12-x-18-inch sheets of good-quality white or light-colored construction paper
Pens and pencils
Art supplies
Overhead projector or chalkboard

Lesson Motivator

1. Construct an example of the story cube (see instructions at end of lesson) but leave the sides blank. Show it to the students and explain that it is an invitation to respond to a book. The blank sides need to be filled with thoughts and feelings about a special book.

2. Show the class what you mean by passing around a cube that you have completed based on a favorite picture book. Explain your reactions, both intellectual and emotional, as expressed through simple illustrations, a favorite quotation, a personal connection with the story, and your idea of why the author might have written the book, as depicted on various sides of your finished product.

3. Spend a short time discussing reader response with the students. Remind them that they are one critical piece in making meaning from a story. The author and his or her words, along with the illustrators and their artistic interpretation of a tale, provide additional pieces to the reading puzzle. What is important to remember is that readers bring their backgrounds of varied life experiences to a book and those backgrounds add a distinct flavor to the way a reader interprets the words penned by an author.

4. Tell the students that because reading is a transaction between the reader and an author, it is as if a slightly new version of the story is read every time a different person picks up that book. No wonder there isn't just one interpretation of a book, as many of us were once taught, because each of us sees the story cast in the light of our own life experiences. Remind the students that discussing stories based on individual perspectives can be enlightening for everyone in the class.

5. Emphasize to the readers that they are not to fear being right or wrong when offering their responses to what they have just read. Individual reflections will be honored in the classroom.

6. Focus the students' attention on *Tea with Milk*. Explain that it is based on Allen Say's mother's memories.

7. Ask students to listen for the differences and similarities between their personal cultural beliefs and those represented in the book. Tell them that you will be discussing their personal responses to this piece of literature, both intellectual and emotional, after the story is completed.

Suggestions for Teaching the Lesson

- Read the book to the class, pausing to let the listeners study the pictures for a short time. Once the story is done, encourage responses.

- As students react, ask them to decide if their response is an intellectual one or an emotional one. Reinforce the fact that we respond to what we read in both ways. You might discuss the differences between Japanese cultural beliefs and those commonly held in the

United States. How might students feel if they were in May's shoes? Do they have similar conflicts between family cultural beliefs and what they believe is important? In their opinion, what is the best way to resolve such differences? *Tea with Milk* should prompt a lively dialogue between classmates.

- Draw the students' attention to the array of books assembled for their individual reading. Request help from the librarian or learning center director to gather thought-provoking, wonderfully written picture books. Highlight as many of them as time allows, then let the students browse. Each student should select a title that is personally appealing, return to a comfortable area, and read.

- Suggest that readers use scratch paper to record their responses to the book once it is completed. They could also work in pairs, discussing the titles they have read with another classmate and thinking out loud about what the book has to say. Then have them begin on their story cubes to take their personal responses from private to public in an attractive and perceptive way. Knowing that their thoughts and feelings will be published is one way to encourage students to stay fully engaged with their reading. Engagement is further facilitated because students are able to choose a book of particular interest to them and will have an opportunity to reflect upon its relevance to their lives. If they are not engaged in their reading, asking for quality responses from students is futile.

- When a number of the students are ready to create their cubes, present a brief mini-lesson using the chalkboard or overhead, on which you will have put the directions for completing the story cube. Have students take turns using a dozen or so previously prepared tagboard patterns to make their own cubes on construction paper of their choice. Students should lightly number the squares as designated:
  1. Title and author of the book the student has read
  2. Favorite scene or part
  3. Key quote or idea
  4. A brief answer to "What do you think the author was trying to say in this book?"
  5. A sentence or two about an experience the student has had that is similar to one in the book
  6. Reader's choice (have students complete this side as desired)

- Before cutting out the cube, students should fill in the squares as noted. They can add simple, appealing artwork before finally assembling the cube. After they cut out the square, have them fold along the lines to shape the cube. Next they should fold the tabs under and add a little glue or tape to hold the sides in place so that a cube is formed.

- Students may choose to discuss their cubes in small groups. An attractive way to display the completed shapes is to arrange five of them into a mobile, using hangers for the base and colored thread to attach the squares. Hang each completed mobile from the ceiling for optimal viewing. The squares can also be displayed attractively on a shelf so that class members can pick each one up and study it. In addition, each reader can briefly book-talk his or her book and share a favorite side of the cube with the class.

Evaluation

- Create a simple rubric for this activity based on class input. Because it is unfair to grade subjective responses, criteria can include neatness, the thought that went into the cube, the accuracy of spelling and sentence construction, and the quality of a short book talk if that becomes a part of sharing the cube with the class.

- On a sheet designated for each student, make anecdotal notes about the effort and quality of thinking that was exhibited during this response activity. Note whether the student is able to work through this type of activity independently or if he or she achieves better results by talking through thoughts with a classmate. You are not making a positive or negative assessment but rather just noting insights about the student as a reader.

- Meet individually with students to discuss observations and abilities that each student is acquiring. Make personal evaluation a part of the conference by asking the reader to assess his or her progress. Build additional strategy development for students from this growing base.

Extensions

- Take this activity to the lower grades. Older students can partner with younger students, read a book together, and complete the cube. The upper-grade student is there for guidance rather than to interpret the book or alter a child's personal response to it. Have students share the results with the rest of the class.

- Give students who like to talk about what they are reading an opportunity to read a novel together and use "buddy" journals. In these journals, they write back and forth to each other about their reactions to what they have read during silent reading in class or at home the night before.

- Have each student keep his or her own journal in which to record thoughts. Have students exchanges journals and write back to their partners, then return the journals to the owners. This reading-responding cycle should continue.

- If buddy journals are used on a wider scale, gather a few journals at a time to monitor the reading-writing process. Jot down a constructive, positive comment on an appropriate page periodically and date your entries. This monitoring process shows that you find journaling to be a valuable use of time. It also tends to keep the written conversation focused on the book at hand.

- In a response journal or as a piece of narrative writing, have students pen thoughts about a personal experience triggered by one of the books read recently.

Suggested Titles for Independent Reading and Research

Bahous, Sally. *Sitti and the Cats: A Tale of Friendship.* Illustrated by Nancy Malick. Niwot, Colo.: Roberts Rinehart Publishers, 1997.

Berkeley, Laura. *The Seeds of Peace.* Illustrated by Alison Dexter. New York: Barefoot Books, 1999.

Coerr, Eleanor. *Sadako.* Illustrated by Ed Young. New York: Putnam, 1993.

Davol, Marguerite. *The Paper Dragon.* Illustrated by Robert Sabuda. New York: Atheneum, 1997.

Fleming, Virginia. *Be Good to Eddie Lee.* Illustrated by Floyd Cooper. New York: Philomel, 1993.

Hearne, Betsy. *Seven Brave Women.* Illustrated by Bethanne Andersen. New York: Greenwillow, 1997.

Hoffman, Mary. *Amazing Grace.* Illustrated by Caroline Binch. New York: Dial, 1991.

———. *Clever Katya: A Fairy Tale from Old Russia.* Illustrated by Marie Cameron. New York: Barefoot Books, 1998.

Howard, Elizabeth Fitzgerald. *Virgie Goes to School with Us Boys.* Illustrated by E. B. Lewis. New York: Simon & Schuster, 2000.

Lacapa, Kathleen, and Michael Lacapa. *Less Than Half, More Than Whole.* Flagstaff, Ariz.: Northland Publishing, 1994.

Lears, Laurie. *Ian's Walk: A Story about Autism.* Illustrated by Katen Ritz. Morton Grove, Ill.: Albert Whitman, 1998.

Matthews, Caitlin. *The Blessing Seed: A Creation Myth for the New Millennium.* Illustrated by Alison Dexter. New York: Barefoot Books, 1998.

Mayer, Mercer. *Shibumi and the Kitemaker.* New York: Marshall Cavendish, 1999.

Myers, Walter Dean. *Harlem.* Illustrated by Christopher Myers. New York: Scholastic, 1997.

Polacco, Patricia. *The Bee Tree.* New York: Philomel, 1993.

Robb, Laura. *Music and Drum: Voices of War and Peace, Hope and Dreams.* Illustrated by Debra Lill. New York: Putnam, 1997.

Savageau, Cheryl. *Muskrat Will Be Swimming.* Illustrated by Robert Hynes. Flagstaff, Ariz.: Northland Publishing, 1996.

Shange, Ntozake. *White Wash.* Illustrated by Michael Sporn. New York: Walker, 1997.

Sikundar, Sylvia. *Forest Singer.* Illustrated by Alison Astill. New York: Barefoot Books, 1999.

Soros, Barbara. *Grandmother's Song.* Illustrated by Jackie Morris. New York: Barefoot Books, 1998.

Wood, Douglas. *Grandad's Prayers of the Earth.* Illustrated by P. J. Lynch. Cambridge, Mass.: Candlewick Press, 1999.

Wyeth, Sharon, Dennis. *Something Beautiful.* Illustrated by Chris K. Soentpiet. New York: Delacorte, 1998.

Story Cube Pattern

Enlarge pattern to easily fit a 12-x-18-inch piece of construction paper. Each square will measure $3\frac{1}{2}$ inches by $3\frac{1}{2}$ inches. Tabs to be folded under for construction will go at the top and on the side squares. Tabs measure $\frac{1}{2}$ inch each. Fold along the solid lines to create a cube shape.

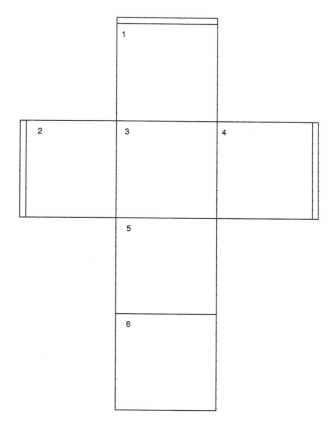

Section III

Working with Expository Text Structures

EXPOSITORY TEXT: AN OVERVIEW

How does the brain work? Why are the kachinas so important to the Hopi people? How does the lead get into a pencil? How fast do hummingbirds' wings move? Questions, questions! The road to most of the answers is paved with expository text—fact-filled content-area textbooks and millions of fascinating informational books from quality picture books to weighty tomes. Many a reader can get lost in the world of expository books as easily as others become wrapped up in a novel. In fact, in most libraries the shelf space devoted to these informational volumes is much greater than that set aside for fictional titles. Imagine how that space will continue to grow in light of the way knowledge is expanding exponentially.

Although wise teachers integrate narrative books into the curriculum to add depth to the topic under study, the standard educational fare continues to be the textbook. It is filled with expository text coupled with explanatory charts, tables, pictures, and diagrams. Bold-faced type often signals the reader that successive chunks of information within a chapter are related. Filled with vocabulary unique to the subject being discussed and concepts that are often abstract, this text structure is designed to convey information in a much different format than that of the narrative text structure so familiar in fictional offerings. The latter is easier to understand because it typically has a beginning, a middle, and an end—a structure very familiar to readers. The author's purpose in this case is to form a partnership of sorts with the reader, transporting him or her to fictional but believable times and places through a well-wrought plot and memorable characters.

Expository text, however, can be more confusing to unravel because the information may be presented via a number of formats, including description, problem and solution, question and answer, comparison and contrast, cause and effect, a time-order sequence, or the listing of particular attributes. Research underscores the fact that understanding how expository text is structured will help readers comprehend it. By modeling various strategies to decode the text and providing time for invaluable practice of those strategies, teachers will be giving students practical tools to use for the rest of their lives.

One such tool is the graphic organizer, which comes in a number of formats. Put simply, a graphic organizer is a map or graph that summarizes the information to be learned. It can show relationships between ideas being studied as well. This visual representation of information matches the brain's schema well because it aids learners in integrating new knowledge with the old. Such organizers might be in the shape of an outline, an anticipation guide, a semantic map, or a chart helping students understand comparison and contrast. There is more to being able to understand the text, of course. To cement knowledge, students should do something with the knowledge they are acquiring. In addition to group or class discussions, they can write about what they have just learned, create a riveting display on a topic, or give a speech to the class using information recently gathered. Examples of several practical graphic organizers and valuable extension activities follow in the suggested lessons.

Uncovering and organizing the facts presented within a textbook or informational book can be an adventure rather than a bewildering task if teachers take the time to teach the appropriate strategies. The goal is to prepare strategic readers who know that they need to vary their rate of reading depending upon the complexity of the materials at hand. These readers use metacognition, aware that they are in charge of their learning and need to recognize when understanding is failing. Then they can choose a strategy to help them get back on track. They know how to evaluate their learning and ask, "What is not working here and what am I going to do about it?" Strategic readers remain undaunted by expository text structures because wise teachers have prepared them well. Armed with the best tools available to ferret out and connect facts, learners will be able put that information to use in any arena of their lives.

Lesson 20

Expository Text Structure

SKILL: Examining Clustering

CULTURE OF FOCUS: Italian

Materials

American Too, by Elisa Bartone; illustrated by Ted Lewin (Lothrop, Lee & Shepard Books, 1996)
Copies of the "Clustering Practice Sheet" (see end of lesson) or pattern guides on listing and clustering
Scratch paper
Pens and pencils
Chart paper, overhead projector, or chalkboard

Lesson Motivator

1. Ask students to take a few minutes to think about what it means to be an American. What might be some advantages? Disadvantages?

2. Brainstorm together, recording answers on the chalkboard, overhead, or chart paper. Go back through the ideas listed and group related items together.

3. Using a pattern like the one on the "Clustering Practice Sheet" at the end of this lesson, demonstrate how the main thought could be placed at the center, with related ideas radiating around the outside. This is called clustering. It is a useful way to coordinate details when studying expository or nonfiction materials. It is also a helpful technique when organizing thoughts before a writing assignment.

4. Model an example of clustering using a topic with which the students are familiar. Perhaps they can look at the weather and its effect on daily events where they live. If snow is central to the winter season, put *snow* in the oval on the chalkboard and have students suggest details to surround this topic. Lunch period or a typical school day might be other topics upon which students could elaborate.

5. Introduce the book for the day's lesson, *American Too,* setting the tone by explaining the time period, the topic covered, and that the story actually happened, before beginning the story.

Suggestions for Teaching the Lesson

- Read through the book, stopping to discuss points students seem particularly interested in. Allow time to chat about the book and student reactions before continuing the lesson.

- Explain that the comprehension skill to be taught or reviewed is that of organizing details or relating items to one another by using clustering, as mentioned in the introduction to the lesson. In textbooks, signal words for upcoming details that are important to remember include "for example" or "characteristics are." Clustering helps a reader to define or describe an object, event, or concept. In this book, students will be going back and looking at different events that celebrate Rosina's life as an Italian even though she has decided that she no longer wants to be different from everyone else.

- Students will need notebook paper and the guided practice sheets. Read the first five pages of the story again. Have students write down on notebook paper behaviors or beliefs in Rosina's life that she wants to change. For example, she wore a red coral horn around her neck to ward off the evil eye.

Apparently she was superstitious and believed that anything red would protect her. Her doll had an Italian name, Alessandra, but she changed its name to Meghan O'Hara. In an oval, write *changes* and encircle it with the changes that students have noted.

- Direct students' attention to the practice sheets. Look at the categories to be detailed, which will eventually form clusters of information. Although other main topics could be chosen, for the sake of practice use behaviors, foods, traditions, and the feast. As you reread the rest of the book, have students jot down details around the appropriate category.

- Once the story is completed, compare guided practice sheets, going from category to category and filling in a duplicate on the overhead or on large chart paper to be saved for reference when students tackle this skill on their own.

- When you are certain that students understand clustering and how important this particular text structure is in aiding their comprehension of expository materials, give them an opportunity to practice the skill with a book of their own choosing. They may work individually, in pairs, or in trios.

Evaluation

- Review the completed practice sheets to assess students' understanding. Give them additional practice in the day's social studies or science assignment.

- Solidify students' understanding by using this skill in a content area later in the week. Point out that in a textbook, students might use headings or subtopic headings in dark print for their categories or items at the center of their cluster formation.

Extensions

- Have students ask questions at home about their ancestors and their family tree. They might like to bring in old photographs or an item that has long been in the family to share with the class. Depending on the item, it may be wise to have a parent bring in the item and relate a family story about it. Countries where families originated could be identified on a world map.

- Present a mock telephone conversation with the main character in the book, having two students role-play the call. Talk about ways to maintain one's heritage and celebrate it while still being part of a new culture.

- If possible, have a "taste-fest," savoring some of the items described in the book.

- Have students act out this story using simple props. Artistic students may enjoy creating a backdrop of Little Italy with the Statue of Liberty somewhere in the background.

- Have students interview a person from the Italian culture and share their insights with the class. They should also make a personally decorated thank-you note or card and mail it to the person interviewed.

- Have other students research Italian folktales and present a book talk on one to the class.

Suggested Titles for Independent Reading and Research

Ammon, Richard. *An Amish Wedding.* Illustrated by Pameal Patrick. New York: Atheneum, 1998.

Ancona, George. *Barrio: Jose's Neighborhood.* San Diego, Calif.: Harcourt Brace, 1998.

———. *Pablo Remembers: The Fiesta of the Day of the Dead.* New York: Lothrop, Lee & Shepard Books, 1993.

Bartone, Elisa. *Peppe the Lamplighter.* Illustrated by Ted Lewin. New York: Lothrop, Lee & Shepard Books, 1993.

Brown, Tricia. *Konnichiwa! I Am a Japanese-American Girl.* Illustrated with photographs by Kazuyoshi Arai. New York: Henry Holt, 1995.

Cha, Dia. *Dia's Story Cloth: The Hmong People's Journey of Freedom.* Illustrated by Chue Thao Cha and Nhia Thao Cha. New York: Lee & Low, 1996.

Hoyt-Goldsmith, Diane. *Arctic Hunter.* Illustrated with photographs by Lawrence Migdale. New York: Holiday House, 1992.

————. *Celebrating Chinese New Year.* Illustrated with photographs by Lawrence Migdale. New York: Holiday House, 1998.

Moyse, Sarah. *Chinese New Year.* Brookfield, Conn.: Millbrook Press, 1998.

O'Connor, Karen. *Dan Thuy's New Life in America.* Minneapolis, Minn.: Lerner, 1992.

Peters, Russell M. *Clambake: A Wampanoag Tradition.* Illustrated with photographs by John Madama. Minneapolis, Minn.: Lerner, 1992.

Pinkney, Andrea. *Bill Pickett, Rodeo-Ridin' Cowboy.* Illustrated by Brian Pinkney. San Diego, Calif.: Gulliver/Harcourt Brace, 1996.

Roessel, Monty. *Kinaaldá: A Navajo Girl Grows Up.* Minneapolis, Minn.: Lerner, 1993.

Sneve, Virginia Driving Hawk. *The Cherokees.* Illustrated by Ronald Himler. New York: Holiday House, 1996.

————. *The Navajos.* Illustrated by Ronald Himler. New York: Holiday House, 1993.

————. *The Seminoles.* Illustrated by Ronald Himler. New York: Holiday House, 1994.

Towle, Wendy. *The Real McCoy: The Life of an African-American Inventor.* Illustrated by Wil Clay. New York: Scholastic, 1993.

Wesley, Valerie. *Freedom's Gifts: A Juneteenth Story.* Illustrated by Sharon Wilson. New York: Simon & Schuster, 1997.

Clustering Practice Sheet

Clustering Using *American Too,* by Elisa Bartone

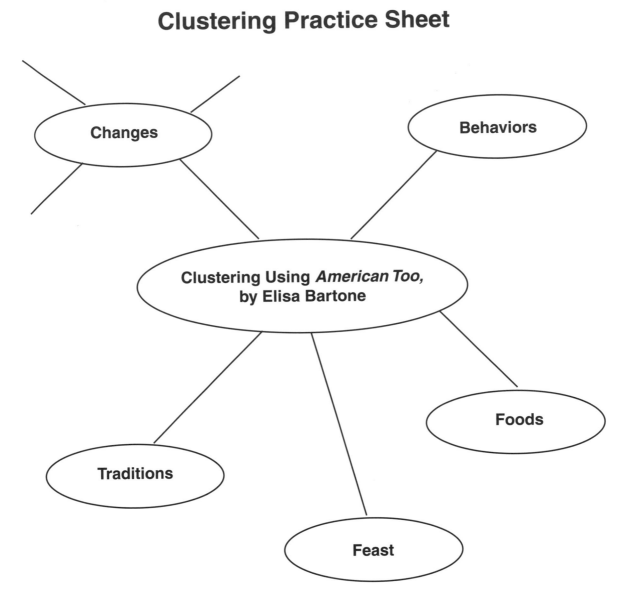

Clustering Practice Sheet

Changes

Behaviors

Clustering Using *American Too,*
by Elisa Bartone

Foods

Traditions

Feast

Lesson 21

Using Biographies and a Positive-Negative Graph to Inspire Writing

SKILL: Developing a Graph to Organize Personal Writing

CULTURE OF FOCUS: African American

Materials

> *Women of Hope: African Americans Who Made a Difference,* by Joyce Hansen (Scholastic, 1998)
> Scratch paper for note-taking
> Pens and pencils
> Butcher or chart paper
> Graph paper for constructing positive-negative graphs
> Colored pencils or fine-line markers
> Posterboard or materials to be used to display the final product
> Overhead projector or chalkboard

Lesson Motivator

1. Ask the students to take out their journals or a piece of notebook paper. They should spend the next few minutes thinking about someone whom they consider to be a hero or heroine. That person may be someone the student knows personally or an individual often seen in the public eye. To stimulate thinking, initiate a brief dialogue about what a hero or a heroine is.

2. Write comments down on the board or overhead. One query to foster thinking is: What does a person do to earn the distinction of being a hero or heroine? Another is: What characteristics or qualities seem to be inherent in these potential role models?

3. Have students return to their personal journals or notebook paper to pursue individual lines of thinking. After a designated time, ask students to discuss what they have written.

4. As students reveal their personal heroes or heroines, list the names, the accomplishments, and the distinctive characteristics that these people display. Based on careful thinking, students must justify their choices with solid arguments supporting the hero/heroine status that their person has earned.

5. Select a woman from *Women of Hope,* showing her picture and then reading about her. As you read, ask the students to list the characteristics or qualities that earned that woman a right to be in this book.

6. Compare the new list with the one generated. Viewing all the information together, encourage the students to form a generalization or two about what a hero/heroine is.

7. Write the students' ideas on butcher paper to be posted for easy viewing during the remainder of the lesson. Tell the class that in their upcoming work they will be proving those generalizations or supporting them with additional information.

Suggestions for Teaching the Lesson

- Read another selection from *Women of Hope.* This time, ask students to jot down notes on the positive and negative factors in this woman's life.

- In addition, have students pinpoint any other distinctive qualities that they ascertain about this specific woman. Once you have completed the reading selection, list students' contributions on the board under the categories "positive factors," "negative factors," and "qualities of a heroine."

- Discuss with the class how they feel about the negatives that have been noted. In their opinions, might the difficult experiences have actually been the fuel to propel the individual to reach heroine status?

- Ask students to reflect on something negative that has happened in their lives. Over time, how did that event fit into the picture of their lives, up to this point at least? After some thinking time, generate a class discussion on the impact of negative factors in their lives. Are they better because of it? Was there a valuable lesson to be learned? Should negative experiences be an excuse not to excel? Why or why not? This could prove to be a lively discussion! At the conclusion of this talk time, request that students watch for and examine the effects that negative events have had on the people they will eventually be researching.

- Hand out practice sheets of 8 1/2-x-11-inch graph paper. Explain that although graphing skills are usually the domain of other subject areas such as math, science, or social studies, they also can be integrated into reading and writing in an interesting way. In her book *Seeking Diversity: Language Arts for Adolescents,* Linda Rief describes the graphing process as a way to generate materials for a student's personal writing. It can easily be adapted for this lesson.

- Have the students go back to their list of positive and negative events in the life of one of the heroines you have just shared. Ask learners to put an asterisk next to the event that was the most positive and the one that was the most negative, and then rank those that are remaining.

Review each category and see if a consensus can be reached, at least as far as the asterisked items. Then list the positives and the negatives on the board for reference.

- Working on the overhead or chart paper, model the following process while the students do likewise on their chart paper. Draw a line on the horizontal axis through the middle of the graph paper, as depicted in the "Sample Positive-Negative Graph" diagram at the end of this lesson. Label that line "Years." The years can be grouped as childhood, adolescence, twenties, thirties, and so forth. The designation will depend on how specific the information is that students will glean from their reading. In future research this line might better be labeled "Age" when the students develop their own personal graphs. From that line upward, write the numbers +1, +2, +3, +4, and +5 after discussing how far apart to space them on the graph paper. Students should leave several graph lines between each number to allow for a little writing and a small drawing near each graph dot. Write "Positive" along the edge of that line, the vertical axis. From the middle line downward, write the negative numbers from -1 to -5, writing "Negative" on that line.

- On this practice sheet there will only be a few events to depict. Review the basics of working with graphs to be certain students remember how to record the information. Then have students plot or chart the positive and negative events on the graph, matching approximate year and intensity of the event. If an event was a major, life-altering situation, it might be ranked at a positive or negative 5, depending on the event. If is was just a little good, or a little discomforting, it might be ranked at a plus or minus 1. Students can confer in small groups to decide on the strength of the event during this practice session. They should connect the first dot plotted to the second, the second to the third, and so forth, as the diagram indicates.

- Next, have students write a few key words to explain the placement of each dot. Using colored pencils or fine-line markers, they should draw or sketch a small, simple picture next to the plotted dot to illustrate that event.

- Once the practice graph is completed, talk about the values of constructing a visual picture of a person's life like this one. Certainly, it can prove to be an interesting overview. It also can help the investigation of a person's life by getting the thought processes flowing as a student begins to wonder what else might be interesting about the hero/heroine. How could the gaps on this particular chart be filled in? In addition, this is a visual aid to the writing process because it helps students organize their thinking, putting life events in order before they place pen to paper to write.

- Ask for questions and clarify any confusion about the use of graphs to record or to analyze important events in a person's life.

- Book-talk biographies or autobiographies from a collection of books about potential heroes and heroines from numerous cultures. These will be the fodder for future investigations of some fascinating individuals. Students may choose one of these people to scrutinize further or they may select an ancestor, relative, or family friend. There is a fascinating listing of more outstanding women from a variety of fields at the conclusion of *Women of Hope* that students might use as a reference.

- Student researchers will start with a well-crafted picture book biography or autobiography, an excellent introduction to the person whom they consider to be a hero or heroine. Then they will seek out more advanced materials to get a broader picture of that person. They should be cautioned to read critically and to compare the information they are gathering from various resources. If they come up against contradictions, discuss how they might resolve the problem. For the next part of this lesson they should read, carefully gather data until their curiosity about the individual is satisfied, and then go back through their notes to ferret out the important positive and negative factors. In the process, they should also list qualities that emerge that set this person apart from others and earn him or her the distinction of being considered a hero or heroine.

- After data collection, the next step is to create an appealing, neatly done positive-negative graph on the individual, complete with tiny illustrations or sketches as appropriate. This work becomes a rough draft of a different sort from which to write a poem or a short paper on the emerging hero/heroine, the final stage of the lesson.

- Polished written work plus a picture or photo if it is possible to get one, should be artfully displayed in poster format. A unique overview of the person's life, the neatly done graph, should be included as well.

- Spend some time over several mornings or afternoons celebrating the heroes and heroines in the students' lives. End the sharing session by listing the criteria that made every person special.

- As a wrap-up activity, check the generalization(s) made at the beginning of this lesson and adjust them as needed. Focus a discussion on those qualities and then reinforce them by designing a banner to encircle the room. Highlighting these attributes for everyone to ponder day after day may inspire students to assimilate a few into their own lives.

Evaluation

- Work with the students ahead of time to establish the criteria for evaluation of a project that is this time-consuming. Obviously, the writing process used in the classroom would be a part of this, but there is the addition of the graph. The teacher may insist on neatness, accuracy, and a specific number of bits of information on the graph for a certain grade. What do students think of these criteria?

- Include criteria on the quality of the presentation about the hero or heroine to the class. Clear speaking, obvious knowledge of the hero or heroine, and an inviting poster should be considered.

- Prepare a handout of the evaluation criteria to be placed in writing folders. When the students complete this project, they should evaluate themselves first, giving careful thought to the quality of their efforts and the resulting product. Conference individually with each student and add your thoughts on the work. Between the two of you, a valid assessment will be achieved.

Extensions

- Students can use the graph approach to write an autobiography. In getting started with this project, Linda Rief asks her students to list 21 of the best things that have ever happened to them. After giving them time to think, she asks them to turn their notebook paper over and list 17 of the worst things that have ever happened to them. Next they are to review

each list and mark the three most positive and the three most negative things with asterisks. Finally, they decide which other events were quite significant.

- The next step is to have students turn to the chart, plotting and graphing the events as they did for the previous lesson. They should illustrate the graphs neatly, adding color with colored pencils or fine-line markers. Using the selected incidents, students can write a poem about their lives based upon elements in the graph or write a longer autobiography. Display the polished writing and appealing graph together on a bulletin board or in a class album highlighting each person in the class.

- At another time during the year, pair up students to write each other's biographies following the same format.

- Have students write a poem about an exemplary role model.

- Ask students to write a newspaper article about a hero or heroine, addressing the key questions: who, what, where, when, and why.

- Have students interview a classmate in the role of hero or heroine in a format like that used in a popular television talk or news show, such as *20/20*.

Suggested Titles for Independent Reading and Research

Adler, David A. *A Picture Book of Simon Bolivar*. Illustrated by Robert Casilla. New York: Holiday House, 1992.

Brighton, Catherine. *Nijinsky: Scenes from a Childhood of a Great Dancer*. New York: Doubleday, 1989.

Bruchac, Joseph. *A Boy Called Slow: The True Story of Sitting Bull*. Illustrated by Rocco Baviera. New York: Philomel, 1994.

Coleman, Evelyn. *The Riches of Oseola McCarty*. Illustrated by Daniel Minter. Morton Grove, Ill.: Albert Whitman, 1998.

Coles, Robert. *The Story of Ruby Bridges*. New York: Scholastic, 1995.

Cooper, Floyd. *Coming Home: From the Life of Langston Hughes*. New York: Philomel, 1994.

Crews, Donald. *Bigmama's*. New York: Greenwillow, 1991.

Demi. *Buddha*. New York: Henry Holt, 1996.

———. *Chingis Khan*. New York: Henry Holt, 1991.

Feelings, Tom. *Black Pilgrimage*. New York: Lothrop, Lee & Shepard Books, 1972.

Ferris, Jeri. *Native American Doctor: The Story of Susan LaFlesche Picotte*. Minneapolis, Minn.: Carolrhoda, 1991.

Fradin, Dennis Brindell. *Hiawatha: Messenger of Peace*. New York: McElderry, 1992.

———. *Sacagawea: The Journey to the West*. Illustrated by Nora Koerber. New York: Silver Press/Simon & Schuster, 1997.

Glassman, Bruce. *Wilma Mankiller: Chief of a Cherokee Nation*. New York: Rosen/Blackbirch Press, 1992.

Golenbock, Peter. *Teammates*. Illustrated by Paul Bacon. San Diego, Calif.: Gulliver, 1990.

Grimes, Nikki. *A Dime a Dozen*. Illustrated by Angelo. New York: Dial, 1998.

Hearne, Betsy. *Seven Brave Women*. Illustrated by Bethanne Andersen. New York: Greenwillow, 1997.

Hilts, Len. *Quanah Parker*. San Diego, Calif.: Gulliver, 1987.

King, Martin Luther, Jr. *I Have a Dream*. Various illustrators. New York: Scholastic, 1997.

Krull, Kathleen. *Wilma Unlimited: How Wilma Rudolph Became the World's Fastest Woman*. San Diego, Calif.: Harcourt Brace, 1996.

Lester, Julius. *Black Cowboy, Wild Horses: A True Story*. Illustrated by Jerry Pinkney. New York: Dial/Penguin, 1998.

Lindbergh, Reeve. *Nobody Owns the Sky: The Story of "Brave Bessie" Coleman*. Illustrated by Pamela Paparone. New York: Candlewick Press, 1996.

Livingston, Myra Cohn. *Let Freedom Ring: A Ballad of Martin Luther King, Jr.* Illustrated by Samuel Byrd. New York: Holiday House, 1992.

Medearis, Angela Shelf. *Princess of the Press: The Story of Ida B. Wells-Barnett*. New York: Lodestar/Dutton, 1997.

Meltzer, Milton, ed. *Frederick Douglass: In His Own Words*. Illustrated by Stephen Alcorn. San Diego, Calif.: Harcourt Brace, 1994.

Mochizuki, Ken. *Passage to Freedom: The Sugihara Story*. Illustrated by Dom Lee. New York: Lee & Low, 1997.

Morris, Juddi. *Tending the Fire: The Story of Maria Martinez*. Flagstaff, Ariz.: Rising Moon, 1997.

Orgill, Roxane. *If I Only Had a Horn: Young Louis Armstrong*. Illustrated by Leonard Jenkins. Boston: Houghton Mifflin, 1997.

Paul, Ann Whitford. *All by Herself*. Illustrated by Michael Steirnagle. San Diego, Calif.: Browndeer/Harcourt Brace, 1999.

Pinkney, Andrea D. *Bill Pickett: Rodeo-Ridin' Cowboy*. Illustrated by Brian Pinkney. San Diego, Calif.: Gulliver/Harcourt Brace, 1996.

———. *Dear Benjamin Banneker*. Illustrated by Brian Pinkney. San Diego, Calif.: Gulliver/Harcourt Brace, 1994.

———. *Duke Ellington: The Piano Prince and His Orchestra*. Illustrated by Brian Pinkney. New York: Hyperion, 1998.

Provensen, Alice. *My Fellow Americans: A Family Album*. San Diego, Calif.: Harcourt Brace/Browndeer Press, 1995.

Rief, Linda. *Seeking Diversity: Language Arts for Adolescents*. Portsmouth, N.H.: Heinemann, 1992.

Ringgold, Faith. *If a Bus Could Talk: The Story of Rosa Parks*. New York: Simon & Schuster, 1999.

Sabin, Louis. *Roberto Clemente: Young Baseball Hero*. Illustrated by Marie DeJohn. New York: Troll, 1992.

Say, Allen. *El Chino*. Boston: Houghton Mifflin, 1990.

Schroeder, Alan. *Ragtime Tumpie: The Life of Josephine Baker*. Illustrated by Bernie Fuchs. Boston: Little, Brown, 1989.

Scordato, Ellen. *Sarah Winnemucca: Northern Paiute Writer and Diplomat*. New York: Chelsea House, 1992.

Stanley, Fay. *The Last Princess: The Story of Princess Ka'iulani of Hawai'i*. Illustrated by Diane Stanley. New York: Four Winds Press, 1991.

Turcotte, Mark. *Songs of Our Ancestors: Poems about Native Americans*. Illustrated by Kathleen S. Presnell. Chicago: Children's Press, 1995.

Turner, Robyn Montana. *Faith Ringgold*. Boston: Little, Brown, 1993.

Winter, Jeanette. *Diego*. New York: Knopf/Borzoi Books, 1991.

———. *Josefina*. San Diego, Calif.: Harcourt Brace, 1996.

Wisniewski, David. *Sundiata: Lion King of Mali*. New York: Clarion, 1992.

Zhang, Song Nan. *A Little Tiger in the Chinese Night: An Autobiography in Art*. Montreal: Tundra Books, 1993.

Zhensun, Zheng, and Alice Low. *A Young Painter: The Life and Paintings of Wang Yani: China's Extraordinary Young Artist*. New York: Scholastic, 1991.

Sample Positive-Negative Graph

The sample graph shows how to set up the initial graph and how events might look once they have been plotted. A symbol or simple picture would illustrate each event. Each event can be explained as well rather than being generic, as these samples are. The birth of a sibling, a broken bone, or a move to a nicer neighborhood could be the specific events. Graphs should fill the paper, so there will be quite a bit of room to include events and illustrations.

Sample Positive-Negative Graph

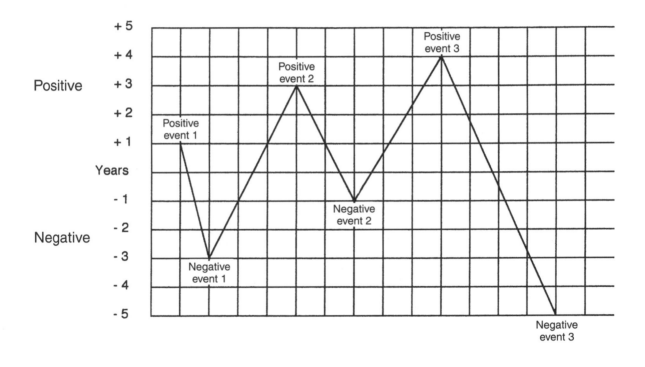

Lesson 22

Examining an Expository Text Structure

SKILL: Using a Venn Diagram to Explore Comparison and Contrast

CULTURE OF FOCUS: Mexican American

Materials

Pablo Remembers: The Fiesta of the Day of the Dead, by George Ancona (Lothrop, Lee & Shepard Books, 1993)

Two lunch-sized paper bags, one filled with small items representing Halloween, the other filled with items related to the celebration of the Day of the Dead; both tied securely with appropriately colored yarns

Guided practice sheets

Large Venn diagram on chart paper

Pens and pencils

Video: *El Dia de los Muertos: The Day of the Dead* (Institute of Texan Cultures, 1991; 21 minutes; 800-776-7651, (optional)

Lesson Motivator

1. Explain to the class that they are going to have an opportunity to broaden their cultural understanding by learning about a particularly interesting celebration that begins on October 31. Numerous students will probably be speculating that it is Halloween. Hand the paper bag with the Halloween items to one student in class and have him or her open it.

2. As the items are shown to the class, ask students to think silently about what popular holiday they represent. Write the identified items in the border of the chart paper or on the chalkboard and then identify the holiday.

3. Next, have another student open the second bag. Again, show each item to the class. For example, a large bakery roll might represent the traditional pan de muertos, or bread of the dead. A cardboard skeleton, a picture of a decorated sugar skull, a tortilla or tamale, several marigolds (flowers of the dead), or a small basket of nuts might be included as clues to the culture and the celebration.

4. Tell the class that these items represent quite a different celebration from Halloween. Ask for guesses. Jot down these items as well. If the students do not know about the Day of the Dead celebration, give them the following brief background and show the informative video *El Dia de los Muertos: The Day of the Dead.*

5. Assure the students that this is not a frightening festival, despite the presence of skeletons. It is a time for Hispanic family members to honor those who have died and to celebrate their lives in the process, remembering them with love. It is a holiday with roots going back to the Aztec, Mayan, and other pre-Hispanic peoples.

In Mexico today, people have somewhat different attitudes toward death than those typical in the United States. They view death with a little humor, shaking their heads at our inevitable fate. Through the fiesta of the Days of the Dead, families gather together to share memories, prepare favorite foods for their loved ones, clean and decorate gravesites, prepare an altar, and attend mass, all making the loss of a loved one more bearable. Different communities may celebrate in slightly different ways. The festival includes October 31 (All Hallows Eve), November 1 (All Saints Day), and November 2 (All Souls Day). By reading the growing number of books available, students can come to understand this Hispanic tradition rather than misunderstand or fear it.

Suggestions for Teaching the Lesson

- Draw the students' attention to the Venn diagram (see end of lesson) at the front of the class. Explain that this graphic organizer is handy to use when comparing and contrasting two items, issues, or ideas. It is an aid to comprehension, whether materials being used are expository or narrative in nature. Label one side of the diagram "Halloween" and the other side "The Days of the Dead," showing students that the outside area of the circles is where they record differences between the two celebrations. The area of overlap is where similarities are noted. Looking at the lists of items on the board, have students suggest where they should be recorded on the diagram and what their relationship is to the holiday.

- Take about 10 minutes for students to brainstorm on notebook paper. They should organize their thoughts, thinking of the purpose or origin of Halloween, activities, items, or events associated with the holiday, and then do the same (as much as they are able to, at this point) for the fiesta of the Days of the Dead. Have them hold on to these papers while they listen to you read *Pablo Remembers*. As they learn about the celebration, they may wish to add notes to their papers.

- Once the book is completed, discuss what students have learned and their reactions to this special celebration. Answer questions that arise or write them down to be researched later. It would be ideal to have an informed guest speaker in the room at this time to answer

questions, so that misconceptions will not have time to form.

- Return to the large class diagram. Ask students to volunteer one or two items that are different and one or two that are the same. Students could come to the front of the room and write them on the diagram themselves. Then, let the rest of the class complete the diagram on a guided practice sheet on their own using the additions on the class diagram.

- Have students write a paragraph comparing and contrasting these two events. List the following signal words on chart paper or tagboard to be placed where students can refer to them easily. Students may even want to copy them, add to the list as they find other words that are useful, and keep them handy in their writing folders.

different	the same as	to contrast/in contrast	although/but
alike	however	either … or	similar
on the one hand …		on the other hand	different from

- Model how you would begin a paragraph by giving the students four or five sentences to show what this would look like. You might begin by discussing the similarities between the two holidays and then give students an idea for a topic sentence to begin writing about the differences if they need that additional guidance. Writers may opt to complete the paragraph you began or start one of their own. They should work with a partner to edit their work and turn in a relatively clean copy to be reviewed by you.

- Starting with a fresh guided practice sheet, have students compare and contrast a personal family holiday with that of the Days of the Dead. They should follow the same procedure, ending with a polished piece of writing.

- Students may choose to "publish" this writing on a piece of tagboard with illustrations or pictures reflecting their cultural event, or opt for other creative presentations.

Evaluation

- Review the students' work on the Venn diagrams and their understanding of comparing and contrasting as exhibited by their writing. List three specific points you will be looking for in their writing, such as indenting paragraphs, capitalizing proper names, and using adjectives to make their writing especially interesting. This will help students focus on particular aspects of their writing. Schedule mini-conferences with students who may need additional support.

- Use this same lesson in science or social studies throughout the year to strengthen the skills and transfer the learning across the curriculum.

Extensions

- Invite parents to share their stories about cultural traditions in the family. Videotape their visits so that students can enjoy them at a future date.

- Have students make simple picture books about their traditions or celebrations, complete with colorful illustrations. These should be shared with children in the younger grades as part of a cultural or ethnic festival.

- Have students fill a basket or a bag with items that represent their celebrations and show them as they read their polished writing to the class.

- Other students can research the roots of their traditions and present their findings in an innovative way to the class. For example, one student could be a news reporter and interview several students on their findings.

- Have students write a poem to present their cultural information.

- Present everyone's personal celebrations on a mural using a long length of chart paper. Each artist should sign the part he or she created. Poems should be typed and displayed at the appropriate part of the mural. Display the mural on a wall outside the classroom.

Suggested Titles for Independent Reading and Research

Ancona, George. *Barrio: Jose's Neighborhood.* San Diego, Calif.: Harcourt Brace, 1998.

———. *Fiesta USA.* New York: Lodestar, 1995.

Carmichael, Elizabeth, and Cloe Sayer. *The Skeleton at the Feast: The Day of the Dead in Mexico.* Austin: University of Texas Press, 1991.

Chambers, Catherine. *All Saints, All Souls, and Halloween.* New York: Raintree/SteckVaughn, 1997.

Hoyt-Goldsmith, Diane. *Day of the Dead: A Mexican-American Celebration.* New York: Holiday House, 1995.

Lasky, Kathryn. *Days of the Dead.* Illustrated with photographs by Christopher G. Knight. New York: Hyperion, 1994.

Luenn, Nancy. *A Gift for Abuelita: Celebrating the Day of the Dead.* Illustrated by Robert Chapman. Flagstaff, Ariz.: Rising Moon/Northland Publishing, 1998. (fiction)

Silverthorne, Elizabeth. *Fiesta! Mexico's Great Celebrations.* Illustrated by Jan Davey Ellis. Brookfield, Conn.: Millbrook Press, 1992.

Venn Diagrams

When using the Venn diagram to compare and contrast time periods, regions, cultures, or other choices, list the differences in the outer area of the circles. The similarities are to be written in the area where the circles overlap.

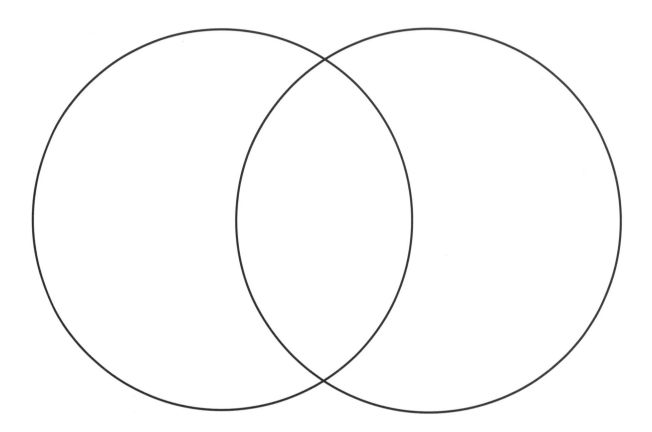

Lesson 23

Understanding Expository Text

SKILL: Working with Cause and Effect

CULTURE OF FOCUS: Hawaiian

Materials

The Last Princess: The Story of Princess Ka'iulani of Hawaii, by Fay Stanley (Four Winds Press, 1991)
Copies of the guided practice sheet "Cause and Effect with Expository Text" (see end of lesson)
Music from Hawaii
Pens or pencils
Map of United States

Lesson Motivator

1. Play a tape or CD of music from Hawaii quietly as students prepare for class. It might be fun to have small cups containing a piece of fresh pineapple, a chunk of coconut, and a macadamia nut on each student's desk as well. Based on the clues they see, hear, and taste, ask learners to name the setting of the book being used for the day's lesson.

2. Have a volunteer point out the Hawaiian Islands on a map of the United States. To assess prior knowledge, invite students to contribute what they know about this country. Give a short overview of this most recent addition to the United States or additional background knowledge as needed.

Suggestions for Teaching the Lesson

- Tell the class that you will be working with cause and effect. Knowledge about this way of arranging text will be valuable in aiding students with understanding both narrative and expository text in daily reading. Remind or teach the class that the cause-and-effect structure describes an event or a problem and then explains the resulting consequences or effects. Give several concrete examples directly related to the students' lives. For example, on the way to school that morning, the school bus driver came to a stop sign (cause). The effect of seeing that sign was to stop the bus and wait for traffic to clear before continuing. Another example is an alarm ringing at 6:30 A.M. (cause), which alerted a student that it was time to get up, which he or she did (effect). Ask students for several additional examples and write them on the board, clearly identifying which is the cause and which is the effect.

- Reinforce students in their efforts to work with cause and effect by telling them that research has shown that readers who understand and use an author's organizational pattern as they read can recall more at the conclusion of their reading than those who do not.

- Continue the lesson by explaining that today's book is nonfiction, or expository text. It is a factual account of the life of a lovely young woman who was the last princess in Hawaii. As you read the book, you will be asking students to listen for cause-and-effect relationships in the story. They will be supported in their observations by a guided practice sheet.

- Hand out copies of the guided practice sheet "Cause and Effect with Expository Text." Ask the students to listen to the first page of the book and complete the cause for number 1. To determine the cause, they should look at the effect and ask themselves, What happened to create this result? or What needed to happen first? Check to be certain that answers are on target before going on. As students contemplate the effect for number 2, they should ask themselves, What happened as a result of this action? Check that response and ask if there are any questions before continuing.

- Read the remainder of the book. Have students continue to fill in the sheets as you read. To keep up interest and to monitor comprehension, stop periodically to chat about an illustration or get reactions from students about what is happening in Ka'iulani's life.

- At the conclusion of the book, spend as much time as needed talking about the story and students' reactions to this young woman's short life. Then go back through the guided practice sheets, asking for volunteers to contribute the appropriate cause or effect. Answers will vary somewhat, but there should be a sensible cause-and-effect relationship. Clear up any misunderstanding before asking students to continue with independent practice.

- From a selection of books in the classroom, have students pick out titles of personal interest and develop their own cause-and-effect sheets. They may like to work in pairs, which encourages dialogue and often makes reading and comprehension much more interesting. Pairs should monitor their learning, checking to see if they clearly understand cause and effect as they work together.

Evaluation

- Monitor the second set of practice sheets to see if students understand this text structure. Follow up on another day with a review of cause-and-effect situations to be certain students retain what they have learned.

- A natural transition of these skills to reinforce learning is into science

and social studies materials, where cause and effect is a common text structure in content-area textbooks.

Extensions

- Apply the text-structure worksheets to a future social studies or science lesson to demonstrate how an understanding of cause and effect helps with comprehension across the curriculum.

- Bring in a travel video of the Hawaiian Islands so that students can learn more about this part of the United States, a popular vacation destination.

- Send students out into the Internet world to glean information about the Hawaiian Islands, famous people who live or have lived there, or areas of personal interest. Have them try to find their names in Hawaiian.

- Have students research Hawaiian fabric designs. They can work with the art teacher to learn how to do a simple batik design on muslin, replicating Hawaiian prints. Display the completed work attractively on the walls outside the classroom or on a classroom bulletin board.

- Compile the information students have learned on Hawaii and make an attractive big book about the state.

Suggested Titles for Independent Reading and Research

Ancona, George. *Earth Daughter: Alicia of Acoma Pueblo.* New York: Simon & Schuster, 1995.

Brewster, Hugh. *Anastasia's Album.* Illustrated with photographs. New York: Hyperion, 1996.

Bruchac, Joseph. *A Boy Called Slow: The True Story of Sitting Bull.* Illustrated by Rocco Baviera. New York: Philomel, 1994.

Coerr, Eleanor. *Sadako.* Illustrated by Ed Young. New York: Putnam, 1993.

Cooper, Floyd. *Coming Home: From the Life of Langston Hughes.* New York: Philomel, 1994.

———. *Mandela: From the Life of the South African Statesman.* New York: Philomel, 1996.

Dingle, Derek T. *First in the Field: Baseball Hero Jackie Robinson.* New York: Hyperion, 1998.

Golenbock, Peter. *Teammates.* Illustrated by Paul Bacon. San Diego, Calif.: Harcourt Brace, 1990.

Hansen, Joyce. *Women of Hope: African Americans Who Made a Difference.* New York: Scholastic, 1998.

Hoyt-Goldsmith, Diane. *Buffalo Days.* Illustrated with photographs by Lawrence Migdale. New York: Holiday House, 1998.

———. *Migrant Worker: A Boy from the Rio Grande Valley.* Illustrated with photographs by Lawrence Migdale. New York: Holiday House, 1996.

Lazo, Caroline. *Arthur Ashe.* Minneapolis, Minn.: Lerner, 1998.

Maruki, Toshi. *Hiroshima No Pika.* New York: Lothrop, Lee & Shepard Books, 1980.

Morris, Ann. *Dancing to America.* Illustrated with photographs by Paul Kolnik. New York: Dutton, 1994.

Murphy, Claire Rudolf. *A Child's Alaska.* Illustrated with photographs by Charles Mason. Seattle, Wash.: Alaska Northwest Books, 1994.

Pinkney, Andrea Davis. *Duke Ellington: The Piano Prince and His Orchestra.* Illustrated by Brian Pinkney. New York: Hyperion, 1998.

Sis, Peter. *Follow the Dream: The Story of Christopher Columbus.* New York: Alfred A. Knopf, 1991.

Stanley, Diane. *Joan of Arc.* New York: Morrow, 1998.

Tillage, Leon Walter. *Leon's Story.* Illustrated by Susan L. Roth. New York: Scholastic, 1997.

Uchida, Yoshiko. *Journey to Topaz.* Illustrated by Donald Carrick. San Francisco, Calif.: Creative Arts, 1985.

Welch, Catherine A. *Margaret Bourke-White: Racing with a Dream.* Minneapolis, Minn.: Carolrhoda, 1998.

Wisniewski, David. *Sandiata: Lion King of Mali.* New York: Clarion, 1992.

Guided Practice: Cause and Effect with Expository Text

Directions: Fill in the blanks explaining either cause or effect.

Title of book: *The Last Princess: The Story of Princess Ka'iulani of Hawaii*
Author: Fay Stanley

Cause	Effect
1.	1. Princess Ka'iulani's life was like a fairy tale when she was young.
2. Princess Ruth gave little Ka'iulani 10 acres of land on the island of O'ahu as a christening gift.	2.
3. Princess Likelike died after seeing Ka'iulani's future.	3.
4.	4. The princess was quite seasick on her way to England.
5.	5. The letters sent from school at Great Harrowden Hall were happy and carefree.
6. Hawaii was desired by several countries because of its location and fertile lands.	6.
7. Over the years the *haoles* became very powerful.	7.
8.	8. Ka'iulani traveled to Washington to speak to President Grover Cleveland.
9. A group of angry young Hawaiians took matters into their own hands.	9.
10. The Hawaiian monarchy was finished, which greatly changed the lives of its citizens.	10.
11. The United States annexed Hawaii after President Cleveland left office.	11.
12. At a wedding party, Ka'iulani rode unprotected in a driving rainstorm.	12.

Lesson 24

Getting Meaning from Expository Text Structures

SKILL: Using Problem and Solution

CULTURE OF FOCUS: South African (Zulu)

Materials

Shaka, King of the Zulus, by Diane
    Stanley and Peter Vennema
    (Morrow, 1988)
Copies of the guided practice sheet
    "Problems and Solutions" (see
    end of lesson)
World map
Additional books for practice

Lesson Motivator

1. Ask the students to do a quickwrite, taking no more than 10 minutes to jot down the chores or jobs for which they are responsible at home. Tell them to also explain what happens when they neglect those responsibilities.

2. At the end of the quickwrite, invite students to discuss their chores and what the consequences are if they forget to do them.

3. Read the first page of *Shaka, King of the Zulus.* Ask the students to predict what might be coming next. Confirm or correct their predictions by reading the second page of the story.

4. Quickly preview the book, introducing Shaka, a brave, powerful, renowned Zulu leader. Zero in on the setting of this story by inviting a student to locate South Africa on a world map, pinpointing Zululand down at the tip of the country.

Suggestions for Teaching the Lesson

- Before continuing in the book, tell the class that they are going to be learning or reviewing a text structure that focuses on identifying problems and finding their solutions. Being able to discover the problem and then read for the solution is an excellent skill to have to improve the comprehension of both narrative and expository materials. Learners will be applying this skill to a fascinating biography of a seemingly fearless leader. This text structure is just as it sounds: The author presents a problem of some type and students read to find the solution or solutions.

- Refer students to the two pages of the book that have just been read. Ask them to identify the first problem and the solution. They will mention the fact that Shaka's wandering attention has resulted in the death of a sheep. The solution is not a simple one. Becoming more attentive to his chores would prevent further scoldings, a logical solution to Shaka's problem. Unfortunately, a second problem develops right on the heels of the first one because his mother, Nandi, defends him. Women did not talk back to their husbands, hence, problem number two. The solution to this double set of problems was to rid the tribe of both offenders. Facing disgrace, Nandi and Shaka are banished from Bulawyo and must return to her own tribe.

- Tell the students to write down problems and their solutions on notebook paper as you read through the remainder of the book. You will discuss their observations as a class once the book has been completed.

- Because this is longer than a typical picture book, you might opt to read half of it, stopping to discuss events in the story, asking for student reactions, comparing and contrasting lifestyles with those of the students, and admiring the lovely artwork. Then you can move to the guided practice work, completing the book later in the day or on the following day before students practice on their own.

- Return to the text structure, handing out the guided practice sheets. Ask students to note the third problem Shaka faces, which is constant ridicule and harassment by the boys in Nandi's clan. The solution is that his mother comforts him and reassures him that one day he will be the greatest chief in the land. Record the students' responses on a model of the guided practice sheet.

- Have students pick six other problems Shaka faces during his life and the solutions that he generates. They should work independently while you circle through the class monitoring their accuracy.

- After an allotted time period, encourage the students to share some of their recorded problems and solutions. Ask them if they see how knowing the way to identify and apply this tool can be particularly useful with some kinds of expository text. Can they give an example or two from reading they have done in the past?

- Once the book is done, take some time to talk about Shaka and his skills as a leader. Have students review some of the things he did to build his troops and make the Zulus a force with which to be reckoned. Continue the discussion by comparing Shaka to other leaders with whom the students are familiar, comparing and contrasting leadership styles.

- Provide a number of intriguing books and fresh guided practice sheets and let the students refine their skills.

Evaluation

- As with the other text structures, review the students' independent practice to assess their understanding of how problem/solution structures work. If you are keeping a checklist of skills mastered for each student, check and date the acquisition of this skill.

- Give the students an opportunity to apply the skill again with appropriate subject matter. Remind the students that to be learned and retained, new skills need review and practice.

Extensions

- Have students who are particularly interested in a leader prepare a report on that individual to be presented to the class. The presentation might be in picture book form, including interviews with people who lived or worked with the leader, or in the form of the individual's diary, explaining day-to-day problems and possible solutions. Another choice might be presenting information in the form of an illustrated timeline.

- Give students the option to write a biography about another classmate, identifying some of the problems and solutions faced in that person's life. Parents, relatives, former teachers, and friends might serve as resources. Once the material is in draft form, the individual can be consulted to see if other information should be included. Photographs would be a wonderful addition to the final product.

- Because picture book biographies or autobiographies only present a segment of an individual's life, students should read several resources on an individual, comparing and contrasting the information in an effort to get as complete a picture as possible. Observations should be shared with the rest of the class, an informative presentation for everyone involved.

- Have students present information about a person in comic strip format, complete with informative conversational bubbles. The carefully sequenced strip may just cover a small portion of the individual's life or give an overview from birth to death. The comic strip can be done on tagboard for durability and then displayed in the classroom reading center for further scrutiny and enjoyment.

Suggested Titles for Independent Reading and Research

Adler, David. *A Picture Book of Sojourner Truth.* New York: Holiday House, 1994.

Bruchac, Joseph. *A Boy Called Slow: The True Story of Sitting Bull.* Illustrated by Rocco Baviera. New York: Philomel, 1994.

Chambers, Veronica. *Amistad Rising: A Story of Freedom.* Illustrated by Paul Lee. San Diego, Calif.: Harcourt Brace, 1998.

Coerr, Eleanor. *Sadako.* Illustrated by Ed Young. New York: Putnam, 1993.

Cooper, Floyd. *Coming Home: From the Life of Langston Hughes.* New York: Philomel, 1995.

Demi. *Buddha.* New York: Holt, 1996.

Hansen, Joyce. *Women of Hope: African Americans Who Made a Difference.* New York: Scholastic, 1998.

Krull, Kathleen. *Wilma Unlimited: How Wilma Rudolph Became the World's Fastest Woman.* San Diego, Calif.: Harcourt Brace, 1996.

Medearis, Angela Shelf. *Princess of the Press: The Story of Ida B. Wells-Barnett.* New York: Lodestar Books, 1998.

Miller, William. *Zora Houston and the Chinaberry Tree.* New York: Lee & Low, 1994.

Mochizuki, Ken. *Passage to Freedom: The Sugihara Story.* Illustrated by Dom Lee. New York: Lee & Low, 1997.

Parks, Rosa, with Jim Haskins. *I Am Rosa Parks.* Illustrated by Wil Clay. New York: Dial, 1997.

Pinkney, Andrea D. *Bill Pickett: Rodeo-Ridin' Cowboy.* Illustrated by Brian Pinkney. San Diego, Calif.: Gulliver/Harcourt Brace, 1996.

———. *Dear Benjamin Banneker.* Illustrated by Brian Pinkney. San Diego, Calif.: Gulliver/Harcourt Brace, 1994.

———. *Duke Ellington: The Piano Prince and His Orchestra.* Illustrated by Brian Pinkney. New York: Hyperion, 1998.

Say, Allen. *El Chino.* Boston: Houghton Mifflin, 1990.

Shange, Ntozake. *White Wash.* Illustrated by Michael Sporn. New York: Walker, 1997.

Stanley, Diane. *Joan of Arc.* New York: Morrow, 1998.

———. *Leonardo Da Vinci.* New York: Morrow, 1996.

Guided Practice: Problems and Solutions

Problems	Solutions

Lesson 25

Using a Timeline

SKILL: Unraveling Content-Area Text

CULTURE OF FOCUS: African American

Materials

Bound for America: The Forced Migration of Africans to the New World, by James Haskins and Kathleen Benson; illustrated by Floyd Cooper (Lothrop, Lee & Shepard Books, 1999)
The Middle Passage, by Tom Feelings (Dial, 1995)
African Beginnings, by James Haskins and Kathleen Benson; illustrated by Floyd Cooper (Lothrop, Lee & Shepard Books, 1998)
Long length of white shelf paper
Pencils
Markers
To Be a Slave, by Julius Lester; illustrated by Tom Feelings (Dial, 1968)
Notebook paper
Chart paper, overhead projector, or chalkboard
String and chalk

Lesson Motivator

1. Take the class outside. Give several students the responsibility of making a long, straight chalk line across the asphalt or concrete. They can keep their line straight by stretching a length of string or twine out along the ground as a guide. It can be held in place by two classmates. Make the line long enough so that everyone in the class will be able to line up comfortably along it. The thick, popular, colored sidewalk chalk might be fun to use for this activity. Students can draw the line in one color and use another color or two for other designations.

2. While the line is being drawn, arrange the rest of the class into large groups based on the year of their birth. You may end up with three, four, or even more groups, depending on the makeup of the class.

3. For the next step, ask for a volunteer to work within each group, arranging classmates in order of their birthdays by months. Line them up single file at this point, with January birthdays first. In the case of several birthdays within the same month, have those students order themselves from earliest in the month to latest.

4. The line-drawers should find their group and get in place accordingly. Write the years represented evenly along the student-drawn line using a different color of chalk (see example below).

1984	1985	1986

5. Ask a student from each group to add the months along the line. Then use arrows and lines to indicate the dates within the months as needed (see example below), depending on how detailed you want the timeline to be. Have students find their spots along the timeline.

```
                    x x x   x x x x x   x x     x        x
         x          x     x x x x x x x x x x x x x x x      x x
    _____
    | | | | | | | | | | | | | | | | | | | | | | | | | | | | | | | |
    J F M A M J J  A S O N D J  F M A M J  J  A S O N D J  F M A  J J
    M
    1984              1985              1986
```

6. Videotape this cooperative effort so that students can see this lineup—a "living timeline"—after they return to class. If a video camera is not available, a few students at a time can step out of line to look at the results.

7. Based on this activity, query the class on one use of the timeline. Can they think of others? In what subject areas might a tool like this be useful? Basically, you are

demonstrating both actively and visually how a timeline can be an aid in organizing various kinds of information.

8. Explain that you will be creating another timeline, this time on paper, based on upcoming reading and research. This one will contain information and illustrations. Return to the classroom and settle in for a thought-provoking introduction to the topic of slavery.

Suggestions for Teaching the Lesson

- Have students take out pens or pencils and notebook paper to be used for a quickwrite. Tell them to listen carefully while you read a vivid quote from a text you have selected. They will be writing their reactions to the quote once you are finished reading. One option is the following quote from *To Be a Slave,* the Newbery Honor Book by Julius Lester:

> To be a slave. To be owned by another person, as a car, house, or table is owned. To live as a piece of property that could be sold—a child sold from its mother, a wife from her husband. To be considered not human, but a "thing" that plowed the fields, cut the wood, cooked the food, nursed another's child; a "thing" whose sole function was determined by the one who owned you.

> —Julius Lester, *To Be a Slave* (New York: Dial, 1968)

- Explain that Lester selected excerpts from nineteenth-century slave narratives and from those gathered by the Federal Writers' Project in the 1930s with an eye to presenting a vivid picture of how slaves felt about the institution of slavery. Emphasize that this is not fictional material.

- Give the students a few minutes to react honestly in writing to the quote. What is their immediate reaction to these words? Prompt with a question such as: "How would you feel if you were suddenly thrust into the lot of a slave?" or "What kinds of feelings does this quote engender?"

- Afterward, open the class discussion by asking for students to voice their feelings. Tell the class that the following lesson will deepen their understanding of the issue of slavery, perhaps raising more questions than it answers. If necessary, they can follow their questions into other avenues of research.

- Continue by plumbing the depths of student knowledge about slavery. When do they think it began? What other cultures used slaves besides the early Americans? Record contributions on the board or on chart paper to be referred to and adjusted as more information is gathered.

- Outline the upcoming steps by directing students' attention to the long piece of wide white shelf paper, which should be taped across a part of the classroom wall where it can remain undisturbed for the duration of this lesson. Place pencils, markers, crayons, or other art materials nearby for easy access. Tell students that after they have gathered enough information, they will be working in small teams on a section of the shelf paper timeline, adding concise bits of pertinent information and illustrating each segment appropriately. Once completed, this visual representation of the institution of slavery can be scrutinized and pondered. This format is certainly different from the "living timeline" they formed. It is a useful tool for future research.

- Next, read "Slavery in History" aloud from the focus book, *Bound for America*. Discuss the two pages with the class, adjusting ideas or dates from the earlier class discussion as necessary. Begin a draft of the timeline on the chalkboard, using the students' draft as a model and for early data collection.

- Have students begin to take their own notes for the timeline, including dates and snippets of pertinent information to tie to the dates. All this initial information will be further researched using the books cited above, the focus book, and the others suggested at the end of this lesson.

- Read the two segments "Africa in 1492" and "Slavery in Africa" (from *Bound for America*), again noting appropriate dates and information on the model timeline. A student recorder or two can facilitate this process.

- Read the remaining topic divisions from the focus book to the class, listing them on the chalkboard or overhead. Are there any topics that might be combined so that six to eight groups can be formed based on the topics? Divide the class into small groups to research a particular topic, letting groups choose the topic of their interest (to the extent that this is possible). Acquaint workers with the materials at hand or send groups to the library, having made arrangements with the librarian ahead of time. Locate an Internet site or two so that some researchers can use that resource. The goal of this part of the lesson is to become as knowledgeable about the topic as possible. This information will eventually be presented to the rest of the class so that everyone can benefit from the reading and research in progress.

- Instruct group members to settle on chunks of gathered information

and corresponding dates they want to record and illustrate on the large sheet of shelf paper that is hanging across one classroom wall. A planner from each group will sit on a committee to lay out all the information, sketching key points into place with pencil. In this way, nothing will be cramped or omitted because students ran out of room.

- After that, other members of each group can add written information as plotted out. Others will illustrate the information appropriately. The emerging result will be an informational pictorial overview of the topic of slavery from its earliest beginnings to a stopping point that has been decided on by the class.

Evaluation

- Ask students to write to you about what they have learned during the time spent investigating slavery. Tell them to focus on four or five skills that they feel they have strengthened during the lesson, such as working cooperatively with others in a group; reading to gather information; summarizing information for use on the timeline; understanding the value of timelines to sequence a large amount of information; and integrating reading, writing, and art into a learning experience.

- Be sure to ask the class how the use of a timeline helped them to understand content-area materials. After students have turned in their personal learning evaluations, discuss this experience with the class, assessing reactions to the project. Conference briefly with individual students, straightening out any difficulties and praising individual efforts. Add the evaluations to portfolios after conferencing.

- Keep the use of this tool to understanding nonfiction materials in use. Include timeline activities in future assignments across the curriculum to review and reinforce learning.

Extensions

- Have students write a newspaper article or an editorial expressing their point of view about the issue of slavery.

- Assign some students to read other books on this topic and compile an annotated bibliography to be used by other classmates interested in reading fiction or nonfiction materials on slavery.

- Bring in a selection of spirituals said to be sung by slaves to discuss and listen to. These were the songs that African Americans used for solace and hope.

- Have students research African-American folktales, looking for the message of hope or courage that might have been underlying the telling of the tale. Have them book-talk three or four of their favorites.

- Help students plan a skit to highlight a segment of a fiction or nonfiction selection. Along those some lines, have them create a reader's theater production by rewriting a moving part of a novel or most of a picture book.

- Have students write a collection of poems on the topic of slavery, with other interested students in the class contributing their efforts. Bind them into a book with compelling illustrations. Share the book with other classes studying the topic of slavery or as a part of the study of early American history.

- Using discarded magazines, have students make a collage that will convey personal feelings about oppression in general. They should use both pictures and words and include an eye-catching caption. They should also explain the resulting artwork. If the entire class engages in the activity, display the completed poster collages in the hallway outside the classroom.

Suggested Titles for Independent Reading and Research

Adler, David. A. *A Picture Book of Sojourner Truth.* Illustrated by Gershom Griffith. New York: Holiday House, 1994.

Altman, Susan, and Susan Lechner. *Followers of the North Star: Rhymes about African American Heroes, Heroines, and Historical Times.* Illustrated by Byron Wooden. Chicago: Children's Press, 1993.

Bial, Raymond. *The Strength of These Arms: Life in the Slave Quarters.* Boston: Houghton Mifflin, 1997.

Chambers, Veronica. *Amistad Rising: A Story of Freedom.* Illustrated by Paul Lee. San Diego, Calif.: Harcourt Brace, 1998.

Edwards, Pamela Duncan. *Barefoot: Escape on the Underground Railroad.* Illustrated by Henry Cole. New York: HarperCollins, 1997.

Hopkinson, Deborah. *A Band of Angels: A Story Inspired by the Jubilee Singers.* Illustrated by Raul Colon. New York: Atheneum, 1999.

———. *Sweet Clara and the Freedom Quilt.* Illustrated by James Ransome. New York: Knopf, 1993.

Johnston, Tony. *The Wagon.* Illustrated by James E. Ransome. New York: Tambourine, 1996.

Lester, Julius. *Black Cowboy, Wild Horses: A True Story.* Illustrated by Jerry Pinkney. New York: Dial, 1998.

———. *From Slave Ship to Freedom Road.* Illustrated by Rod Brown. New York: Dial, 1998.

McCurdy, Michael. *Escape from Slavery: The Boyhood of Frederick Douglass in His Own Words.* New York: Knopf, 1994.

Monjo, F. N. *The Drinking Gourd: A Story of the Underground Railroad.* Illustrated by Fred Brenner. New York: HarperCollins, 1993.

San Souci, Robert D. *The Hired Hand: An African American Folktale.* Illustrated by Jerry Pinkney. New York: Dial, 1997.

Sanders, Scott Russell. *A Place Called Freedom.* Illustrated by Thomas B. Allen. New York: Atheneum, 1997.

Silverman, Jerry. *Just Listen to This Song I'm Singing: African-American History through Song.* Illustrated with photographs. Brookfield, Conn.: Millbrook, 1996.

Thomas, Joyce Carol. *I Have Heard of a Land.* Illustrated by Floyd Cooper. New York: HarperCollins, 1998.

Turner, Ann. *Nettie's Trip South.* Illustrated by Ronald Himler. New York: Macmillan, 1987.

Van Steenwyk, Elizabeth. *My Name Is York.* Illustrated by Bill Farnsworth. Flagstaff, Ariz.: Rising Moon/Northland Publishing, 1997.

Wesley, Valerie. *Freedom's Gifts: A Juneteenth Story.* Illustrated by Sharon Wilson. New York: Simon & Schuster, 1997.

Winter, Jeanette. *Follow the Drinking Gourd.* New York: Knopf, 1988.

Section IV

Word Recognition and Vocabulary-Building Strategies

WORD RECOGNITION: AN OVERVIEW

Our worlds are filled to the brim with words. As if they were building blocks, readers take one after another to eventually build a vast storehouse of personal vocabulary. This acquisition begins when children are just infants, when they try "Mama" and "Dada" and "juice" on for size. It continues through the emergent reader stage and burgeons through the years leading to adulthood. Strategies for unlocking the meaning of more and more difficult combinations of letters are acquired along the way.

This next section addresses a few of those particular strategies. In understanding the process of word recognition, it is important to note that readers learn two aspects of words as they become adept in this area. One piece involves word recognition. The other involves understanding a word's meaning. Researchers indicate that learning occurs simultaneously in both areas. To more specifically explain each piece, word recognition refers to sight words, those words that a student can recognize immediately, then pronounce, and read out loud. Meaning vocabulary covers those words that readers can understand and use appropriately. A third aspect, that of word analysis, involves teaching students how to break words into meaningful parts to ferret out the meaning of a new word. This particular aspect deals with phonics, using letter-sound relationships to sound out a word or structural analysis, where larger meaningful

bits of words are decoded. These three segments of vocabulary development work together to create meaning as students explore reading and writing over the years.

Textbook after textbook explains how research has clearly established a strong relationship between vocabulary and reading comprehension. Basically, the more words a reader knows, the better he or she will be able to understand what is being read. Word numbers reported by researchers are interesting to note. Although the estimates vary somewhat, students learn between 2,700 and 3,000 new words each year. First graders may boast a vocabulary of around 5,000 words. Gathering about seven words a day over the years, high school seniors know approximately 47,000 words by graduation. Those words are best learned in a rich language environment where students see language in action, use quality models for their writing, and have the opportunity to engage in both extensive and intensive reading.

Students can continually increase the number of words they recognize in a classroom setting where wide reading is encouraged. It helps when they are taught how to use context to decipher word meanings and then are given the opportunity to use those skills regularly. These students also have an advantage if they can have access to aids such as the dictionary or a knowledgeable person, and if they receive periodic instruction on word identification strategies. Considering the amazing number of words that students learn year by year, they obviously learn the majority of them on their own. But that process can be facilitated in the classroom. Because there is no one best way to teach new words, try a variety of means to keep words at the forefront of daily activities:

- Build an awareness of words and maintain a high interest through a variety of classroom activities such as those suggested in this volume.

- Use word journals or require that a section of a student's daily journal be devoted to a continuing list of intriguing words.

- Read aloud to students regardless of their ages. Older students can be spellbound by fabulous writing as readily as young children can get caught up in a picture book. Stop periodically when an interesting word is encountered and chat about it.

- When "Literature Circles" are a part of the classroom routine, make students into word detectives, always on the lookout for a great word to discuss with the group.

- Encourage students to use new words in their writing. Using these words on a regular basis leads to ownership.

- Build word walls and change them periodically. The focus might be holidays at one time, a social studies assignment another time, homonyms at still another time. Learners have easy access to words on the wall.

- Invite various people throughout the school and the community to drop in occasionally to celebrate a new word with the class.

The key to building vocabulary and fine-tuning word recognition is to integrate old knowledge with the new in an ever-expanding process of word knowledge. The following activities are a step in doing just that.

Lesson 26

Reviewing Synonyms and Antonyms

SKILL: Practice with Word Opposites

CULTURE OF FOCUS: Mexican/ Mexican American

Materials

Tio Armando, by Florence Perry Heide and Roxanne Heide Pierce (Lothrop, Lee & Shepard Books, 1998)

Collection of books about the Mexican/Mexican-American culture with a focus on family relationships

Copies of the guided practice sheet "Using Synonyms and Antonyms" (see end of lesson)

Lesson Motivator

1. Tell the students you are going to play a word game involving the use of synonyms and antonyms. Explain that synonyms are words that mean almost the same thing. Antonyms are words that mean the opposite thing.

2. Divide the class into four teams. Each team should have a team name that ties into the Mexican or Mexican-American culture. Students should take turns being the scorekeeper and timer if numbers don't work out evenly. Student scorekeepers and timers can rotate onto a team after a period of time and another student can take over the duties, so that everyone has an opportunity to work with these words.

3. Model what you expect before beginning the game. Write a short list of words on the board that have obvious similarities and opposites.

To reinforce the concept that synonyms mean "similar," have the students come up with synonyms for the words on the board first. Then move to antonyms, or opposites, and record student suggestions. Words such as *cold, tall, happy,* and *hungry* can be used. Then begin the game.

4. Give the first team a simple word and ask them to provide a synonym for that word that is appropriate to the grade level with which you are working. For example, the words must be at least five letters long and must be spelled correctly to count.

5. Give team members two minutes to confer and come up with their best effort. If you deem the word acceptable, the team earns a point. If they cannot come up with a quality word or it is misspelled, they get no points.

6. Move to the second team and let them have a try at the previous synonym. If they come up with an acceptable answer, they earn the point and get another turn. After that turn is correctly completed, the third team gets a chance, and so forth. The only time a team gets two turns in a row is when they correct a previous team's error. Each waiting team should be quietly conferring while the team on the spot is coming up with their word, so that all students stay actively involved.

7. Play several rounds, making certain that different members of each team are participating. Then switch to using antonyms and continue until every person seems to have had a chance to contribute or until enough practice time has elapsed to suit you.

8. The team with the highest score is the winner, but all students should get something simple as a prize to deemphasize the competitive aspect. Prizes should be tied into the reading-writing curriculum, such as extra free reading time for the week.

9. After the class has returned to their desks, read the focus book, *Tio Armando.* Ask the students to listen for words or actions that help them to get to know Tio. These will be shared at the conclusion of the book.

Suggestions for Teaching the Lesson

- When *Tio Armando* has been completed, spend some time talking about this warm and special book. Discuss the relationship between Tio and the rest of the family members. Invite students to connect further with the story by sharing incidents that reflect similar relationships with their own relatives and family members.

- Ask students to come up to the board individually and write a word that they came up with that described Tio. Look over the words together and circle the ones that are synonyms. Take one word and brainstorm other synonyms. Switch gears and take another word, this time brainstorming antonyms. Discuss how quickly the picture of the main character changes when you work with words that have opposite meanings.

- Hand out copies of the guided practice sheet "Using Synonyms and Antonyms." The students should circle one choice out of the three words given that is the best synonym for the italicized word in the sentence. (There are several examples providing practice working with antonyms as well.)

- Let students discuss their selections and observations with a partner and then with the whole class to wrap up this part of the lesson.

- Pair up students to read another book of their choice. They should create their own guided practice sheet based on their particular book, including both kinds of words. Pairs should exchange books and sheets, meeting in groups of four at the conclusion of their work to discuss the books and their interesting synonyms and antonyms. For this activity students may choose to work with a thesaurus, a handy tool they should become familiar with for use when editing their personal writing.

Evaluation

- Monitor students' work as they read and develop their worksheets. On a list of skills to be acquired, date and check off the skill of working with synonyms and antonyms when you feel each student understands these categories or words.

- Later in the week, as a quick review, give the class several words in both categories to work with. Remind students to use a thesaurus in their writing. Check periodically to see if the choice of more interesting words is actually improving as a result of this lesson.

Extensions

- Because the focus book is about special family relationships, invite treasured relatives to meet the class. You could have a distinctive event to which these people are invited, or they could come in periodically to visit the class to chat and share something interesting about themselves. Relatives could also just drop in to read a book to the class.

- Students can celebrate a special relative, whether living or deceased, by making a collage of pictures from magazines to remind themselves of that person. After the pictures are in place, they should cut a variety of pertinent words out of the text of magazines and sprinkle them on top of the pictures. They should then glue these in place and add the person's name. Have students share their creation honoring a special person in their lives.

• Work with the idea of antonyms by creating a diamond-shaped poem. Have students create a poem by following the directions at the end of this lesson. They can write poems inside the diamond shape on a lined 5-x-8-inch card. They should write the poem neatly on the lined side of the card and put an appropriate illustration on the blank side of the card, cut out the diamond, and punch a hole near the top of the shape. Four or five of these diamond-shaped poems can be made into a mobile using colorful yarn to attach the diamonds to a coat hanger. Suspended from the ceiling, the poems twist and turn, so that both sides can be appreciated by readers.

Suggested Titles for Independent Reading and Research

Altman, Linda Jacobs. *Amelia's Road.* Illustrated by Enrique O. Sanchez. New York: Lee & Low, 1993.

Ancona, George. *Fiesta Fireworks.* New York: Lothrop, Lee & Shepard Books, 1998.

Belton, Sandra. *May'naise Sandwiches & Sunshine Tea.* Illustrated by Gail Gordon Carter. New York: Four Winds Press, 1994.

Bruchac, Joseph. *Fox Song.* Illustrated by Paul Morin. New York: Philomel, 1993.

Bunting, Eve. *Going Home.* Illustrated by David Diaz. New York: Cotler/HarperCollins, 1996.

Caines, Jeannette. *Abby.* Illustrated by Steven Kellogg. New York: HarperCollins, 1973.

Calhoun, Mary. *Tonio's Cat.* Illustrated by Edward Martinez. New York: Morrow, 1996.

Castaneda, Omar S. *Abuelo's Weave.* Illustrated by Enrique O. Sanchez. New York: Lee & Low, 1993.

Chanin, Michael. *The Chief's Blanket.* Illustrated by Kim Howard. Tiburon, Calif.: H. J. Kramer/Starseed Press, 1997.

Covault, Ruth M. *Pablo and Pimienta.* Illustrated by Francisco Mora. Flagstaff, Ariz.: Rising Moon/Northland Publishing, 1993.

Cowen-Fletcher, Jane. *It Takes a Village.* New York: Scholastic, 1994.

Cowley, Joy. *Big Moon Tortilla.* Illustrated by Dyanne Strongbow. Honesdale, Pa.: Boyds Mills Press, 1998.

Crews, Donald. *Bigmama's.* New York: Mulberry, 1991.

Dorros, Arthur. *Isla.* Illustrated by Elisa Kleven. New York: Dutton, 1995.

Flournoy, Valerie. *The Patchwork Quilt.* Illustrated by Jerry Pinkney. New York: Dial, 1985.

———. *Tanya's Reunion.* Illustrated by Jerry Pinkney. New York: Dial, 1995.

Garay, Luis. *Pedrito's Day.* New York: Orchard, 1997.

Garza, Carmen Lomas. *In My Family/En Mi Familia.* San Francisco, Calif.: Children's Book Press, 1996.

Gilman, Phoebe. *Something from Nothing.* New York: Scholastic, 1992.

Greenfield, Eloise. *Grandpa's Face.* Illustrated by Floyd Cooper. New York: Putnam, 1988.

Hest, Amy. *When Jessie Came across the Sea.* Illustrated by P. J. Lynch. Cambridge, Mass.: Candlewick Press, 1997.

Howard, Elizabeth Fitzgerald. *Aunt Flossie's Hats (and Crab Cakes Later).* Illustrated by James Ransome. New York: Clarion, 1991.

Johnson, Angela. *When I Am Old with You.* Illustrated by David Soman. New York: Orchard/Jackson, 1990.

Joose, Barbara. *Mommu, Do You Love Me?* Illustrated by Barbara Lavallee. San Francisco, Calif.: Chronicle Books, 1991.

Lacapa, Michael, and Kathleen Lacapa. *Less Than Half, More Than Whole.* Flagstaff, Ariz.: Rising Moon/Northland Publishing, 1994.

Luenn, Nancy. *A Gift for Abuelita.* Illustrated by Robert Chapman. Flagstaff, Ariz.: Rising Moon/Northland Publishing, 1998.

Nez, Redwing. *Forbidden Talent.* Flagstaff, Ariz.: Rising Moon/Northland Publishing, 1995.

Polacco, Patricia. *Babushka's Doll.* New York: Aladdin, 1995.

———. *My Rotten Redheaded Older Brother.* New York: Aladdin, 1998.

———. *Thunder Cake.* New York: Philomel, 1990.

Raczek, Linda Theresa. *The Night the Grandfathers Danced.* Illustrated by Katalin Olah Ehling. Flagstaff, Ariz.: Northland Publishing, 1995.

Ringgold, Faith. *Tar Beach.* New York: Crown, 1991.

Roessel, Monty. *Songs from the Loom: A Navajo Girl Learns to Weave.* Minneapolis, Minn.: Lerner, 1995.

Rosa-Casanova, Sylvia. *Mama Provi and the Pot of Rice.* Illustrated by Robert Roth. New York: Atheneum, 1997.

Rosen, Michael. *Elijah's Angel: A Story for Chanukah and Christmas.* Illustrated by Aminah Brenda Lynn Robinson. San Diego, Calif.: Harcourt Brace, 1992.

Soto, Gary. *Too Many Tamales.* Illustrated by Ed Martinez. New York: Putnam, 1993.

Stevens, Jan Romero. *Carlos and the Cornfield.* Illustrated by Jeanne Arnold. Flagstaff, Ariz.: Rising Moon/Northland Publishing, 1995.

———. *Carlos and the Skunk.* Illustrated by Jeanne Arnold. Flagstaff, Ariz.: Rising Moon/Northland Publishing, 1997.

Williams, Sherley Anne. *Working Cotton.* Illustrated by Carole Byard. San Diego, Calif.: Harcourt Brace, 1992.

Guided Practice: Using Synonyms and Antonyms

Read each of the following sentences. Look carefully at each word that is italicized. Then review the three words in parentheses. Circle the word that would be the best synonym for the italicized word, matching the meaning as closely as possible.

1. Tio Armando says that when you have a *big* (loud, brawny, large) family, there is always someone to celebrate, someone to be *happy* (delighted, lucky, casual) about.
2. You to be *young* (light-hearted, a child, timid), I to be *old* (extinct, elderly, dilapidated)!
3. Tio Armando asked me if I could prepare a *banquet* (treat, surprise, feast) for his friends.
4. Rosita is changing and growing so *fast* (firmly, rapidly, faithfully) it is as if she is becoming a *new* (fresh, creative, different) person every day.

Watch how the meaning of a sentence can change when you replace a word with one that has the opposite meaning. In the following sentences, look at the antonym in parentheses following each italicized word. Think about how using the antonym instead of the italicized word would change the meaning of the sentence. Then add an antonym of your own in the blank. Be prepared to discuss your work with a partner or in a small group.

1. We have a *big* (small, _____) family.
2. He is an *old* (youthful, _____) man, *small* (brawny, _____).
3. He *laughed* (grumbled, _____) and said, "A talk about talking!"
4. But you and I, how *lucky* (unfortunate, _____) we are!
5. People waved to him and *smiled* (glowered, _____).

Directions for Creating a Diamond-Shaped Poem

Materials

Lined scratch paper
Pens or pencils
Diamond shape traced on a 5-x-8-inch
index card, lined on one side,
blank on the other
Markers, crayons, or colored pencils

Directions

1. Choose a noun (person, place, or thing) that has an opposite. Write that word on the top line of a sheet of scratch paper. Skip down to the seventh line and write an antonym, or opposite, of the noun.

2. On the second line, write two adjectives describing the first noun.

3. On the third line, write three participles. These are verbs that end in *ing* or *ed.*

4. On the fourth line, write four nouns related to the subject in some way.

The first two of these nouns should refer to the noun on the first line. The second two of these nouns are going to change the tone of the poem. They should refer to the antonym on the seventh line, beginning the transition.

5. On the fifth line, write three more participles, but these should continue to refer to the antonym. If you used the *ing* ending on the third line, use the same ending for the sake of continuity.

6. On the sixth line, write two adjectives referring to the antonym.

7. Proofread your work. Share it with a partner to help with the editing process. Then copy the polished version of your poem onto the lined side of your diamond. Turn the card over and illustrate it. Cut it out and display it so that everyone can enjoy your creativity.

Pattern for Creating a Diamond-Shaped Poem

This will fit nicely on a lined 5-x-8-inch index card.

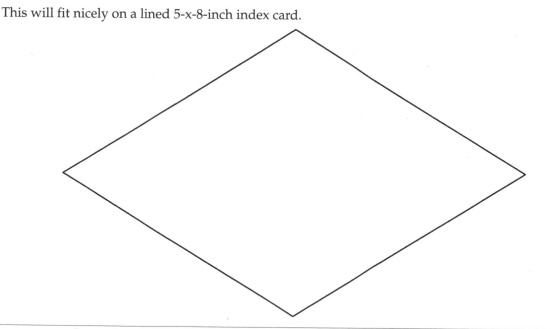

Lesson 27

Understanding the Context

SKILL: Inferring Word Meanings

CULTURE OF FOCUS: Japanese

Materials

Little Oh, by Laura Krauss Melmed (Lothrop, Lee & Shepard Books, 1997)

Student-created chart with the steps to follow to decipher words in context

Examples to put on the board or overhead to teach and model this skill

Printed directions (see below)

Paper to be used for an origami project

Lesson Motivator

1. Tell the students that the lesson ahead is going to teach them how to use the context of a story or informational text to help them figure out the meaning of unfamiliar words. This important skill will help them increase their vocabulary and become more independent readers.

2. Because the story is set in Japan and examines another culture, begin with an art activity that originated in Japan. It is called origami, or paper folding. This skill is practiced by the mother in the upcoming tale, and the students will learn to do it too.

3. Hand out squares of precut paper to be used to make an origami shape. Regular or recycled, foldable gift wrap that has been smoothed free of excess wrinkles, special origami paper, or even Xerox paper can be used. Avoid construction paper, which tends to tear easily as pieces are folded and refolded to create the various origami shapes.

4. Tell the students that the main character in the upcoming story is an origami doll who is destined to have some exciting adventures. You are going to practice the Japanese art of origami together to learn one shape, but students will have the opportunity to try other shapes on their own at a special reading center during free time. Perhaps their creations, too, will come to life and have a story to tell.

5. Follow the directions at the end of this lesson to teach the students to make a frog, a relatively simple shape that ties into the story. For future activities, see the list of suggested titles (also at the end of the lesson) for books that teach a variety of origami shapes.

6. Once this folding project is done, encourage students to bring in other interesting origami shapes to share. Some may want to become experts and learn to fold a shape that they can then teach to other classmates. Setting the frogs out of harm's way, turn to the book and invite students to listen to a story about one origami creation that took on a life of her own.

7. As you read, ask students to jot down several words from the story that they don't know. Remind them that the lesson growing out of this book involves understanding the meaning of a word using other words around it for clues.

Suggestions for Teaching the Lesson

- Before beginning this lesson, select five or six interesting words from the story that students might not know or could be curious about. Jot them down and set them aside to be used at the conclusion of the story. Read the book to the class, stopping to point out interesting bits of culture or to highlight one of your words for them to think about. For example, you could use the word *frolicked*, pointing it out to the students, writing it on the board, and then rereading the paragraph so that students can try to figure out the meaning. Share ideas, clarify the meaning of the word, and then continue the story.

- Once the book is completed, discuss the students' reactions to the story. To facilitate thinking skills, ask the students to discuss the ways in which the author created suspense to keep the reader involved in the story. Talk about the conclusion of the story. Did students expect the ending to be as it was written? Were there clues to let them know this kind of ending was coming? Did the listeners have any strong feelings as they heard the story? What did the author do to make them feel that way?

- Point out that the students can model a story of their own after this one, using the same techniques that the author used, thus emphasizing the point that the authors they read are often the best writing teachers.

- Return to words and the word recognition strategy to be reviewed. Teach the students that context clues are bits of meaning, of information within the text that might help them derive the meaning of a word they don't know. Sometimes there is a restatement of information that explains what a word means.

- Tell the students that there also may be other statements used to compare and contrast information, and the word can be understood through that information. Context includes the words surrounding the unfamiliar word. Go back to the word *frolicked* and highlight how the paragraph gave clues to the meaning of that particular word.

- Continue to model the strategy of using the context to understand the meaning of an unfamiliar word by listing the words on the board that students have selected as the story was read. Add your words as well, if they haven't been identified. Use one of the words to work through the steps below.

- Display on the overhead or a chart the steps to follow to decipher a word using the context:

  1. When encountering an unfamiliar word, continue reading to the end of the sentence or the paragraph to see if the word is important to your understanding of the text. If is isn't, read on.

  2. If you decide that the word is important, reread the sentence or the paragraph, looking for clues to the meaning of the word.

  3. If you are still stumped, try your word analysis skills and look for the base word, prefixes, or suffixes that are familiar to you.

  4. Draw on your phonics skills to try to pronounce the word. Does it sound familiar when you say it aloud?

  5. If you still don't understand the word, refer to the dictionary or ask for help.

  6. Once you have figured out the meaning of the word, read the text again to be sure you understand what the sentence or paragraph is trying to convey.

- Move to one of the students' words and walk through the steps to unlock its meaning. Then divide the students into pairs and let them practice on another word of their choice.

- Invite one or two students to create a copy of a chart to be posted for easy viewing, with the steps in the use of context clues written simply. Students can use the completed chart for reference as they practice this skill in future reading and eventually make it their own.

- Let the students select another tale of Japanese origin, or a book set in Japan in another genre, to read and to practice word recognition using context clues. As they practice and reinforce this new skill, have them keep a list of words they have learned over a period of a week and share them with you during individual student conferences. Encourage students to transfer these skills to the novels that they choose to read on their own or for other assignments.

Evaluation

- As your schedule permits, meet with each reader in the class to discuss his or her word recognition strategies. Each learner will share the list of words recently acquired and demonstrate how to use context clues so that you can tell if the skill has been acquired and mastered.

- Review this skill once or twice during the upcoming weeks to reinforce its importance and to help anyone who is still struggling with it.

Extensions

- Encourage students to practice their skills at origami. Several students can combine their creations to form an attractive mobile to decorate the classroom or the school library.

- Invite students to write a story about one of their origami shapes, working like the author in *Little Oh* to develop an intriguing tale. Have them polish and illustrate it, then read it to the class and store a copy in the classroom library for other readers to enjoy.

- Invite a guest speaker to enlighten the class on Japanese traditions and celebrations. Have students write in their journals about the similarities and differences between their cultural beliefs and those of children in the Japanese culture.

- Assign interested students to research ancient Japanese traditions, contrast them to contemporary beliefs, and present a report with attractive visuals to the class.

- To fine-tune literary skills, ask the class: "Who does the most work?" Ask interested students to return to *Little Oh* to look for ways that the Japanese culture and traditions are expressed in the text and how the illustrator represented them. They should surmise that an author and illustrator work very closely to convey a complete tale that requires both text and pictures to interact smoothly, like a quality partnership.

- Have these students relate their findings to the class and challenge classmates to look for ways other author/illustrator pairs team up to tell the story through the interaction of text and picture.

Suggested Titles for Independent Reading and Research

Biddle, Steve, and Megumi Biddle. *Origami Safari.* New York: Tupelo/Morrow, 1994.

Bunting, Eve. *So Far from the Sea.* Illustrated by Chris K. Soentpiet. New York: Clarion, 1998.

Chinn, Karen. *Sam and the Lucky Money.* Illustrated by Cornelius Van Wright and Ying-Hwa Hu. New York: Lee & Low, 1995.

Coerr, Eleanor. *Sadako.* Illustrated by Ed Young. New York: Putnam, 1993.

Hamanaka, Sheila. *Screen of Frogs: An Old Tale.* New York: Orchard, 1993.

Hong, Lily Toy. *Two of Everything.* Morton Grove, Ill.: Whitman, 1993.

Kodama, Tatsuharu. *Shin's Tricycle.* Illustrated by Noriyuki Ando. Translated by Kazuko Hokumen-Jones. New York: Walker, 1995.

Levine, Arthur A. *The Boy Who Drew Cats: A Japanese Folktale.* Illustrated by Frederic Clement. New York: Dial, 1994.

Long, Jan Freeman, adapter. *The Bee and the Dream: A Japanese Tale.* Illustrated by Kaoru Ono. New York: Dutton, 1996.

Martin, Rafe. *Mysterious Tales of Japan.* Illustrated by Tatsuro Kiuchi. New York: Putnam, 1996.

Mayer, Marianna. *Turandot.* Illustrated by Winslow Pels. New York: Morrow, 1995.

Mayer, Mercer. *Shibumi and the Kitemaker.* New York: Marshall Cavendish, 1999.

Melmed, Laura Krauss. *The First Song Ever Sung.* Illustrated by Ed Young. New York: Lothrop, Lee & Shepard Books, 1993.

Merrill, Jean. *The Girl Who Loved Caterpillars: A Twelfth-Century Tale from Japan.* Illustrated by Floyd Cooper. New York: Philomel, 1992.

Mochizuki, Ken. *Baseball Saved Us.* Illustrated by Dom Lee. New York: Lee & Low, 1993.

———. *Passage to Freedom: The Sugihara Story.* Illustrated by Dom Lee. New York: Lee & Low, 1997.

Montroll, John. *African Animals in Origami.* Wheaton, Md.: Antroll Publications, 1993.

Nakano, Dokuihtei. *Easy Origami.* Illustrated by Eric Kenneway. New York: Puffin Books, 1994.

Namioka, Lensey. *The Loyal Cat.* Illustrated by Aki Sogabe. San Diego, Calif.: Harcourt Brace, 1995.

Nomura, Takaaki. *Grandpa's Town.* Translated by Amanda Mayer Stinchecum. New York: Kane/Miller, 1991.

Paterson, Katherine. *The Tale of the Mandarin Ducks.* Illustrated by Leo Dillon and Diane Dillon. New York: Lodestar, 1990.

Powers, Daniel. *Jiro's Pearl.* Cambridge, Mass.: Candlewick Press, 1997.

San Souci, Robert D. *The Snow Wife.* Illustrated by Stephen T. Johnson. New York: Dial, 1993.

———, reteller. *The Samurai's Daughter: A Japanese Legend.* Illustrated by Stephen T. Johnson. New York: Dial, 1992.

Say, Allen. *Grandfather's Journey.* Boston: Houghton Mifflin, 1993.

———. *Tea with Milk.* Boston: Houghton Mifflin, 1999.

———. *Tree of Cranes.* Boston: Houghton Mifflin, 1991.

Schroeder, Alan. *Lily and the Wooden Bowl.* Illustrated by Yoriko Ito. New York: Doubleday, 1994.

Smolinski, Jill. *Holiday Origami.* Illustrated by Mary A. Fraser. Los Angeles: Lowell House Juvenile, 1995.

Temko, Florence. *Jewish Origami.* Torranace, Calif.: Heian International, 1991.

———. *Origami Magic.* New York: Scholastic, 1993.

Tompert, Ann. *Bamboo Hats and a Rice Cake.* Illustrated by Demi. New York: Crown, 1993.

Uchida, Yoshiko. *The Bracelet.* Illustrated by Joanna Yardley. New York: Philomel, 1993.

Waite, Michael P. *Jojufu.* Illustrated by Yoriko Ito. New York: Lee & Shepard, 1996.

Wells, Ruth. *The Farmer and the Poor God.* Illustrated by Yoshi. New York: Simon & Schuster, 1996.

Yee, Paul. *Roses Sing on a New Snow: A Delicious Tale.* Illustrated by Harvey Chan. New York: Macmillan, 1991.

Yep, Laurence. *The Boy Who Swallowed Snakes.* Illustrated by Jean Tseng and Mou-sien Tseng. New York: Scholastic, 1994.

Directions for Making an Origami Frog

1. Using a 3-x-5-inch index card, fold the top short edge over to meet the left side of the card, beginning with the right corner. This is the beginning of an X. Repeat with the other corner to finish the X. Open the card.

2. Fold the card backward through the center of the X, as indicated.

3. Push down at the middle of the X. Move points A and B to meet together in the middle of the card.

4. Fold the outer corners of the triangle to the top so that it looks like the sketch for step 5.

5. Fold sides A and B into the middle along fold lines as indicated.

6. Fold the bottom edge to the top.

7. Fold the top edge of the front layer to the bottom edge.

8. Turn the shape over and loosen the front and back legs. Now the frog is not flat. Gently tap the back of the frog with your finger and it will hop.

9. Complete your frog by adding some eyes so that it can see where it is going!

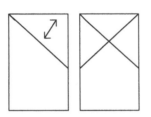

1. Using a 3-x-5-inch index card, fold the top short edge over to meet the left side of the card, beginning with the right corner. This is the beginning of an X. Repeat with the other corner to finish the X. Open the card.

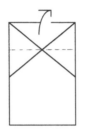

2. Fold the card backward through the center of the X, as indicated.

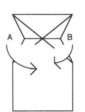

3. Push down at the middle of the X. Move points A and B to meet in the middle of the card.

4. Fold the outer corners of the triangle to the top so that it looks like the sketch for step 5.

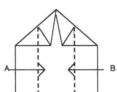

5. Fold sides A and B into the middle along fold lines as indicated.

6. Fold the bottom edge to the top.

7. Fold the top edge of the front layer to the bottom edge.

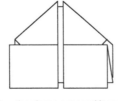

8. Turn the shape over and loosen the front and back legs. Now the frog is not flat. Gently tap the back of the frog with your finger and it will hop.

9. Complete your frog by adding some eyes so that it can see where it is going!

Lesson 28

Using Award-Winning Books by African-American Authors and Illustrators

SKILL: Self-Selecting Vocabulary

CULTURE OF FOCUS: African American

Materials

For a change of pace, rather than using just one focus book, this lesson will make use of several, all by award-winning African-American authors and illustrators.

The Ballad of Belle Dorcas, by William Hooks; illustrated by Brian Pinkney (Knopf, 1990)

John Henry, by Julius Lester; illustrated by Jerry Pinkney (Dial, 1994)

The Dark-Thirty: Southern Tales of the Supernatural, by Patricia C. McKissack; illustrated by Brian Pinkney (Scholastic, 1992)

Ma Dear's Aprons, by Patricia C. McKissack; illustrated by Floyd Cooper (Atheneum, 1997)

A Million Fish … More or Less, by Patricia C. McKissack; illustrated by Dena Schutzer (Knopf/Borzoi Books, 1992)

Mirandy and Brother Wind, by Patricia C. McKissack; illustrated by Jerry Pinkney (Knopf, 1988)

Cendrillon: A Caribbean Cinderella, by Robert D. San Souci; illustrated by Jerry Pinkney and Daniel San Souci (Simon & Schuster, 1998)

The Faithful Friend, by Robert D. San Souci; illustrated by Brian Pinkney (Simon & Schuster, 1995)

Sukey and the Mermaid, by Robert D. San Souci; illustrated by Brian Pinkney (Aladdin Paperbacks, 1996)

The Talking Eggs: A Folktale from the American South, by Robert D. San Souci; illustrated by Jerry Pinkney (Dial, 1989)

Paper
Pens and pencils
Tagboard and markers
Dictionaries

Lesson Motivator

1. Find a dozen or so interesting and unusual words from the books selected for the lesson or from those listed for independent reading. Using dark markers, write each word on a strip of tagboard large enough to be seen by the entire class.

2. Randomly select one student per card and ask them to come to the front of the room. Give several other students dictionaries and place placards on their desks designating them "Word Authorities."

3. Spend some time playing with words. After the students with words have lined up at the front of the classroom, positioned so that all the words can be read, give the rest of the class some time to study the words.

4. Ask for volunteers to read a word they think they can pronounce or that they already know. After the word has been pronounced, one of the "Word Authorities" will verify the pronunciation or correct it as needed based on dictionary consultation. The same student or another volunteer can offer a definition. That, too, can be verified by another "Word Authority" if there is a doubt about the meaning suggested. Someone else can attempt to use the word in a sentence. As the teacher, you may choose to be the judge here.

5. Continue the activity until all the words have been correctly pronounced, defined, and used in a sentence. Before the students are seated, ask them to put themselves in alphabetical order, the final result to be approved by the class. This type of activity reviews

vocabulary and dictionary skills and extends word knowledge in general in a much more interesting way than the standard worksheet approach.

Suggestions for Teaching the Lesson

• Teach the students the importance of learning new words as an ongoing, everyday effort. Your enthusiasm for finding and learning new words will be the best motivator for vocabulary acquisition in your classroom.

• Explain that you are going to be looking for a new word each day for a period of several weeks off and on throughout the year. In this manner, the task will not become tedious. Some words are to be recorded in a reading or writing journal, while others will be selected to be shared with the class daily. Remind students that new words must be used and used again to be permanently acquired.

• Spend a few minutes extolling the virtues of the dictionaries that were a part of the day's motivator. These books are often ignored, possibly because of misuse in boring vocabulary exercises in the past, but they are invaluable in building vocabulary.

• Book-talk the titles selected for the day's lesson. Rather than using the read-aloud format, students should work in small groups with a wonderful collection of titles.

• Tell the class that the skilled authors and illustrators of these particular books are all award-winners. They are going to have the opportunity to work with some especially fine literature reflecting the African-American culture. Learners may be interested to know that Brian Pinkney is Jerry Pinkney's son, that Jerry illustrates books written by his wife, and that his entire family is

involved in the worlds of art and children's literature. They might enjoy looking up information about this creative family on an author/illustrator website in their free time.

• Have students work in pairs or triads to read a book. Having several copies of each title will be beneficial and will permit groups to remain small as students read and share a title together. Students should pick several words to pursue further after reading the book together. Ask them to define the word based on the way it is used in the context of the story. Have them write those words on tagboard, as demonstrated in the motivator, with the context definition written on the back. One reader should double-check the definition in the dictionary before presenting the word to the class.

• After reading their books and selecting their words, each group should read their words to the class, standing in front of the class. Have the class pick one word to pronounce, define, and use in a sentence as the wordplay continues for several days. Each student should record the new word and its definition in a personal reading or writing journal so it will be handy for future reference.

• Tagboard vocabulary, those words used and not used, should be stapled to a bulletin board to be studied and pondered by the class. Assign a creative writing project in which students must use as many of the new words as possible in a short story, a rap, or a poem.

• Continue building vocabulary based on words that the students select from daily reading, making it a word-a-day activity. Rotate the selection so that all students get a chance to share a new word. Write the latest word on colored tagboard and post it in a specific place each day. The student discoverer should teach the class about the word based on dictionary research. You and the students should try to use the word several times throughout the day.

- Have at least three students use the word in a sentence before the class leaves for lunch, and have several more work with it in different ways before heading home at the end of the day. Remind learners again that words must be used or they will not become a part of their growing vocabulary.

Evaluation

- When students select words for study and give their definitions, assess their usage. Discuss whether the definitions were obtained from context or from the dictionary. Monitor the way in which students integrate new words with their prior knowledge, a word-check that can be done via quick conversations with each student.

Extensions

- Send an interested student on a Web search for more information about the authors and illustrators of this collection of books. Useful websites are provided in Appendix III.

- Students should also review pertinent volumes in the Something About the Author series in their school learning center or public library, presenting a verbal thumbnail sketch of an illustrator or author to the class.

- Ask the art teacher if he or she could spend some time with the class, teaching them how to use the scratch-board technique that distinguishes much of Brian Pinkney's artwork. Brian explains it as using a white board that has been covered with black ink. The ink is scratched off with a sharp tool, thus exposing the white underneath. The color is added using oil pastels, which are rubbed into the appropriate scratched areas. The excess color is rubbed away with a product called Liquin. Another approach is to cover white tagboard with a heavy layer of many colors of crayons. The crayons are painted over with India ink. When it is dry, a sharp instrument is used to scratch a drawing onto the surface, scraping away the black ink to reveal the multicolor underneath.

- Have students read other titles by these creative African-American writers. The students should then either book-talk the titles, write lively reviews and post them in the reading center to entice other readers, or create some drama activities related to their favorites.

- Have students prepare a reader's theater script from a lively book and present the production to the class.

- Divide the class into pairs and have each duo role-play a conversation between two characters from different but related books.

Suggested Titles for Independent Reading and Research

Burton, Albert. *Where Does the Trail Lead?* Illustrated by Brian Pinkney. New York: Simon & Schuster, 1993.

Dragonwagon, Crescent. *Half a Moon and One Whole Star.* Illustrated by Jerry Pinkney. New York: Aladdin Paperbacks, 1990.

———. *Home Place.* Illustrated by Jerry Pinkney. New York: Macmillan, 1990.

Kipling, Rudyard. *Rikki-Tikki-Tavi.* Adapted and illustrated by Jerry Pinkney. New York: Morrow, 1997.

Lester, Julius. *Further Tales of Uncle Remus: The Misadventures of Brer Rabbit, Brer Fox, Brer Wolf, the Doodang, and Other Creatures.* Illustrated by Jerry Pinkney. New York: Dial, 1990.

———. *The Last Tales of Uncle Remus.* Illustrated by Jerry Pinkney. New York: Dial, 1994.

———. *More Tales of Uncle Remus: Further Adventures of Brer Rabbit, His Friends, Enemies, and Others.* Illustrated by Jerry Pinkney. New York: Dial, 1988.

———. *The Tales of Uncle Remus: The Adventures of Brer Rabbit.* Illustrated by Jerry Pinkney. New York: Dial, 1987.

Pinkney, Andrea Davis. *Dear Benjamin Banneker.* San Diego, Calif.: Harcourt Brace, 1994.

———. *Hold Fast to Dreams.* New York: Morrow, 1995.

Pinkney, Brian. *The Adventures of Sparrowboy.* New York: Simon & Schuster, 1997.

———. *Jo Jo's Flying Sidekick.* New York: Simon & Schuster, 1995.

———. *Max Found Two Sticks.* New York: Simon & Schuster, 1994.

Pinkney, Gloria. *Back Home.* Illustrated by Jerry Pinkney. New York: Dial, 1992.

———. *The Sunday Outing.* Illustrated by Jerry Pinkney. New York: Dial, 1994.

Lesson 29

Another Tool for Building Vocabulary

SKILL: Previewing Words before a Reading Selection

CULTURE OF FOCUS: Russian American

Materials

A Piece of Home, by Sonia Levitan (Dial, 1996)
Notebook or newsprint for sketching
Pens or pencils
Heavy paper
Tagboard sheets (8 1/2 x 11 inches)
Markers
Collection of books about Russian Americans, Russian folktales, and other titles that address the experience of being an immigrant

Lesson Motivator

1. Set the scene: Each student and his or her family is facing an imminent move. They are going to a country where the language and customs differ markedly from those to which they are accustomed. Because they will travel by air and housing will be cramped, at least initially, personal possessions must be limited to absolute necessities. Beyond basic clothing, each person can only take one treasured item. What will it be?

2. Have the students sketch the items and below them write a few sentences explaining why they have been selected.

3. When the work has been completed, ask for volunteers to come up to the front of the class and share their responses to a difficult situation. Sketches can be tacked along the top of the chalkboard or on a bulletin board for the duration of the lesson.

Suggestions for Teaching the Lesson

- Word games have long been a popular pastime, whether playing Hangman to pass the last few minutes of a class period productively or as a way for students to use free time quietly and constructively. Even on television, programs like *Wheel of Fortune* maintain high audience appeal. Because practice and exposure strengthen and build word recognition skills, dedicate a portion of the classroom reading corner to word games.

- Used games are frequently available at garage sales at greatly reduced prices. Strive for an irresistible selection of games for use during free time or just for a change-of-pace activity when the whole class is involved in polishing spelling and vocabulary skills by applying their word knowledge to wordplay. Popular games like Boggle, Scrabble, and Probe are engaging choices.

- For this particular lesson, create your own word game, which will involve delving into prior knowledge, applying word analysis strategies, spelling practice, vocabulary development, and, at times, a little inventive guessing.

Using heavy paper or tagboard 8 ½ x 11 inches in size, one sheet per letter, write out three to five words that you have selected after prereading the day's reading selection. Suggestions from *A Piece of Home* by Sonia Levitan are *journey, passports, samovars, harness,* and *wrings*. Pick words that are unusual, important to comprehending the story, and that will be excellent additions to the students' growing vocabulary knowledge.

- Use the railing of the chalkboard or a pocket chart that has been adapted to hold larger letter cards. This can also be done on the chalkboard or an overhead transparency by drawing a rectangular shape for each letter as follows:

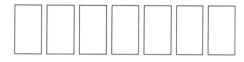

- Place the letters in the correct order, blank sides toward the class. Then, hold up the book to be read, introducing it by title and author. Ask students to predict what the story might be about. After a brief discussion, direct their attention to the words to be discovered. Begin with the first word, giving the students a simple clue to its meaning. Based on their predictions about the book and the clue, they should begin to think about what the word might be. In a predetermined, orderly fashion, have students guess the letters. It may take several turns before enough letters appear to enable students to guess what the word might be. When a student has an idea, he or she should raise a hand and wait to be called upon. Once the vocabulary word is guessed, have the guessing student spell it before the rest of the letters are turned over. Let several students be in charge of double-checking the spelling in the dictionary, taking turns looking up the spelling and reading an appropriate definition to the class. If there is something of interest to point out about the way the word is spelled, draw the students' attention to it briefly and then proceed.

- After all the words have been discovered, tell the students to raise their hands quietly when they encounter the word in the book you are about to read. Before beginning the story, ask if anyone has altered their predictions about the book based on the review of upcoming interesting words. Then share the book with the class.

- Divide students into teams of three. Have them choose a book from those gathered beforehand, read it carefully, and select three to five words from the book. Using the heavy paper or tagboard, they should spell their choices, keeping them from any prying eyes. Following the procedure just described, have the students take turns presenting a book each day along with the vocabulary. Suggested titles listed below reflect tales from Russia and books about other children who have been immigrants to America.

- Have students take turns reading their books aloud after practicing. Oral reading skills are being polished for the readers, and listening skills are being strengthened for the rest of the class. Not only are word recognition skills being enhanced, but so is vocabulary development.

Evaluation

- During this activity, walk from group to group. Select two or three learning behaviors to target and take anecdotal notes on individuals. Are they working cooperatively? How are their oral reading skills? Do they use word "attack" skills appropriately when they encounter an unknown word?

- Schedule a short conference with each student periodically to discuss the learning behaviors you have noted during classroom activities. Target a skill that might need reinforcing and focus each student's attention on useful strategies to apply in the future.

Extensions

- Have students develop a game of their own reinforcing vocabulary or based on the plot of one of the books.

- Create a student version of *Jeopardy*, including rules for quiet and orderly play. If students play this in teams, the classroom noise level is guaranteed to rise. Brainstorm categories as a class and go to work finding new words and reviewing previously learned words. One afternoon a month might be devoted to *Jeopardy*, with a different team of students in charge each time. Work with the students to be certain their categories and words are correct and thought-provoking.

- Use one bulletin board as a "Word Wall for Interesting and Unusual Words." Keep a supply of 5-x-8-inch index cards and markers handy. When students come across an intriguing word, they should write it out and share it with you along with its definition to be certain they understand it. Then they read it to the class, give the definition, and attach it to the "Word Wall" for classmates' future reference.

- Have students keep an eye out for words that have become a part of the English language but are rooted in other countries. They can make an attractive mobile using note cards, yarn, and hangars, one per country, once they have discovered five or six words.

- Read more about the immigrant experience, focusing on nonfiction accounts. Have students role-play being an immigrant, letting the class ask pertinent questions about the experiences several "actors" may have had.

- Have students find out where their ancestors lived and note their homelands on a map of the world. Tie that knowledge into individual projects that can be integrated into the social studies curriculum.

Suggested Titles for Independent Reading and Research

Aliki. *Marianthe's Story, Book One: Painted Words; Book Two: Spoken Pictures*. New York: Greenwillow, 1998.

Bartone, Elisa. *American, Too*. Illustrated by Ted Lewin. New York: Lothrop, Lee & Shepard Books, 1996.

———. *Peppe the Lamplighter*. Illustrated by Ted Lewin. New York: Lothrop, Lee & Shepard Books, 1993.

Brett, Jan. *The Mitten*. New York: Putnam, 1989.

Brown, Tricia. *Lee Ann: The Story of a Vietnamese-American Girl*. Illustrated with photographs by Ted Thai. New York: Putnam, 1991.

Fonteyn, Margot. *Swan Lake*. Illustrated by Trina Schart Hyman. San Diego, Calif.: Harcourt Brace, 1989.

Franklin, Kristine L. *The Wolfhound*. Illustrated by Kris Waldherr. New York: Lothrop, Lee & Shepard Books, 1996.

Helprin, Mark. *Swan Lake*. Illustrated by Chris Van Allsburg. Boston: Houghton Mifflin, 1989.

Hest, Amy. *When Jessie Came across the Sea*. Illustrated by P. J. Lynch. Cambridge, Mass.: Candlewick Press, 1997.

Hoffman, Mary. *Clever Katya: A Fairy Tale from Old Russia*. Illustrated by Marie Cameron. New York: Barefoot Books, 1991.

Joose, Barbara M. *The Morning Chair*. Illustrated by Marcia Sewall. New York: Clarion, 1995.

Kallman, Esther. *Tchaikovsky Discovers America*. Illustrated by Laura Fernandez and Rick Jacobsen. New York: Orchard, 1995.

Kimmel, Eric A. *Baba Yaga: A Russian Folktale*. Illustrated by Megan Lloyd. New York: Holiday House, 1991.

———. *Bearhead: A Russian Folktale*. Illustrated by Charles Mikolaycak. New York: Holiday House, 1991.

Knight, Margy Burns. *Who Belongs Here? An American Story*. Illustrated by Anne Sibley O'Brien. Gardiner, Maine: Tilbury House, 1993.

Kroll, Steven. *Ellis Island: Doorway to Freedom*. Illustrated by Karen Ritz. New York: Holiday House, 1995.

Kuklin, Susan. *How My Family Lives in America*. New York: Bradbury, 1992.

Lemieux, Michele, reteller. *Peter and the Wolf*. New York: Morrow, 1991.

Lurie, Alison. *The Black Geese: A Baba Yaga Story from Russia.* Illustrated by Jessica Souhami. New York: DK Ink, 1999.

Morgan, Pierre. *Turnip: An Old Russian Tale.* New York: Putnam, 1990.

Nelson, Nan Ferring. *My Day with Anka.* Illustrated by Bill Farnsworth. New York: Lothrop, 1996.

O'Conner, Karen. *Dan Thuy's New Life in America.* Minneapolis, Minn.: Lerner, 1992.

Park, Frances, and Ginger Park. *My Freedom Trip: A Child's Escape from North Korea.* Illustrated by Debra Reid Jenkins. Honesdale, Pa.: Boyds Mills Press, 1998.

Polacco, Patricia. *The Keeping Quilt.* New York: Simon & Schuster, 1988.

———. *Rechenka's Eggs.* New York: Philomel, 1988.

Pomeranc, Marion Hess. *The American Wei.* Illustrated by DyAnne DiSalvo-Ryan. Morton Grove, Ill.: Albert Whitman, 1998.

———. *The Hand-Me-Down Horse.* Illustrated by Joanna Yardley. Morton Grove, Ill.: Whitman, 1996.

Rael, Elsa Okon. *What Zeesie Saw on Delancey Street.* Illustrated by Marjorie Priceman. New York: Simon & Schuster, 1996.

Reynolds, Marilynn. *The New Land: A First Year on the Prairie.* Illustrated by Stephen McCallum. Seattle, Wash.: Orca, 1997.

Sorensen, Henri. *New Hope.* New York: Lothrop, Lee & Shepard Books, 1995.

Steptoe, John. *Creativity.* Illustrated by E. B. Lewis. New York: Clarion, 1997.

Surat, Michele Maria. *Angel Child, Dragon Child.* Illustrated by Vo-Dinh Mai. New York: Scholastic, 1983.

Tarbescu, Edith. *Annushka's Voyage.* Illustrated by Lydia Dabcovich. New York: Clarion, 1998.

Vagin, Vladimir. *The Enormous Carrot.* New York: Scholastic, 1998.

Watson, Mary. *The Butterfly Seeds.* New York: Tambourine, 1995.

Winthrop, Elizabeth. *Vasilissa the Beautiful.* Illustrated by Alexander Koshkin. New York: HarperCollins, 1991.

Wolkstein, Diane. *Oom Razoom, or Go I Know Not Where, Bring Back I Know Not What: A Russian Tale.* Illustrated by Dennis McDermott. New York: Morrow, 1991.

Lesson 30

One Plus One = Something

SKILL: Working with Compound Words

CULTURE OF FOCUS: Arabic

Materials

The Storytellers, by Ted Lewin (Lothrop, Lee & Shepard Books, 1998)
If You're Not Here, Please Raise Your Hand, by Kalli Dakos (Four Winds Press, 1990)
Regular (3-x-5-inch) and large (4-x-6-inch) index cards
Crayons, pens, or pencils
Overhead projector or chalkboard
Set of compound word puzzle pieces, enough so that each student in the class receives one puzzle piece

Lesson Motivator

1. Prepare a set of compound word puzzle pieces ahead of time. Write a compound word in large print on a 3-x-5-inch index card using a marker. Divide the word into two pieces by cutting the card like two puzzle pieces (see example below).

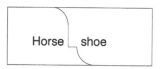

2. Make enough compound word pairs so that each student in the class gets a puzzle piece. Use a selection of words from around the classroom or words that pertain to subjects currently under study. Other word options include:

horseshoe	streetcar
cookbook	campfire
firewood	sidewalk
moonbeam	anyone
airplane	pitchfork
trapdoor	wishbone
somewhere	nobody
overhead	stereotype
classroom	grandmother
cattail	cupcake
armchair	earring
inside	lawnmower
hairspray	notebook
toothbrush	dogwood
nightlight	flapjacks

3. Mix up the pieces thoroughly. Put them in a large coffee can or basket so that students can pick one when the lesson begins.

4. To begin the lesson, read "I Have No Time to Visit with King Arthur," from *If You're Not Here, Please Raise Your Hand.* This particular poem addresses the overuse of worksheets as tools to teach grammar, doing so in an amusing way. It also highlights compound words, a hint about the upcoming lesson.

5. Tell the students there is a clue to the skill to be reviewed in the poem, then move ahead with the lesson. Although the author may not have intended it, there is also a reminder to support the teaching of skills within the realm of good books.

6. Now, pass the container around the room, instructing each student to take a puzzle piece without looking.

7. The students' next task is to move around the room in an effort to find the match for their puzzle piece. Each one is looking for a puzzle-piece partner. Once the match has occurred, student pairs should read their resulting word and sit quietly until all the students and words are matched.

8. Go from pair to pair, having one student read a word while you write

it on the overhead. Ask one student of each pair to use the word in a sentence before continuing on to the next pair.

9. When all the words have been recorded, encourage the students to talk about this list. What is unusual about these words? The students will no doubt quickly detect that they are similar because they are all compound words. Invite someone to define what a compound word is. Their definition should explain that a compound word is made up of two known sight words, or words that are complete in themselves. When combined, they create a new word.

10. Discuss the word analysis that the students might use in deciphering a compound word. In the process of understanding them, the students should break the word apart, recognize each piece, and then blend the pieces together. Sometimes these blended words are concrete and easy to understand *(baseball, sunshine)*, whereas others are more abstract *(insight, brainstorm).* In the latter case, explain to readers that they should use the context of the sentence to help them with the word's meaning.

11. Finally, point out that the day's lesson involves working with compound words. As they listen to the upcoming story, ask students to pick out clues in the story to help them identify the culture depicted and details that reveal the setting. They also should jot down any compound words that they hear to be added to the list at the conclusion of the story.

Suggestions for Teaching the Lesson

• Read the focus book, *The Storytellers,* which conveniently contains a compound word in the title. Stop periodically to discuss the various occupations depicted in the story and how they compare to or contrast with those in the United States. When the story is completed, ask for students' comments or reactions. Can they identify the country depicted in the story? What culture is being recognized? What do they think of the occupation of storyteller? Are they familiar with storytellers in this country? What other cultures can they think of that also have storytellers?

- Ask for a list of the compound words the students found as they listened. The list should include the following:

grandfather	firewood
lambskins	cobblestones
countless	bathtubs
doorway	rooftop
sunlight	inlaid
craftsmen	teapot
horseman	everyone
storyteller	

- Add these to the words already listed on the overhead. Talk through the resulting list of words. Circle a few of the words that are easy to understand because their meanings are clearly represented by the word parts, such as *lambskins, baseball,* and *bathtubs.* Then look through the list of words again for some whose meanings are more abstract. Draw a square around words such as *cattail* or *brainstorm.* Talk about how the two words in these terms combine to form quite a different meaning.

- Check on word analysis skills by asking how students figure out the meaning of such a word when they encounter it during reading. They might suggest that they use the context of the sentence to figure out the meaning or they may continue to read but check the meaning in the dictionary at a later time.

- Assign each pair of students a task to complete. Using scratch paper and a pen or pencil, they are to

take three to five minutes to brainstorm as many compound words as they can think of that have not already been used.

- When the time is up, students should write a nonsense story using as many of the compound words as they can from their list and those provided on the overhead. Give students about 15 minutes to work on the writing part of the assignment. You are not looking for polished writing, but rather just some creative use of compound words. Move about the room, monitoring progress and prompting writers as needed.

- When the designated time is up, ask for several volunteers to read their stories. The class will surely enjoy the sharing of this amusing creative writing.

- For further practice, send pairs to find a picture book of their choice to read together. The books collected ahead of time can reflect the Arabic cultures, other titles written or illustrated by Ted Lewin, and titles from a variety of other cultures. As they read, direct students' attention to any compound words they encounter. Have them decide if they are concrete or abstract in the way they are used. Once students have completed the book, have them select a word from the book to illustrate.

- Wordplay adds variety to the daily routine and makes learning new words an appealing process. In this case, students cannot use written words. Instead, they must draw a picture of each of the pieces of the word, connected by a plus sign, on one side of a 4-x-6-inch index card or other suitable material. On the other side, they should draw the meaning of the word. For example, if a pair were working with *cupcake,* they would draw the picture of a cup + a cake on one side of the card. On the other side, they would draw a cupcake.

- Once the drawings are completed, students can come to the front of the room and let the rest of the class guess their compound words from the pictures they have drawn. Because markers tend to bleed through the cards, colored pencils or crayons are best suited for this activity.

Evaluation

- For this activity, focus on several learning behaviors. How do students work cooperatively in pairs? Does each person in the pair contribute equally to the brainstorming, writing, and drawing activities? As a quick review, make up an overhead with sentences that contain compound words from several of the books used by the students.

- Have student volunteers come up to the front of the room, read the sentence on the overhead, and circle the compound words. Periodically, in upcoming lessons or reading activities, stop to identify several compound words to keep word recognition skills finely honed.

Extensions

- Set up a time when a small team of your students can go to another classroom to teach those students about compound words. They can begin their mini-lesson with a definition of compound words, put several examples on the chalkboard or overhead, and then present their picture cards for class members to try to guess. The lesson can conclude with the students reading their favorite picture book. Listeners should note a few compound words to discuss at the conclusion of the story.

- Invite a group of students to create a bulletin board, with interesting compound words as one part and

some wordplay as another part. They might have a segment for silly questions focusing on compound words and their meanings. For instance, one query would be, "If we have a chairman, why don't we have a deskman?" or "If we have outside and inside, why don't we have outfit and infit?" Each sentence could be illustrated to extend the fun.

- If students have a writing notebook, ask them to devote a page to new compound words that they discover in their reading. Encourage them to use those that fit appropriately in some of their future writing assignments.

- Interested students can make a small collage of compound words on posterboard using different word parts snipped from newspapers, posters, advertisements, and magazines. Share with the class and, later, arrange collages attractively on a wall outside the classroom.

Suggested Titles for Independent Reading and Research

Bahous, Sally. *Sitti and the Cats: A Tale of Friendship.* Illustrated by Nancy Malick. Boulder, Colo.: Roberts Rinehart Publishers, 1997.

Bartone, Elisa. *American Too.* Illustrated by Ted Lewin. New York: Lothrop, Lee & Shepard Books, 1996.

———. *Peppe, the Lamplighter.* Illustrated by Ted Lewin. New York: Lothrop, Lee & Shepard Books, 1993.

Birdseye, Tom. *Soap! Soap! Don't Forget the Soap! An Appalachian Folktale.* Illustrated by Andrew Glass. New York: Holiday House, 1993.

Casler, Leigh. *The Boy Who Dreamed of an Acorn.* Illustrated by Shonto Begay. New York: Philomel, 1994.

Cowley, Joy. *Big Moon Tortilla.* Illustrated by Dyanne Strongbow. Honesdale, Pa.: Boyds Mills Press, 1998.

Dakos, Kalli. *If You're Not Here, Please Raise Your Hand: Poems about School.* Illustrated by G. Brian Karas. New York: Four Winds Press, 1990.

Heide, Florence Parry. *The Day of Ahmed's Secret.* Illustrated by Ted Lewin. New York: Mulberry, 1990.

London, Jonathan. *Ali: Child of the Desert.* Illustrated by Ted Lewin. New York: Lothrop, Lee & Shepard Books, 1997.

McKissack, Patricia C. *Ma Dear's Aprons.* Illustrated by Floyd Cooper. New York: Atheneum, 1997.

Nez, Redwing T. *Forbidden Talent.* Flagstaff, Ariz.: Northland Publishing, 1995.

Pinkney, Andrea. *Duke Ellington.* Illustrated by Brian Pinkney. New York: Scholastic, 1998.

Rose, Deborah Lee. *The People Who Hugged the Trees.* Illustrated by Birgitta Saflund. Niwot, Colo.: Roberts Rinehart Publishers, 1990.

Say, Allen. *Tea with Milk.* Boston: Houghton Mifflin, 1999.

Sikundar, Sylvia. *Forest Singer.* Illustrated by Alison Astill. New York: Barefoot Books, 1999.

Stevens, Jan Romero. *Carlos and the Squash Plant.* Illustrated by Jeanne Arnold. Flagstaff, Ariz.: Northland Publishing, 1995.

Surat, Michele Maria. *Angel Child, Dragon Child.* Illustrated by Vo-Dinh Mai. New York: Scholastic, 1983.

Tseng, Grace. *White Tiger, Blue Serpent.* Illustrated by Jean Tseng and Mou-sien Tseng. New York: Lothrop, Lee & Shepard Books, 1999.

Lesson 31

Is It Their, They're, *or* There— Break *or* Brake?

SKILL: Understanding Homonyms

CULTURE OF FOCUS: Native American

Materials

Buffalo Dreams, by Kim Donner
    (Westwinds Press, 1999)
Student journals
Markers
Roll of cash register receipt tape
5-x-8-inch index cards
List of homonyms (see end of lesson)
One or two practice sentences to
    introduce the lesson
Overhead transparency or chalkboard
Collection of Native American tales
    from a number of different tribes

Lesson Motivator

1. If possible, bring in an authentic dreamcatcher or make one according to the directions at the end of *Buffalo Dreams.* Holding the dreamcatcher up in front of the class, ask if anyone has ever seen one. Do they know what it is? If students do not know what a dreamcatcher is, ask them to speculate.

2. Begin the day's lesson with a short writing session in student literature journals. Give them two options about which to write. One is to discuss the dreamcatcher. What is it? Where did it originate? How would they use it if they had one?

   The other writing option is to respond to the following quote from the story you will soon be reading to them: "Maybe magic doesn't make you do something special. Maybe you do something special and it makes magic." What might that mean?

3. After a short period to write, ask students to share their responses to either of the prompts. At this point, read the author's note to fill in background knowledge about dreamcatchers and also to explain the origins of the myths behind this story.

4. Prepare the class to listen to *Buffalo Dreams* to see how magic is explained within the context of this story.

Suggestions for Teaching the Lesson

• Focus the students for listening to the story by discussing the cover. What is unusual about it? Certainly the white buffalo is notable, but they might also see the white buffalo shapes repeated in the clouds. Ask the class if they have ever seen a white buffalo on family travels. Because they are rare, it is highly probably that no one will have been fortunate enough to have seen one. Have they ever spent a few imaginative minutes looking for shapes in the clouds? If so, they already have something in common with the main character of the story.

• As you read the story, stop periodically to talk about family events. Ask students how this family is alike or different from their families. Have they gone camping like this family? Continue reading after connecting listeners to the story through background experiences.

- When the story has been concluded, ask the students for reactions. What would they have done in a similar situation? Despite some different beliefs or practices, does one family behave much like another? Just what did magic have to do with this story? Were the students thinking as Sarah was or were they thinking along different lines?

- After discussing this beautifully written story, tell the students that you are going to use it to focus on some interesting words called homonyms. To give them a clue about what makes these words unusual, you are going to ask them to don an imaginary editor's hat. Next, they are to listen to a sentence like the following one: "If the whether is just write, I plan to sale my knew boat this weekend." Ask the fledgling editors if they can detect any major errors in this sentence just by listening to it. They should not find any mistakes because it does make sense when heard.

- Write the sentence on the overhead or on chalkboard. Read it aloud again. Ask the students if they can pick up on any errors once they see the sentence written out. As the hands go up, invite corrections. One word and one student at a time, request students to come up to correct a word they find to be wrong. They should cross out the word that has been used incorrectly, write the appropriate one above it, and explain the difference between the two words.

- Chat about how confusing a message can be if the wrong words are used. Then ask the class why they couldn't find any errors when hearing the sentence but could find many mistakes once they

could see it. You are encouraging learners to voice the fact that homonyms are words that sound alike but are actually different. Write the word *homonym* on the board or overhead, repeat the definition, and move into some practice time with homonyms.

- Write a collection of sentences from the story on different sheets of notebook or writing paper, one sentence at the top of each sheet. Use the papers to divide students into triads or groups of four to practice finding and using homonyms. Some sample sentences are:

  1. The next day, when the tribe awoke, their village was surrounded by a herd of buffalo. (*their, by, herd*)

  2. "Not for two weeks. But by then, my dreamcatcher will be ready to display there. See?" (*not, for, two, but, by, be, to, there, see*)

  3. Joe galloped through the campground as Sarah looked for a place to hang her dreamcatcher for the night. (*through, for, to, night*)

  4. Changing shapes wouldn't be too handy at school, but being able to hear and answer dreams or to save people in trouble—those were powers she thought anyone would like to have! (*be, too, but, to, hear, or, in, would*)

  5. They hung the dreamcatcher from just the right branch. (*right*)

  6. "I'm still only me. I don't think I can do anything special, even though I touched a white buffalo." (*I, do*)

  7. The dreams flowed that night, out of hearts, past the trees, across the hills, and floated through one certain dreamcatcher. (*night, past, through, one*)

8. As two braves hunted the plains for game to save their starving tribe, they were amazed to see a beautiful woman approach them. (*two, plains, for, to, their, see*)

- Each triad or foursome should take the sheet of paper, locate a word in the sentence that qualifies as a homonym, and write the matching homonym. Have them write a phraselike definition of each word and then go on a quest for more of the same. From a collection of picture books and, later, personal reading materials, they should begin to collect homonyms, sharing their findings within their group.

- Rather than making a bulletin board of words, try something different. Each group will write their homonyms on the chalkboard, discussing them as they go. Duplicates will be eliminated. When the last group has added theirs, bring out the role of cash register tape. The tape is a novel writing material to have on hand for timelines or other change-of-pace writing assignments. One group at a time, have the students write their homonyms on the tape in large, legible letters, rolling the loose end up neatly as they go. Different colored markers might be used to add color to the tape. After the last group is done, it's time to post the tape.

- The goal is to ring the room with homonyms by using this tape, taping it securely to the wall. Encourage students to check the tape periodically to review the ring of words and as a reminder to check the meaning of the words they are using in their writing.

- When they find a new pair of words, students should print them neatly on a fresh length of cash register receipt tape. As they add new words, they should unwind the tape a little more. Review the new words periodically, having the student who contributed a pairing (or a threesome) use each word in a sentence to remind the class of the different meanings.

- **Note:** Purchase a box of the tapes from a discount store and share the cost with several other teachers in the building as a more economical way to add variety to the writing program.

- In addition to this assignment, encourage students to collect homonyms in their daily reading. One amusing resource they will enjoy browsing through is *The Alphabet from Z to A*, by Judith Viorst (see list of suggested titles below).

Evaluation

- Have the students select a dozen homonyms that they particularly like. They should use them in a short paragraph or in well-conceived sentences to demonstrate their understanding of the words.

- Note their grasp of knowledge in their writing portfolios or on an ongoing checklist of acquired skills.

Extensions

- Play "Around the World" to review a variety of homonyms. A starter list of homonyms follows this lesson. Prepare a series of short sentences on a sheet or two of paper. Put 5-x-8-inch index cards with appropriate homonym choices on them in the correct order, numbered to match the sentences. Read the sentences to the students.

- Hold up a 5-x-8-inch card with the homonym options printed on it. The first student to pick the correct word to fit the meaning of the sentence goes on to the next person. This works best when the challenger can stand behind the student being challenged, who is seated. If the seated student answers fastest and is correct, he or she replaces the challenger and moves on to the next student, proceeding around the room until you deem the activity at an end.

- Create a card game like "Go Fish" using homonym pairs.

- Working with a knowledgeable person, create a dreamcatcher decorated with meaningful personal mementos.

Suggested Titles for Independent Reading and Research

Bierhorst, John, ed. *The Dancing Fox: Arctic Folktales.* Illustrated by Mary K. Okheena. New York: Morrow, 1997.

Bruchac, Joseph. *Between Earth and Sky: Legends of Native American Sacred Places.* Illustrated by Thomas Locker. San Diego, Calif.: Harcourt Brace, 1996.

Bunting, Eve. *Moonstick: The Seasons of the Sioux.* Illustrated by John Sandford. New York: HarperCollins, 1997.

Dabcovich, Lydia. *Polar Bear Son: An Inuit Tale.* New York: Clarion, 1997.

Field, Edward. *Magic Words.* Illustrated by Stefano Vitale. New York: Gulliver, 1998.

French, Fiona. *Lord of the Animals: A Miwok Indian Creation Myth.* Brookfield, Conn.: Millbrook Press, 1997.

Goble, Paul. *Remaking the Earth: A Creation Story from the Great Plains of North America.* New York: Orchard, 1996.

Goldin, Barbara Diamond. *Coyote and the Fire Stick: A Pacific Northwest Indian Tale.* Illustrated by Will

Hillenbrand. San Diego, Calif.: Harcourt Brace, 1996.

———. *The Girl Who Lived with the Bears.* Illustrated by Andrew Plewes. New York: Gulliver, 1997.

Hauseman, Gerald. *Eagle Boy: A Traditional Navajo Legend.* Illustrated by Cara Moser and Barry Moser. New York: HarperCollins, 1996.

Hulpach, Vladimir. *Ahaiyute and Cloud Eater.* Illustrated by Marek Zawadzki. San Diego, Calif.: Harcourt Brace, 1996.

Jones, Jennifer Berry. *Heetunka's Harvest: A Tale of the Plains Indians.* Illustrated by Shannon Keegan. Niwot, Colo.: Roberts Rinehart Publishers, 1994.

Kinsey-Warnock, Natalie. *The Fiddler of the Northern Lights.* Illustrated by Leslie W. Bowman. New York: Cobblehill, 1996.

Morin, Paul. *Animal Dreaming: An Aboriginal Dreamtime Story.* San Diego, Calif.: Harcourt Brace, 1998.

Nelson, S. D. *Gift Horse: A Lakota Story.* New York: Harry N. Abrams, 1999.

Normandin, Christine, ed. *Echoes of the Elders: The Stories and Paintings of Chief Lelooska.* New York: DK Ink, 1997.

———. *Spirit of the Cedar People: More Stories and Paintings of Chief Lelooska.* New York: DK Ink, 1998.

Osofsky, Audrey. *Dreamcatcher.* Illustrated by Ed Young. New York: Orchard, 1992.

Pollack, Penny. *The Turkey Girl: A Zuni Cinderella Story.* Illustrated by Ed Young. Boston: Little, Brown, 1996.

Rodonas, Kristina. *Follow the Stars.* New York: Marshall Cavendish, 1998.

VanLaan, Nancy. *Shingebiss: An Ojibwe Legend.* Illustrated by Betsy Bowen. New York: Houghton Mifflin, 1997.

Viorst, Judith. *The Alphabet from Z to A (with Much Confusion on the Way).* Illustrated by Richard Hull. New York: Atheneum, 1994.

A Starter List of Homonyms

add-ad
aid-aide
aisle-I'll-isle
ant-aunt
ate-eight
awl-all
bale-bail
ball-bawl
base-bass
be-bee
bear-bare
beat-beet
blue-blew
board-bored
bolder-boulder
bough-bow
bowled-bold
boy-buoy
break-brake
bred-bread
browse-brows
by-bye-buy
cent-scent-sent
cheap-cheep
climb-clime
cord-chord
course-coarse
creek-creak
days-daze
deer-dear
dew-do-due
die(d)-dye(d)
doe-dough
earn-urn
faint-feint
fair-fare
feet-feat
fined-find
flee-flea
flower-flour
for-fore-four
fourth-forth
fowl-foul
gait-gate
great-grate
guest-guessed
hair-hare
haul-hall
heard-herd
heel-heal
heir-air

here-hear
hey-hay
hi-high
hole-whole
horse-hoarse
hour-our
hymn-him
I-eye-aye
in-inn
its-it's
knew-new-gnu
know-no
lead-led
leak-leek
lie-lye
lone-loan
made-maid
male-mail
mane-main
maul-mall
maze-maize
meet-meat
might-mite
mist-missed
morn-mourn
need-knead
night-knight
not-knot
oh-owe
one-won
ore-or
our-hour
pair-pear-pare
pale-pail
past-passed
paws-pause
peddle-pedal
peek-peak-pique
peel-peal
plane-plain
pole-poll
pour-poor
praise-prays
rain-reign-rein
rap-wrap
red-read
reed-read
right-write
ring-wring
road-rowed-rode
role-roll

root-route
rot-wrought
sail-sale
see-sea
seem-seam
sell-cell
seller-cellar
serial-cereal
sheer-shear
shone-shown
shoo-shoe
side-sighed
sight-site-cite
so-sew-sow
sole-soul
son-sun
sore-soar
stare-stair
steak-stake
steel-steal
straight-strait
sum-some
sweet-suite
tacks-tax
tail-tale
tea-tee
there-their-they're
threw-through
thrown-throne
tide-tied
time-thyme
to-too-two
tow-toe
vein-vane-vain
vice-vise
wail-whale
waist-waste
wait-weight
wave-waive
way-weigh
we'd-weed
we've-weave
wear-ware-where
week-weak
whet-wet
would-wood
wrote-rote
you-yew
your-you're

Section V

Sparking an Interest in Poetry

POETRY: AN OVERVIEW

One of poetry's many gifts is that its offerings come in all shapes and sizes, rhymes, and beats. Even the most resistant student will succumb to poetry's wiles if given enough of an opportunity to graze on the offerings.

Narrative poetry is one type that appeals to most students. It may relate a relatively short story within its lines. Other narrative poems are longer, however, coupled with vibrant illustrations to fill the pages of an entire picture book. In contrast, lyric poems, often only a dozen or fewer lines long, succinctly express an intense feeling or thought, or describe a mood to draw forth an emotional response from the reader. For those with a keen ear, poems also hold music to be savored.

There are pictures within poetry, too, vivid images created by word painters who select just the right words and assemble them in just the right combinations to leave lasting impressions on the mind's eye. Some selections paint humorous or nonsensical scenes while others will offer a quieter vision.

Not to be missed are the emotions touched on within poetry. Verses may make us laugh outright, while some poems even touch a raw spot hidden from prying eyes. Readers of all ages harbor such spots. Occasionally a poem slips in, catching the reader unaware. Eyes well up, tears slip over. Most certainly, poets celebrate laughter and pain, life's sunshine and rain.

Poems are a legacy bequeathed by clever, talented wordsmiths. With time, concerted effort, a critical eye, and years of practice, poets can pick a few critical words to portray a vast range of places, people, emotions, and things in quite a different way than we are accustomed to viewing them. The results cover a plethora of topics from fire-breathing toasters, the woes of homework, lost love, found love, embarrassing moments, and life's routine events from birth to death. Some subject matter is a part of the real world, although other poets take us to places that are wonderfully imaginary. With such wonders to share, no child should be without poetry, no classroom empty of its sounds. No classroom walls should be bereft of a weekly poem, nor should an array of appealing books be missing from bookshelves.

From their earliest days, children ought to be exposed to poetry for the joy of it. Take frequent poetry breaks to recharge the learning atmosphere in your classroom. Teach students to use the tools of poetry, to understand the terms with impossible spellings such as *onomatopoeia, alliteration,* or *cinquain.* They should write poetry, sometimes learning from patterns to scaffold their attempts and later, to create verse in free-flowing lines. They should be given the freedom to play with words in the way in which their favorite poets play, mixing and matching the sounds to please the ear and the mind. Let learners dabble in words that can traipse tantalizingly over the tongue, some sensible, others pure nonsense. Challenge them to try a concrete poem, where the subject of the poem dictates its shape while the words fill in the rest of the visual image. There is a poet in every child just waiting to be nourished. Remember, though, that those efforts could be forever stilled because of the fear of being graded. Perhaps only a few selections chosen by the poet might go into a portfolio to showcase.

Make poetry a part of classroom life by sharing your favorites, thereby modeling your enjoyment. You will find that it is contagious. Have routine "Poetry Shares" in which students may volunteer to read a well-practiced favorite to the class. Always have an assortment of books in the classroom containing a variety of poetry, from collections to single volumes. Add new titles from the learning center periodically. Be sure to show the students where other collections are shelved in the school learning center or library so that they can check them out at their leisure. Invite the parents, local business people, the principal, other teachers, cafeteria workers, and school maintenance people in from time to time to share their personal favorites, confirming to learners that poetry is for everyone. Careful exposure over time can make poetry as natural as breathing and instill a love of poetry that will flourish year after year.

Lesson 32

Put a Poem in Your Pocket and a Picture in Your Mind

SKILL: Writing a Poem Using a Picture as a Prompt and Creating a Poetry Pocket Book

CULTURE OF FOCUS: African American

Materials

Brown Angels: An Album of Pictures and Verse, by Walter Dean Myers (HarperCollins, 1993)

Glorious Angels: A Celebration of Children, by Walter Dean Myers (HarperCollins, 1995)

Collection of old photographs or pictures of a variety of children from magazines, mounted on colored paper like photographs in an album

Overhead projector

Scratch paper

Pens or pencils

Lesson Motivator

1. As students enter the room for class, or at the beginning of the class, ask them to browse through a collection of pictures spread out on a table at the front of the room. Have them each choose one that is particularly appealing for one reason or another and take it back to their desks.

2. Display an interesting picture of a child on a transparency and ask the students to speculate about the picture. Who might this child be? Where might he or she live or have lived? What age? What family circumstances? Where might he or she be now? Write down the speculations and observations to be used after reading *Brown Angels.*

3. Talk about the value of photographs in general and question students about why an album of family pictures could be an important addition to their lives. Then introduce one of Myers's books by reading his introduction to that book. If possible have several copies of the book available so that students can pass them around to study the photographs as you read a selection of the poems.

Suggestions for Teaching the Lesson

- Using *Brown Angels,* choose several of the poems that you enjoy and read them to the class. Put one on a transparency so that the whole class can see it. Read it aloud to the class and then read it together several times. This is a wonderful opportunity to hear the rhythms and rhymes in Myers's poems. Students may share Jeannie's giggles as they read "Jeannie Had a Giggle." The poem describes an experience to which they all can probably relate.

- Ask the class to listen for the rhyme, rhythm, and sounds of these poems. As young children, they were probably raised on the verses of Mother Goose, simple songs, cultural music, and other familiar poetry filled with these three items. Tell them to experiment with these three elements of poetry as they write poems about people for the upcoming writing experience.

- Ask the students to study the photograph or picture they previously selected. Have them ask themselves the same kinds of questions you covered during the motivator. In this way they are gathering information that may eventually become a part of a poem they are going to write about the picture. You could work with the picture on the overhead, writing and creating a poem about that child right along with the students. Share your ideas and struggles to get the words right as you enthusiastically model the writing process. An excited model is a powerful motivator.

- Give students creative time, walking around to monitor their thinking processes and asking pertinent questions to help the students along. Encourage them to read through a copy of *Brown Angels* themselves, studying the pictures and verse while getting ideas for the way they might like to write a poem. Give them time to browse through *Glorious Angels*, which takes a broader look at children from many different cultures through fabulous photographs and beautiful poetry. These books should be fuel for writing because they are so wonderfully crafted.

- Have students follow the established class writing process to draft and polish a poem to be displayed in a class book or on the bulletin board. Share those poems in small and large groups, enjoying each student's creativity.

- Take the process one step further by encouraging poets to bring in a family photo, one showing a relative from years past or a current family member. After they gather the necessary information from family members, have the students write poems about the photographs, then polish them. They may either read the poems aloud as they are completed or save them for a special afternoon or morning poetry reading.

Evaluation

- Set the standards for quality writing ahead of time, noting the specific skills you will be monitoring. If the poems are to be enjoyed in a book or on a bulletin board, spelling, punctuation, and content should be evaluated.

- Note whether each student follows the procedures designated by the writing process, jotting down a few anecdotal notes as appropriate.

- Add student-selected copies of poetry to portfolios throughout the year to show growth in writing.

Extensions

- Refer students to Myers's *Glorious Angels*, which celebrates children of many nationalities. Challenge students to write a poem about children in general or to celebrate one special aspect of childhood in a particular culture. Then have them polish and publish the poems.

- Involve students in poetry from the first thing in the morning until the buses line up to take them home. Start the day with a humorous poem from a collection by Jack Prelutsky, *A Pizza the Size of the Sun,* or from Shel Silverstein's *A Light in the Attic* (see list of suggested titles below). Even those who are completely turned off to poetry can scarcely resist these verses.

- Read a poem about animals or insects in science from a selection such as Jack Prelutsky's *The Beauty of the Beast: Poems from the Animal Kingdom* or celebrate heroes in social studies or history by reading from Susan Altman and Susan Lechner's *Followers of the North Star: Rhymes about African American Heroes, Heroines, and Historical Times.* Your enthusiastic support of poetry throughout the curriculum will go a long way toward making learners into lifelong lovers of poetry.

- Encourage the students to sign up to read some poems they have discovered. The rules are that the poem must be appropriate for the classroom and that students must have practiced reading it aloud so that they can do so with ease. You may start the day with the poem, break for lunch with a student's poem, or read the selected poem individually and then together before leaving the classroom for the day.

- Reserve a portion of one bulletin board or a corner of the classroom for a poetry corner. Keep a spirited and appealing collection of anthologies, books by a single poet, and poetry that works across the curriculum, as well as poetry written by the students. Personal poetry can go into a class anthology after the poems have been displayed and thoroughly appreciated for a week or two. Slip poems into a clear plastic sleeve, one backing another in each sleeve, and store them in a wide three-ring binder ready for reading and pondering by classmates. Include in the poetry corner a tape recorder or CD player, headphones, and audiotapes or CDs of poets reading their own works.

- Stimulate interest in building a personal poetry collection by creating a pocket book. Learners can follow the directions at the end of this lesson to make a book in which to keep poems that they have copied because they like them, along with poetry they have written. The cover of the book might be lightweight tagboard or a supple paper that will withstand frequent openings and closings. The number of pages inside the book may be designated either by you or the poet. Each pocket should be labeled and hold writings about an idea or concept such as friendship, family, animals, school, emotions, the Earth, and so forth, depending on the interests of the student. Poems from these collections should be shared periodically at poetry time throughout the week.

- Send poets "on the road" throughout the year with their collections and let them read several poems to students in lower grades to pique

their interest in poetry, demonstrating the richness there is in poetry.

Suggested Titles for Independent Reading and Research

Adoff, Arnold. *I Am the Darker Brother: An Anthology of Modern Poems by African Americans.* Illustrated by Benny Andrews. New York: Simon & Schuster, 1997.

Altman, Susan, and Susan Lechner. *Followers of the North Star: Rhymes about African American Heroes, Heroines, and Historical Times.* Illustrated by Byron Wooden. Chicago: Children's Press, 1993.

Angelou, Maya. *Now Sheba Sings the Song.* Illustrated by Tom Feelings. New York: Puffin, 1994.

Berry, James. *Everywhere Faces Everywhere.* Illustrated by Reynold Ruffins. New York: Simon & Schuster, 1997.

Bryan, Ashley. *Ashley Bryan's A B C of African American Poetry.* New York: Atheneum, 1997.

Carlson, Lori Marie. *Sol a Sol: Bilingual Poems.* Illustrated by Emily Lisker. New York: Henry Holt, 1998.

Feelings, Tom. *Soul Looks Back in Wonder.* New York: Puffin, 1999.

Field, Edward. *Magic Words.* Illustrated by Stefano Vitale. San Diego, Calif.: Gulliver, 1998.

Grimes, Nikki. *Hopscotch Love: A Family Treasury of Love Poems.* Illustrated by Melodye Benson Rosales. New York: Lothrop, Lee & Shepard Books, 1999.

Heide, Florence Perry. *Oh, Grow Up! Poems to Help You Survive Parents, Chores, School, and Other Afflictions.* Illustrated by Nadine Bernard Westcott. New York: Orchard, 1996.

Johnson, Angela. *The Other Side: Shorter Pieces.* New York: Orchard, 1998.

Nye, Naomi Shihab, selector. *The Tree Is Older Than You Are: A Bilingual Gathering of Poems and Stories from Mexico, with Paintings by Mexican Artists.* New York: Simon & Schuster, 1995.

Paul, Ann Whitford. *All by Herself.* Illustrated by Michael Steirnagle. San Diego, Calif.: Browndeer/Harcourt Brace, 1999.

Philip, Neil, selector. *Earth Always Endures: Native American Poems.* Illustrated with photographs by Edward S. Curtis. New York: Viking, 1996.

Prelutsky, Jack. *The Beauty of the Beast: Poems from the Animal Kingdom.* Illustrated by Meilo So. New York: Alfred A. Knopf, 1997.

———. *A Pizza the Size of the Sun.* Illustrated by James Stevenson. New York: Greenwillow, 1996.

Robb, Laura. *Music and Drum: Voices of War and Peace, Hope and Dreams.* Illustrated By Debra Lill. New York: Philomel, 1997.

Silverstein, Shel. *Falling Up.* New York: HarperCollins, 1996.

Soto, Gary. *Canto Familiar.* Illustrated by Annika Nelson. San Diego, Calif.: Harcourt Brace, 1995.

Spivak, Dawnine. *Grass Sandals: The Travels of Basho.* Illustrated by Demi. New York: Atheneum, 1997.

Directions for Making a Pocket Book

Figure 1

Although the size may vary, it is best if each student makes a large pocket book that can be used throughout the first half of the year. A second one can be constructed later in the year to hold additional poetry. Begin with a sturdy sheet of paper or lightweight tagboard measuring 12 x 18 inches. Standard construction paper is colorful but it tends to tear along the creases when it is used frequently, so it is not the best choice for bookmaking projects. Fold the cover in half, matching the 12-inch sides. You now have a book cover measuring 9 x 12 inches (see figure 1). Set the cover aside.

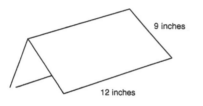

Figure 2

The pages or pockets will be formed using the same size paper but in white or a neutral color. Each page must measure the same size, so the folding must be done carefully, matching the pages as they are completed. Take one sheet and fold the bottom edge up toward the middle, 6 to 6 1/4 inches, as illustrated (see figure 2).

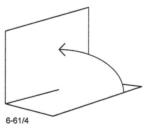

6-61/4
inches

Figure 3

Next, fold the sheet back, smooth sides against each other. The "pocket" is now on the outside (see figure 3). Depending on the number of pages desired for the completed book, make additional pages. Rather than making a book too thick, students may choose to make several books, each with a larger overall theme, as the school year progresses and their collections of poems increase in size.

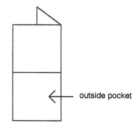

outside pocket

Figure 4

Place the pages inside the cover with the open edges fitting into the crease of the cover. The folded edges of each page will face outward toward the edge of the book, as shown (see figure 4). Secure the pages with a stapler, stapling them in several places.

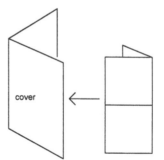

cover

Figure 5

Decorate the cover, write in the appropriate categories—one per pocket on the inside of the book (see figure 5), add artistic embellishments as desired, and begin to celebrate poetry with a "Poetry Pocket Book".

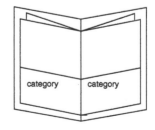

category   category

Lesson 33

Choral Reading

SKILL: Listening for the Music in Poetry

CULTURE OF FOCUS: All

Materials

Bein' with You This Way, by W. Nikola-Lisa; illustrated by Michael Bryant (Lee & Low, 1994)
Overhead projector, chart paper, or chalkboard

The following books contain poems that could be read like a reader's theater or as poems for two or three voices:

Followers of the North Star: Rhymes about African American Heroes, Heroines, and Historical Times, by Susan Altman and Susan Lechner; illustrated by Byron Wooden (Children's Press, 1993): "James Armistead," "Harriet Tubman," "Rosa Parks," "Benjamin Banneker," "Escaped Slave," and "Muhammad Ali"
Meet Danitra Brown, by Nikki Grimes; illustrated by Floyd Cooper (Mulberry, 1994): "Purple," "Culture," and "Stories to Tell"
… I Never Saw Another Butterfly: Children's Drawings and Poems from Terezin Concentration Camp (1942–1944), edited by Hana Volavkova (Schocken Books, 1993): "At Terezin," "It All Depends on How You Look at It," and "The Butterfly"

Collect books of poetry featuring various cultures as a resource for poems that can be read in pairs, small groups, or as a large group. Some suggestions are included in this lesson, but enjoy the quest for finding additional rhythmic poetry for students to read aloud.

Note: As you and eventually your students select poems to be read aloud, look for those that have a definite rhythm, have a clear

rhyming format or sounds that are appealing to reader and listener, use language in a unique way to present ideas, stimulate the imaginations of the listeners, and evoke vivid sensory images. Avoid poetry that is didactic, seeming primarily to teach a lesson rather than to enrich the senses of the reader or reciter. A sound test is to read the poem aloud yourself several times as you assess its appropriateness for choral reading.

Lesson Motivator

1. Read "Dance Poem" from *Sing a Soft Black Song,* by Nikki Giovanni, aloud to the class (see list of suggested titles at end of lesson).

2. Have the students just listen to the words and the rhythm. Read the poem again, asking the students to clap along to the beat of the poem. Explain that poetry is an interesting form of writing in that it often has a much more distinct rhythm than most narrative writing. Isn't it a challenge for poets to create a word picture with so few words?

3. Put the poem on the overhead and divide the class into four groups. Assign each group one stanza of the poem and read through it, all joining in for the last verse.

4. Read the poem through again after the initial practice and listen to the flow of the words. This is an excellent opportunity to comment on how practice is critical to the smooth delivery and interpretation of a poem.

5. To illustrate how much fun poetry can be, play a little with several poems, such as David McCord's "The Pickety Fence" or "Song of the Train," from *One at a Time: His Collected Poems for the Young,* or "Clickbeetle," by Mary Ann Hoberman, which can be found in *The Random House Book of Poetry for Children,* an excellent classroom resource. These poems are not specifically multicultural in nature, they are just good examples of what a joy poetry can be. They also present

the perfect opportunity to teach a mini-lesson on sound patterns and their importance as an element of poetry. In this case, the focus is on alliteration.

6. Write *alliteration* on the board along with its definition: a pattern of sounds. It refers to the repetition of the initial consonant sounds of words that are close together. Invite students to watch and listen for the effect of alliteration in the following poems.

7. Put each of the poems on a large chart or on the overhead so that they can be seen by the entire class. Read through a poem aloud once so that the students can listen to the words and the rhythm. Then read it together.

8. Finally, divide the class into two parts and read the poem like a round. Start the first group, let them read the first two lines, then indicate when the second group should come in. Watch the expressions on the faces of the readers. Students across grade levels love this wordplay.

9. Pick up the pace and read the poem in a round a second time, letting the students savor the fun of poetry. Challenge them to look for other poems that would work in a round as they encounter poetry in the upcoming weeks.

Suggestions for Teaching the Lesson

- Involve readers in the toe-tapping *Bein' with You This Way.* Prepare tagboard signs to hold up with the following phrases on them: "Uh-huh!," "Mm-mmm," and "Ah-ha!"

- Pick three students from the class and have them stand nearby as you read the story. When you read the appropriate words, quickly point to the student with the correct sign. He or she should

hold it up and the class should respond by reading it aloud. This may take a little choreographing ahead of time but should be fun as the story and the students become intertwined.

- Turn this book into a reader's theater or narrative for many voices. Using a number of paperback copies of the book or rewriting the story in sections for individual readers, put everyone to work with a part to read. Practice going through the book individually and in unison as parts direct. Students who have some of the characteristics being described should read those lines. After practicing until the presentation is perfect, visit another classroom in the building and celebrate diversity through a lively rendition of *Bein' with You This Way.* An activity such as this integrates reading, listening, and speaking in a meaningful and memorable manner.

- Work with materials that have been collected ahead of time for the lesson, giving students suggestions about what poems might be read aloud in pairs, threesomes, or as a group. Students will quickly make their own appropriate suggestions as they learn to interpret their poems. Encourage them to practice their poetry using the punctuation to help them with pauses, inflection, and expression until the can read without a hitch. When they are confident, it is time to perform their work for the class. Choral reading is an excellent way to strengthen reading aloud in front of the class because students are not forced to perform alone but have companions with them as they present their poems.

- Ask students to continue to look for poems with strong rhythm and interesting words and acceptable content that can be read chorally. Use those discoveries in class from time to time to keep skills in choral reading polished and in fine form.

Evaluation

- For an activity such as this, maintain anecdotal records with a focus on student interest, involvement in the activity, and cooperation with classmates. Post a short checklist for student reference and evaluation use that includes items such as the following:

  1. Student uses his or her voice appropriately to express the sounds and the mood of the poem and enhance its emotional impact.

  2. Reader appears confident as he or she delivers a smooth oral reading, indicating the evidence of practice.

  3. Reader uses punctuation in the poem (if present) to interpret pauses and expression.

  4. Reader clearly enunciates each word, works with the rhyme scheme, and flows with the rhythm to deliver a poem that delights listeners.

  5. There is evidence of growth in the reader's ability to orally interpret a poem.

- Make video snippets of students as they perform in a small group and keep these as part of ongoing portfolios.

Extensions

- Form poetry troupes and encourage students to polish their choral reading skills through presentations at various functions throughout the school year. A trip to a nearby nursing home is another possibility.

- Tape record the poetry readings, print out the poems, and send them to a lower-grade classroom for their reading center. The materials should be moved from classroom to classroom after a designated time period.

- Have students illustrate a favorite poem, making a large poster that can be displayed while students recite the poem.

- Have students write and perform original poetry. One of their efforts should include alliteration, as discussed in this lesson. Often school districts have poetry contests. Post the guidelines and encourage students to submit entries.

Suggested Titles for Independent Reading and Research

Altman, Susan, and Susan Lechner. *Followers of the North Star: Rhymes about African American Heroes, Heroines, and Historical Times.* Illustrated by Byron Wooden. Chicago: Children's Press, 1993.

Berry, James. *Classic Poems to Read Aloud.* Illustrated by James Mayhew. New York: Kingfisher, 1995.

Bruchac, Joseph, and Jonathan London. *Thirteen Moons on a Turtle's Back: A Native American Year of Moons.* Illustrated by Thomas Locker. New York: Philomel, 1992.

Giovanni, Nikki. *Spin a Soft Black Song.* Illustrated by George Martins. New York: Hill and Wang, 1985.

Glaser, I. J. *Dreams of Glory: Poems Starring Girls.* Illustrated by Pat Lowery Collins. New York: Atheneum, 1995.

Grimes, Nikki. *Hopscotch Love: A Family Treasury of Love Poems.* Illustrated by Melodye Benson Rosales. New York: Morrow, 1999.

———. *Meet Danitra Brown.* Illustrated by Floyd Cooper. New York: Mulberry, 1994.

Hamanaka, Sheila. *All the Colors of the Earth.* New York: Morrow, 1994.

McCord, David. *One at a Time: His Collected Poems for the Young.* Illustrated by Henry B. Kane. Boston: Little, Brown, 1986.

Prelutsky, Jack, selector. *The Random House Book of Poetry for Children.* Illustrated by Arnold Lobel. New York: Random House, 1983.

Rosen, Michael, selector. *Classic Poetry: An Illustrated Collection.* Illustrated by Paul Howard. New York: Candlewick Press, 1997.

Viorst, Judith. *If I Were in Charge of the World and Other Worries: Poems for Children and Their Parents.* Illustrated by Lynne Cherry. New York: Aladdin, 1981.

———. *Sad Underwear and Other Complications: More Poems for Children and Their Parents.* Illustrated by Richard Hull. New York: Atheneum, 1995.

Yolen, Jane, ed. *Street Rhymes from around the World.* Illustrated by 17 international artists. Honesdale, Pa.: Boyds Mills Press/Wordsong, 1992.

Lesson 34

Reading, Writing, and the Poetry Connection: A Look at Narrative Poetry

SKILL: Writing Narrative Poetry

CULTURE OF FOCUS: Mexican American

Materials

Calling the Doves (El Canto de las Palomas), by Juan Felipe Herrera (Children's Book Press, 1995)
Collection of picture books and/or anthologies that exemplify narrative poetry
"Pop quiz" (see below)
Scratch paper
Pens and pencils

Lesson Motivator

1. Tell the class they are going to have a pop quiz. Those two words usually rivet students' attention on the teacher, don't they? They are to take out pens or pencils and a piece of notebook paper.

2. After they read the following sentences on the chalkboard or on a prepared overhead transparency, have the students respond with "true" or "false" and write one or two sentences to justify their answer. The "quiz" should look something like this:

   • Poetry helps us to become better listeners.

   • Reading and writing poetry can help to expand our vocabulary.

   • Reading poetry silently and aloud will improve our reading skills.

   • If I write poetry, I will become a better writer.

   • Reading and writing poetry can help me learn to think better.

   • Poetry is really fun!

3. Of course, the answer to all the statements is "true," but students may not agree. Take time to discuss the pop quiz after students have completed their work. Listen to their reactions and let students know you appreciate their willingness to share them. Then explain why poetry is such a valuable part of the classroom lives of these readers and writers. Tell them to be prepared because poetry will be interwoven throughout the curriculum all year long! You already know what they will learn: that students who are immersed in poetry grow in so many directions, both as readers and as writers, and for some, that growth is introspective as well.

4. Introduce narrative poetry, a non-intimidating form of poetry that tells a story. Research shows that this form of poetry is a favorite of most children. Sometimes it rhymes, sometimes not, but there is always a quiet rhythm to the lines. In a narrative poem you have the same elements as you do in a story—including characters, setting, a simple plot, and a theme—very carefully written. As with most poetry, narratives beg to be read aloud because the music of their words underscores the story and becomes quite a special listening experience.

5. Although the award-winning focus book, *Calling the Doves,* does not have distinct rhymes, ask the students to listen for the rhythm and flow of the story. They will have an opportunity to work with other narratives that do have a rhyme when they pour over books collected for their inspection.

Suggestions for Teaching the Lesson

- No matter what kind of poetry you are reading to your class, remember that enthusiasm is contagious. An inspired teacher who shows his or her love for poetry by reading with verve and a sparkle in the eye will do more to foster the love of poetry than can be imagined. Students who are reluctant to touch poetry may need to be convinced of its entertainment value before they allow it anywhere near their hearts. If you feel that you need some moral support in your endeavors, consult the list of resources available in Appendix II.

- Read *Calling the Doves* to the class after explaining to the students that Herrera is one of the most prominent Mexican-American poets writing today. He is an award-winning author who has written five books, in addition to being an actor, a musician, and a professor at California State University. Students enjoy knowing a little background about an author or illustrator. Point out the awards this particular book has earned: the 1996 Hungry Mind Review Children's Book of Distinction, Smithsonian Notable Book for Children, and the Ezra Jack Keats Book Award.

- Because this book is written in both English and Spanish, it would be a boon if you could have someone who is fluent in Spanish partner with you to read the book to the class in two languages.

- Once the book is completed, discuss the picture of the life of a migrant worker that is depicted. Go through the book, highlighting the characters, setting, plot line, and theme. Talk about what the listeners learned about each family member. Have the students tie the book to their own lives as they think about members of their families. What might those members be best at that could be included in a poem about their families? Discuss ensuing contributions briefly. Then point out that this book is a narrative poem that relates a long story. Narratives can also relate a single incident or an episode. Look for examples of each of these.

- Once you have completed the discussion about the focus book, read several selections from *Where the Sidewalk Ends* or *A Light in the Attic,* by Shel Silverstein (see list of suggested titles at end of lesson). Not only will you elicit some chuckles, but you will illustrate what you mean when you say a narrative can just highlight a single event.

- Give the class plenty of time to read and reread a variety of narratives, sharing the ones they like with classmates. Set aside time during this immersion in narratives to talk about what students are noticing as they study the books at hand. When you feel they are saturated by quality poetry, move to the writing stage.

- Divide the students into teams of three to work on writing a short narrative first and then, if they work cooperatively together, to take on writing a longer narrative that they will illustrate and present to the class in picture book format. Talk about the importance of every word in a poem, going back to study one or two good examples.

- Advise students to write a rough draft and then go back and scrutinize the words. They should use a thesaurus to locate the most meaningful words to get their ideas across. To test the sense of their poems, have students read their drafts to another classmate or a teacher in another class who has a fresh set of ears for listening.

- After the class has tackled a short narrative, set the parameters for the longer narrative. Put the framework on the board for students to follow. The narrative must tell a story. That means it needs vivid characters, and a distinct plot with an inviting beginning, a middle, and a strong conclusion. There must be a setting, which probably will be addressed only briefly. Students should include a theme as well. To that end, they should discuss why they want to write the narrative. Is there a message they want to convey?

Evaluation

- Work together to create a checklist for use in evaluating the narrative once it is completed. Include such items as:

  —Does the narrative tell a story?
  —Can you identify the setting, characters, a conflict, a beginning, middle, and end, and a theme?
  —Are spelling and punctuation correct?
  —Has careful attention been paid to word selection?
  —Is the work neatly presented?
  —Is the artwork carefully done and appropriate for the poem?

- The team of poets should evaluate their work first, then conference with you so that they can receive your insights.

Extensions

- Have the students illustrate the narratives using collage, a medium that won the Caldecott Committee's attention in *Harlem*, by Walter Dean Myers and his son Christopher. Invite students to study the media and styles in the classroom collection of narratives and try something different than they usually do.

- Display a collection of the short narratives or a group of the longer picture book narratives in the library

or learning center for students throughout the school to enjoy.

- Make a "Big Book" of shorter narratives or of appropriate picture book narratives and take the books into primary grade classrooms for a "Poetry Read." This is a wonderful way to support the joys of poetry across the grades.

Suggested Titles for Independent Reading and Research

Aardema, Verna. *Bringing the Rain to Kapiti Plain.* Illustrated by Beatriz Vidal. New York: Dial, 1981.

Aliki. *Marianthe's Story—One: Painted Words, Two: Spoken Memories.* New York: Greenwillow, 1998.

Berry, James, ed. *Classic Poems to Read Aloud.* New York: Larousse Kingfisher, 1995.

Bruchac, Joseph, and Jonathan London. *Thirteen Moons on Turtle's Back: A Native American Year of Moons.* Illustrated by Thomas Locker. New York: Philomel, 1992.

Clifton, Lucille. *Everett Anderson's Friend.* Illustrated by Anny Grifalconi. New York: Henry Holt, 1992.

de Regniers, Beatrice Schenk, Eva Moore, Mary Michaels While, and Jan Carr, eds. *Sing a Song of Popcorn: Every Child's Book of Poems.* New York: Scholastic, 1988.

Gilman, Phoebe. *Something from Nothing.* New York: Scholastic, 1992.

Greenfield, Eloise. *For the Love of the Game: Michael Jordan and Me.* Illustrated by Jan Spivey Gilchrist. New York: HarperCollins, 1997.

Hamanaka, Sheila. *All the Colors of the Earth.* New York: Morrow, 1994.

Highwater, Jamake. *Songs for the Seasons.* Illustrated by Sandra Speidel. New York: Lothrop, Lee & Shepard Books, 1995.

Hughes, Langston. *The Dream Keeper and Other Poems.* Illustrated by Jerry Pinkney. New York: Alfred A. Knopf, 1994.

Lauture, Denize. *Father and Son.* Illustrated by Jonathan Green. New York: Philomel, 1992.

Lindbergh, Reeve. *Nobody Owns the Sky: The Story of "Brave Bessie" Coleman.* Illustrated by Pamela Paparone. Cambridge, Mass.: Candlewick Press, 1996.

Longfellow, Henry Wadsworth. *Hiawatha.* Illustrated by Susan Jeffers. New York: Dial, 1983.

McLerran, Alice. *The Ghost Dance.* Illustrated by Paul Morin. New York: Clarion, 1995.

Medearis, Angela Shelf. *Dancing with the Indians.* Illustrated by Samuel Byrd. New York: Holiday House, 1991.

Milnes, Gerald. *Granny Will Your Dog Bite? and Other Mountain Rhymes.* Illustrated by Kimberly Bulcken Root. New York: Alfred A. Knopf, 1990.

Myers, Walter Dean. *Harlem.* Illustrated by Christopher Myers. New York: Scholastic, 1997.

Prelutsky, Jack. *A Pizza the Size of the Sun.* Illustrated by James Stevenson. New York: Greenwillow, 1996.

Shaik, Fatima. *The Jazz of Our Street.* Illustrated by E. B. Lewis. New York: Dial, 1998.

Silverstein, Shel. *A Light in the Attic.* New York: HarperCollins, 1981.

———. *Where the Sidewalk Ends.* New York: HarperCollins, 1974.

Stevenson, Robert Louis. *My Shadow.* Illustrated by Ted Rand. New York: Putnam, 1990.

Tagore, Rabindranath. *Paper Boats.* Illustrated by Grayce Bochak. Honesdale, Pa.: Boyds Mills Press/Caroline House, 1992.

Thomas, Joyce Carol. *Gingerbread Days: Poems.* Illustrated by Floyd Cooper. New York: Harper, 1995.

———. *I Have Heard of a Land.* Illustrated by Floyd Cooper. New York: HarperCollins, 1998.

Turcotte, Mark. *Songs of Our Ancestors: Poems about Native Americans.* Illustrated By Kathleen S. Presnell. Chicago: Children's Press, 1995.

Winter, Jeanette. *Follow the Drinking Gourd.* New York: Alfred A. Knopf, 1988.

Lesson 35

Plying a Poet's Tools

SKILL: Using Figurative Language

CULTURE OF FOCUS: African American

Materials

I Have Heard of a Land, by Joyce Carol Thomas; illustrated by Floyd Cooper (HarperCollins, 1998)

January Rides the Wind: A Book of Months, by Charlotte F. Otten; illustrated by Todd L. W. Doney (Lothrop, Lee & Shepard Books, 1997)

Scratch paper

Pens or pencils

4-x-6-inch index cards

Set of building tools (hammer, screwdriver, measuring tape, etc.)

Preassembled "poet's toolbox" (see below)

Overhead projector or chalkboard

Suitable collection of poetry books for reference and independent reading (see list at end of lesson)

Lesson Motivator

1. Bring in a handyman's toolbox or a simple carpenter's tool kit assembled in a way that you like. It might be a carpenter's tool belt, a carpenter's "apron" with some handy tools in it, or a small tool kit with some basics that you use around the house.

2. As class begins, ask the students to talk about the prompt: What is it? What is it used for? What kinds of tasks might they need it for? Transition from that tool kit to one that poets might use, which you have put together ahead of time. In a box or clear plastic container nearby have paper, pens, pencils, erasers, a dictionary, a thesaurus, and some large note cards with the following words on them: *simile, metaphor,* and *personification.*

3. Take the items out, chat about them, and then query the students about who might need a kit with these kinds of items in it. Once students have ascertained that a writer or poet might need such a kit, explain that the activities ahead will focus on poetry. Students will take a close look at how poets use language to say so much with so few words, and read a variety of wonderful poetry.

4. Zero in on the vocabulary for the day's lesson, the three aspects of figurative language, which are handy tools for the poet to use. Discuss the fact that figurative language helps the writer create meaning that goes beyond the literal meaning of the words used, enabling a reader to see or feel things in fresh ways. If they understand how figurative language works, they will be able to dig more deeply into poems of their choice and develop a greater appreciation for the poets.

5. Hold up the three index cards from the poet's toolbox once again and

check student knowledge by asking for a definition of each of the terms. Reteach and review the terms as needed:

Simile: Poets use similes to make direct comparisons between objects. The words *like* and *as* are used in similes. In *January Rides the Wind,* note the way the animals' tails are described:

January rides the wind,
sideswipes deer and rabbits.
(great use of personification)
Their white tails billow
like pillowcases on the line.

Brainstorm commonly used similes that students hear from time to time or provide additional examples:

- He runs like the wind.

- Her eyes are as blue as the sky.

- The rain ran like tears down the windows.

Metaphor: Using this tool is a little more complex because it involves making an implied comparison without using the words *like* or *as.* Find examples ahead of time by noted poets or make up your own. An example is:

Night
is black tissue paper
stretched tightly from horizon to horizon.
Stars,
night's glitter,
sparkle hopefully from edge to edge.

Again, find a number of examples to read through, discuss, and post for future reference.

Personification: This is the process of giving an inanimate object ideas, or giving things human characteristics. Plants, animals, and ordinary, everyday items look quite different when given human thoughts and feelings. Use the vivid example describing the month of March from the supplementary focus book, *January Rides the Wind:*

March eats the winter;
icicles drip from its mouth
to fall on secret gardens.
Crocuses wake,
stain the melting snow with gold.

6. After reading other examples, ask for questions. Then, to check for understanding, try this segment of the upcoming focus book and ask the students which of the tools have been used here:

I have heard of a land
Where the earth is red with promises
Where the redbud trees catch the light
And throw it in a game of sunbeams
*   and shadow*
Back and forth to the cottonwood trees.

(personification)

7. Spend a few minutes reviewing the words and giving additional examples of each so that the class has a clear idea of what powerful writing tools they can be. Let students study them for a few minutes and then move on to the focus book for the lesson.

Suggestions for Teaching the Lesson

- Set the background for understanding this narrative poem by reading or telling the class the information on the front and back inside flaps of the focus book. Also point out that the quality of this writing earned an award for the author, the Coretta Scott King Award.

- Read through the book once, asking the students to just savor the beauty of the language and think about the experience described by the author.

- Take time to chat about the book and relish student reactions. Read the author's note at the conclusion of the book; it is a mini–history lesson in itself.

- Pick several passages that illustrate the three terms and put them on the chalkboard or overhead.

Examine them together and be certain the students know how they work before setting forth to find other examples on their own:

Simile:
where the flapjacks spread out
big as wagon wheels

Metaphor:
earth is red with promises
the stake is life and the work
that goes into it

Personification:
where the cottonwood trees are
innocent

syrup is honey stirred thick by
a thousand honeybees

• Working with metaphors may require more attention than the other two elements. Make the lessons as practical as possible before trying to find examples of them in a book. Have students get out paper and pencils. Ask them to focus on a special person in their lives, a good friend, a parent, or a much-loved relative. Put several of the following prompts on the overhead or board, add others of your own, and let the students work with them a bit. Remind them that a metaphor involves an implied comparison:

1. If your person were a season of the year, which one would he or she be? Write a few lines.

2. If your person were weather, what kind of weather would you choose? Write a few lines.

3. If this person were music, what type of music would most closely fit? Write a few lines.

4. If this person were a building, what kind of building might that be? Write a few lines.

5. If this person were a geographical feature, what feature is the most suitable? Write a few lines.

• Have students share their work with a partner and reflect on the process of trying to write a metaphor together. Finally, return to a class discussion to assess understanding of this tool and the others.

• At this point, invite students to read poetry from the books listed at the end of this lesson. Let them savor the poetry for the joy of reading it. Tell them to keep their writer's eye peeled for use of the three tools and to jot down examples that particularly appeal to them on note cards designated for each term, or in their writer's notebooks.

• After immersing themselves in poetry, have students begin a poetry workshop. Start with something simple like describing the weather for the day with appropriate figurative language. Armed with their tools, students should try their hands at other options. One way to begin and to take the worry out of having to write a poem on demand is to begin with an object to prompt a flow of thoughts. Assemble a variety of common classroom items, such as an eraser, chalk, a transparency, paper clips, a tattered book, a thumbtack, a trash can, and the janitor's broom. Add intriguing items from home or from garage sales, such as an old doorknob, rusty nails, a discarded lampshade, tools from that tool kit, a trowel, a packet of flower seeds, and a sponge. Display the items on a table and have the students select an object that particularly appeals to them. They should write about it poetically, plying their tools of imaginative writing to make that object something more than it seems.

• Have the students play, edit, polish, and share the results. They should exchange items, add new ones, and begin again. Those students who don't want to use the prompts can just let poetic thoughts spill out. Continue the poetry workshop until you deem that it is time to change the pace.

To publish, students can write their favorite effort neatly on an index card and display it with the item, if they have used one of the prompts, or alone if they have followed their own thoughts.

Evaluation

- Give the students a review sheet with one or two poems on it. Have them identify any similes, metaphors, and uses of personification. Check the results to see if students understand these three tools. Ask them to show you examples of the use of each one in their writing in the upcoming weeks. Encourage students to keep in their portfolios several examples of poems they have written.

- Conference individually with each student to evaluate grasp of poetry, feelings of competence when writing it, and plans for future efforts.

Extensions

- Have students make a poetry banner to decorate the classroom or the hallway outside the door. The banner might include copies of favorite poems that the students have found, or it might be a place to publish poetry they have written themselves. Decorate the banner with student artwork too.

- Make a big book of poetry filled with poems that would appeal to younger children. A rotating group of students can take it to classrooms and read the book aloud.

- Pass out crayons or markers and crisp, white paper. Read a poem to the class and let them respond by drawing their feelings, explaining in art what the poem means to them.

- Encourage students to investigate the websites dedicated to poetry, beginning with those listed in Appendix III. After polishing their own originals, they may publish them on a student site.

- After reading a wide variety of kinds of poetry, vote as a class on the students' favorite one. Make a bulletin board filled with some of their favorites, describing the contest, the results, and why the winner emerged as it did.

- Invite students from a high school English class or students from a nearby college to come in and share some of their appropriate, original work. Students can pair up with a high school or local college student to become poetry partners, reading and writing together.

- Add extra greenery to the classroom or a wall outside the classroom door by growing a poetry tree. Have the students make the trunk and branches out of construction paper. Each leaf should contain a favorite poem. Have students gather the poems and cover the tree over a period of time.

- Have students read a selection of well-practiced, lively poems onto a tape and send it to a lower-grade classroom along with illustrated copies of the poems. This would be a popular addition to the reading corner.

- Have students get involved in an Internet Pen Pal Program and periodically exchange poems with pen pals.

Suggested Titles for Independent Reading and Research

Adoff, Arnold. *I Am the Darker Brother: An Anthology of Modern Poems by African Americans*. Illustrated by Benny Andrews. New York: Simon & Schuster, 1997.

———. *My Black Me: A Beginning Book of Black Poetry*. New York: Puffin, 1995.

Alcaron, Francisco A. *Laughing Tomatoes and Other Spring Poems (Jitomates Risueños y Otros Poemas de Primavera)*. Illustrated by Maya Christina Bonzalez. Chicago: Children's Book Press, 1997.

Begay, Shonto. *Navajo: Visions and Voices across the Mesa*. New York: Scholastic, 1995.

Berry, James, ed. *Classic Poems to Read Aloud*. New York: Larousse Kingfisher, 1995.

———. *When I Dance*. San Diego, Calif.: Harcourt Brace, 1991.

Bruchac, Joseph. *The Earth under Sky Bear's Feet: Native American Poems of the Land*. Illustrated by Thomas Locker. New York: Putnam, 1995.

Bryan, Ashley. *Sing to the Sun: Poems and Pictures*. New York: HarperCollins, 1992.

Cullinan, Bernice, ed. *A Jar of Tiny Stars: Poems by NCTE Award-winning Poets*. Honesdale, Pa.: Wordsong/ Boyds Mills Press, 1996.

de Paola, Tomie. *Tomie de Paola's Book of Poems*. New York: Putnam, 1988.

Esbensen, Barbara Juster. *Echoes for the Eye: Poems to Celebrate Patterns in Nature*. Illustrated by Helen K. Davie. New York: HarperCollins, 1996.

———. *Who Shrank My Grandmother's House? Poems of Discovery*. Illustrated by Eric Beddows. New York: HarperCollins, 1992.

Giovanni, Nikki. *The Genie in the Jar*. Illustrated by Chris Raschka. New York: Henry Holt, 1996.

———. *The Sun Is So Quiet*. Illustrated by Ashley Bryan. New York: Henry Holt, 1996.

Greenfield, Eloise. *Night on Neighborhood Street*. Illustrated by Jan Spivey Gilchrist. New York: Puffin, 1991.

Hamanaka, Sheila. *All the Colors of the Earth*. New York: Morrow, 1994.

Hudson, Wade, ed. *Pass It On: African American Poetry for Children*. Illustrated by Floyd Cooper. New York: Scholastic, 1993.

Hughes, Langston. *The Dream Keeper and Other Poems*. Illustrated by Jerry Pinkney. New York: Alfred A. Knopf, 1994.

Janeczko, Paul B., ed. *The Place My Words Are Looking For*. New York: Bradbury, 1990.

Mora, Pat. *Confetti: Poems for Children*. Illustrated by Enrique O. Sanchez. New York: Lee & Low, 1996.

Myers, Walter Dean. *Brown Angels: An Album of Pictures and Verse*. New York: HarperCollins, 1993.

———. *Glorious Angels: A Celebration of Children*. New York: HarperCollins, 1995.

———. *Harlem*. Illustrated by Christopher Myers. New York: Scholastic, 1997.

Nye, Naomi Shihab. *The Tree Is Older Than You Are: A Bilingual Gathering of Poems and Stories from Mexico*. Illustrated with paintings by Mexican artists. New York: Simon & Schuster, 1995.

Rogasky, Barbara, selector. *Winter Poems*. Illustrated by Trina Schart Hyman. New York: Scholastic, 1994.

Rosenberg, Liz, ed. *The Invisible Ladder: An Anthology of Contemporary American Poems for Young Readers*. New York: Henry Holt, 1996.

Shaik, Fatima. *The Jazz of Our Street*. Illustrated by E. B. Lewis. New York: Dial, 1998.

Siegen-Smith, Nikki, comp. *A Pocketful of Stars: Poems about the Night*. Illustrated by Emma Shaw-Smith. New York: Barefoot Books, 1999.

Soto, Gary. *Canto Familiar*. Illustrated by Annika Nelson. San Diego, Calif.: Harcourt Brace, 1995.

———. *Neighborhood Odes*. Illustrated by David Diaz. San Diego, Calif.: Harcourt Brace, 1992.

Steele, Susanna, and Morag Styles, eds. *Mother Gave a Shout: Poems by Women and Girls*. Illustrated by Jane Ray. Volcano, Calif.: Volcano Press, 1991.

Thomas, Joyce Carol. *Brown Honey in Broomwheat Tea*. Illustrated by Floyd Cooper. New York: HarperCollins, 1993.

Wong, Janet S. *Good Luck Gold and Other Poems*. New York: McElderry, 1994.

Section VI

Pulling It All Together

PULLING IT ALL TOGETHER:
AN OVERVIEW

....

Teachers know all too well that there is never enough time in a classroom day. How do they accomplish everything they would like to do and still leave room for the joy of learning? First there are the students with their varying needs, abilities, and interests. Then there are the requirements of the district curriculum, which realistically could take a year and a half to cover. Add to that the students' growing interests—those days when they want to spend more time on their intriguing science experiments, when they want to build kites, not just read a story about them, and when a field trip simply makes more sense than a test as a way to cement learning. One can't forget the mandatory bus evacuation drills, the fire drills that pop the bubble of a magical, teachable moment, the flu, district standardized tests, and so forth. Finally, just when you think you've got it right, a new class appears on the horizon and it is time for change. There simply isn't enough time.

Juggling schedules with an eye to quality learning and deep understanding of subject matter is tough. One way to meet those challenges inherent in creating and maintaining a positive, productive classroom environment is to integrate subjects when it makes good learning sense. Teach across the curriculum, practicing newly taught reading skills in science, social studies, math, art, music, and/or P.E. Life outside the classroom has never required problem-solving responses to events that occur in boxlike isolation through-

out a day. Life inside the classroom must mirror real-life demands.

The judicious teacher will eke out time for inner and outer reflections and will emulate what day-to-day life requires, allowing students to practice necessary skills inside the classroom. In that light, the following lessons take a reading skill and put it to work with multicultural materials that will enrich learning in numerous ways across subject matter. But it isn't just the suggested materials and procedures that make learning exciting and foster understanding; it is the teacher who orchestrates the classroom routine to rewrite the symphony of learning for a different group of players year after year. Each of you deserves a standing ovation.

Also, keep in mind the following thoughts from educators that substantiate interdisciplinary teaching:

- Teaching across subjects focuses on the processes of learning more than on the resulting products. Products are still important, of course, but they do not drive learning.

- This approach breaks down subject matter boundaries and offers students integrative learning opportunities, a better way to make permanent connections.

- Although district curricular requirements are still important, there is more attention on the learner, whose interests, varying needs, and different abilities really should be the heart of the curriculum anyway.

- Working across the curriculum stimulates self-directed discoveries and investigations as individuals become fired up about a problem, issue, event, or personal insight.

- Such learning helps students build relationships between ideas and concepts, which facilitates deeper understanding of subject matter.

- There is a more reasonable opportunity to build on individual background knowledge and move each learner ahead as he or she integrates new learning with the old.

- There is time to revel in cultural differences and similarities.

- Students can be supported and encouraged as they stretch and take some learning risks.

- Students develop as independent learners, become more responsible and self-directed through individual, paired, small group, and large group activities.

- Learners can see the "why" behind classroom activities much more readily instead of continually having to memorize the "what."

- Each student in the classroom better assimilates learning because each has more time to investigate and then to reflect upon discoveries through discussions with classmates, journaling with the teacher, or just mulling over new thoughts introspectively.

Please enjoy the following learning opportunities, adapting them to fit your classroom and your teaching styles as you energize yourself and your students.

Lesson 36

Examining the Role of Action Verbs

SKILL: Improving Writing across the Curriculum

CULTURE OF FOCUS: All

Materials

The Jazz of Our Street, by Fatima Shaik
(Dial, 1998)
Notebook paper for every student
Pencils or pens
Large piece of butcher paper that will
become part of an action verb
word wall
Overhead projector and transparencies
Kites Sail High: A Book about Verbs, by
Ruth Heller (Scholastic, 1988)

Lesson Motivator

1. Prepare a display of objects that move or make intriguing noises. Place them on a table at the front of the room so that the students can see them. Include objects such as a top that spins, a baby rattle, an aluminum pie pan, small chimes, keys on a key chain, pencils in a box that roll loosely, a watch or small clock that ticks loudly, several sheets of tissue paper, a golf ball, a small wind-up toy, a globe on a stand, a yo-yo, a rainstick that rattles, or one or two percussion instruments from the band room.

2. Find enough objects so that students, divided into groups of three, can choose one, take it to a quiet area, and work with it.

3. Model the activity, which students will complete in triads. For example, begin with a basketball. Show it to the students and have them identify it. Then put it to work—roll it across the table, bounce it rhythmically, and dribble it quickly.

4. When you are done, ask volunteers to describe what you have just done with the ball, what they saw and heard. Write their responses on the chalkboard or overhead. Hopefully, they will use several action verbs to describe what they have seen. Take a large sheet of paper and ask the students to listen this time. Slowly crumple up the paper, rustling and rattling it a great deal. Ask students to supply words to describe what they saw and heard. Add these words to the previous list.

5. Explain that the day's activities will involve looking at interesting ways to add vitality to their personal writing and to enrich their writing in other subjects just by changing some worn-out verbs. Those verbs will be replaced by lively, action-describing verbs. Put a sentence on the overhead and then show students how much more interesting it is to read with some changes. For example:

   • The people talked about their problem.

   • Talk encircled the room, bounced off walls, rising and falling in pitch until the problem was resolved.

6. As a quick review of what this part of speech entails, read Ruth Heller's book *Kites Sail High.* Put a few copies in the writing center for easy reference.

7. Remind students to focus on words that denote an action of some type in the upcoming work. Invite a representative from each group to come up to the table, select an item, and take it back to their group for close scrutiny.

8. Have students use pencil and paper to write down as many action verbs as they can that are triggered by the item they have selected. Challenge them to use several of the verbs in sentences before returning to the entire group to share.

9. Convene the class as a whole. One by one, each triad should display the item they have chosen. Have them quickly review the list of verbs they generated along with an impressive sentence or two. Take samples of verbs and sentences. A student recorder can write down the action verbs on a large piece of chart paper while you record a sample sentence from each group on the overhead.

10. Ask if there are other verbs that popped into anyone's head before going to the next item and next group. Finally, take some time to scrutinize the sentences and comment on unusual verbs. Once the activity is completed, you have set the stage for listening to the read-aloud title, *The Jazz of Our Street*, whose text moves with musical rhythms.

Suggestions for Teaching the Lesson

• Read the book through once, just to hear the rhythm of the words and for students to enjoy the slice of life depicted. Chat about the images the book evokes and any personal experiences it triggers. Then have the students listen again, this time writing down words that could serve as action verbs in a future writing assignment. List those verbs on the wall chart once the book is completed. Verbs students might choose include:

pounding	run	greet
dropped	stopped	calls
tell	talk	gather
celebrate	follow	dance
jumping	squawks	honks
shout	coo	chuckle
cracking	sways	slapping
scraping	growl	rumble
snap	shake	shimmy
leaping	beat	spills

• Have students return to their groups of three and read another book, enjoying the glimpse into that particular culture and watching

how the author uses the verbs. During a second reading, they should write down verbs that show action.

• When the class gathers to discuss their books and new verbs, have each group tell about their book in a brief book talk. In the process they will cite the title, author, and illustrator, giving a quick three- or four-sentence synopsis of the plot. They can also engage in a short critical review about what particularly appealed to them about the book.

• The students should then share one of their action verbs by acting it out. Once the rest of the class guesses the word, one representative from the group will add it to the growing list of verbs on the chart paper. Each student in the triad should be active, just like the verbs, all three taking a part in covering the various sharing and investigating activities.

• End the lesson by asking students to quietly review the action verbs listed on the chart for future reference. They should pick several that particularly appeal to them and try them in an experimental sentence. These words will become a part of a temporary verb word wall. They should also be transferred to students' writing folders for handy use.

• Finally, have students focus on their writing folders to apply what they have just practiced. They should select a piece that they would like to improve, with the goal of exchanging some of the lifeless verbs for those that add more vitality to the piece. Remind students to return to their word lists to find exciting verbs for writing assignments in social studies.

Evaluation

• Circulate from group to group as they interact with interesting objects. Using anecdotal note-taking, quickly note behaviors that indicate engagement and cooperation. Later, in the large group when students share, do the same students always have their hands raised?

- Take quick notes on the students who are not participating. Watch them in future large group activities to see if there is a pattern of not contributing. Work to include every learner at an opportune time if there are some who rarely respond. Finally, as the next piece of writing appears and you conference with that author, talk about how the verbs have changed, asking the writer to point out those changes. Make a note about writing progress for the student's writing portfolio.

Extensions

- Play a game of Charades with the students, focusing on acting out new action verbs.

- Encourage students to watch for writing that is particularly effective and ask them to share their discoveries with the class. Authors make fabulous role models. Have students read segments from novels or picture books aloud or write out quotes and post them on an "Action Verb" bulletin board.

- Invite students to take a poem that is quiet in tone and change the verbs to create a new and much different version. They should illustrate it and display the completed transformation on a bulletin board (properly citing the original poet, of course).

- Have students write a news article about an event in history, using action-packed verbs to bring the event to life.

- When completing an assignment in social studies, make one of the criteria the use of such strong

verbs that the people and the place are vividly portrayed. Certainly, adjectives help with this, but keep the focus on fresh, strong verbs.

- Challenge the students to write up a science experiment using verbs that describe the results as vividly and realistically as possible.

Suggested Titles for Independent Reading and Research

Bartone, Elisa. *American Too.* Illustrated by Ted Lewin. New York: Lothrop, Lee & Shepard Books, 1996.

Bunting, Eve. *Smoky Night.* Illustrated by David Diaz. San Diego, Calif.: Harcourt Brace, 1994.

Coles, Robert. *The Story of Ruby Bridges.* Illustrated by George Ford. New York: Scholastic, 1995.

Doner, Kim. *Buffalo Dreams.* Portland, Oreg.: Westwinds Press, 1999.

Johnston, Tony. *Alice Nizzy Nazzy, the Witch of Santa Fe.* Illustrated by Tomie dePaola. New York: Scholastic, 1995.

———. *The Tale of Rabbit and Coyote.* Illustrated by Tomie dePaola. New York: Putnam, 1994.

Keams, Geri. *Grandmother Spider Brings the Sun: A Cherokee Story.* Illustrated by James Bernardin. Flagstaff, Ariz.: Northland Publishing, 1995.

Krupinski, Loretta. *Best Friends.* New York: Scholastic, 1998.

Leaf, Margaret. *Eyes of the Dragon.* Illustrated by Ed Young. New York: Lothrop, Lee & Shepard Books, 1987.

Mayer, Marianna. *Turandot.* Illustrated by Winslow Pels. New York: Morrow, 1995.

McCully, Emily Arnold. *Beautiful Warrior: The Legend of the Nun's Kung Fu.* New York: Scholastic, 1998.

McDermott, Gerald. *Zomo, the Rabbit: A Trickster Tale from West Africa.* New York: Scholastic, 1992.

Pinkney, Andrea Davis. *Duke Ellington.* Illustrated by Brian Pinkney. New York: Scholastic, 1998.

Smucker, Barbara. *Selina and the Shoo-Fly Pie.* Illustrated by Janet Wilson. New York: Stoddart Kids, 1998.

Thomas, Joyce Carol. *I Have Heard of a Land.* Illustrated by Floyd Cooper. New York: HarperCollins, 1998.

Lesson 37

Author! Author! Participating in an Author Study of Patricia Polacco

SKILL: Participating in an Author Study

CULTURE OF FOCUS: Russian and Irish

Materials

Babushka's Doll, by Patricia Polacco (Aladdin Paperbacks, 1995)
Video: *Patricia Polacco: Dream Keeper* 23 minutes, $39.95 (Philomel, 1996)
Wide selection of titles by Patricia Polacco (see list of suggested titles following the lesson)
Paper and pencils for planning
Medium-sized cardboard cartons (one per group)
Construction paper
Markers, paints, and other imaginative materials to make an author display

Don't miss the following informative article on questioning strategies as related to Patricia Polacco and her work: Patricia L. Bloem and Anthony L. Manna, "A Chorus of Questions: Readers Respond to Patricia Polacco," *The Reading Teacher* 52 (1999): 802–808.

Lesson Motivator

1. Explain that students will be engaged in an author study to learn more about a specific talented writer and illustrator. Upon completion of this author study, they will be able to work in groups to learn about another author of their choice.

2. If it is possible to locate it, show the video *Patricia Polacco: Dream Keeper* to introduce the author/illustrator and her books. Another option would be to visit the following website, a fascinating one for teachers and students alike: "Kay Vandergrift's Learning about the Author and Illustrator Pages," at: http://www.scils.rutgers.edu/special/kay/author.html.

Another site is: http://www. patriciapolacco. com.

3. If you have the equipment to show the Vandergrift site on a large screen for the entire class to enjoy, do so. Show the students around the site and then move to Patricia Polacco's web page. Several sites can be accessed from this page. Survey the sites, demonstrating how interesting they are and what excellent resources they can be for future research, then return to the partially completed example of an author display (described below).

4. Unveil an author display that you have begun about Patricia Polacco. Point out the classroom collection of her books that you have gathered previously from the library or learning center. You can purchase a three-sided display board in several sizes from a craft or office supply store to be used as the background for the display.

5. A less expensive way to create a backdrop for this motivational display is to construct it using a medium-sized cardboard box. Cut off one side of the box and one set of endflaps. Open the box to form a three-sided display, supporting the display on the bottom endflaps. For relatively little expense, students can also develop a pleasing overview of any popular author's or artist's work as part of their assignments later in the lesson.

6. Include the following types of things in the Polacco display: a short biography based on information in the reference set *Something about the Author,* available in most public libraries, or facts gleaned from the website; an annotated list of a selection of her books (one-line annotations are sufficient); snippets of quotes from some of

her books; a list of interesting or surprising facts, titled "Did You Know?"; and a diorama depicting a scene from a favorite Polacco book.

7. Have students help complete this display, in small groups each in charge of one of the items. Because of student involvement, the interest level should be high at this point.

Suggestions for Teaching the Lesson

- Read one of your favorite titles written and illustrated by Patricia Polacco. The focus book suggested here highlights the relationship between a young girl and her Babushka, or Russian grandmother, and relates a lesson about selfishness in a charming manner.

- Upon completion of the story, discuss the book and illustrations with the class. Point out that authors can often be the best teachers when it comes to showing readers how to become good writers. Ask students to pay attention to what Polacco does to make her stories move along as they read other books she has written. How does she hold the reader's interest in book after book?

- Spend some time with the students enjoying Polacco's artwork, which is characterized by strong lines. Point out that her favorite media seem to be pencils, colored marking pens, and acrylics. Draw the students' attention to the way she sets up her illustrations. She frequently leaves white space, "negative space" as it is referred to by artists, around many of her pictures as an effective way to set them off.

- Have students read through the collection of books you have gathered working in groups of three or four. As each group completes a title, they should list it under specific categories that you have designated ahead of time. Tape sheets of chart paper conveniently around the room with a topic at the top of each. If the book basically

addresses that topic, a student should write the title on the sheet. It is possible that a book might fit on several sheets. Examples of topics to include are problems in growing up, family relationships, the importance of reading, and childhood fears.

- Have each group decide what common threads tie many of the books together, aside from the fact that they were all written and illustrated by the same person. For instance, readers may discover that most of the stories are based on family history. They may perceive that in numerous books there is a young child and an elderly adult. Animals of one kind or another also appear in Polacco's illustrations. The style of artwork may be another thread that ties the books together. These observations should be noted and discussed when the class gathers as a whole to go over what they have learned.

- Move on to incorporating some analysis of literature as you ask students to think critically about how this author writes. Within their groups they should discuss what makes these stories interesting and the characters memorable. Each group should read each book twice, once to thoroughly enjoy the story and a second time to look critically at the way the author uses words. How does she develop a plot? How does she make her characters memorable and real? How does Polacco celebrate her Russian/ Jewish/Irish ancestry? Add ideas to a list on chart paper to be shared with the class as a whole.

- Discuss with the class the author's craft and what skills they may try in their future writing as a result of having Patricia Polacco as their "teacher." Share the observations in a large group discussion.

- After a general class discussion about Patricia Polacco and her works and the completion of the author display, introduce other multicultural authors. Give a short book talk on an appealing book an author has written or illustrated. Regroup students based on their interest in a particular author or illustrator so that they can delve into that person's books. Let them orchestrate an author study from scratch, conducting research, reading a variety of books, and creating an inviting author display.

• Each group should present their author study to the class. To pique the interest of other readers in the school, the completed displays should be showcased in the learning center or library. They might even become traveling displays, complete with the accompanying books. A group can take their author study to another classroom, present it, and leave it for several weeks so that the students in that classroom can become acquainted with a new author or illustrator before it travels on.

Evaluation

• Monitor the group work and ascertain whether each student is a contributing member. Are all students reading? Discussing?

• When students divide into groups to begin their own author studies, design a rubric for them to use as they work. They may help to develop the rubric after having been involved in this model lesson, assigning appropriate point values to each section. Such a rubric could include the following three areas and various points under each area:

Research:
1. Students provide enough material about the author's or illustrator's background to make the presentation lively and interesting.
2. Students read a representative number of the author's or illustrator's books.
3. Students bring an appealing number of books to class as

part of the display and for classmates' future reading.

Presentation:
1. Every member in the group has a part in the presentation.
2. It is obvious that each member has gained knowledge about the author or illustrator.
3. The display is neatly done.
4. The display is original, attractive, and interesting.
5. The biographical information is clearly written.

Group Interaction:
1. One student was the leader who organized work sessions and made certain everyone's ideas were heard and respected.
2. All members did their share of the work.
3. Each member contributed thoughts on what worked, what needed improvement, and how valuable he or she thought the project was as a learning tool.

• Be certain to make time to meet with each group, go over their rubric, and give feedback as needed.

Extensions

• After reading a variety of Polacco's books, have students play a version of Twenty Questions. One student should come to the front of the room with a specific title in mind. The rest of the class must attempt to narrow the field of possibilities, trying to guess the title in question. One student at a time should ask a question about the book that can only be answered by a yes or a no response, until clever guessing leads to the answer.

• Divide the class into two teams and play Charades, with students acting out the title of a book for teammates to guess.

• Have students write and illustrate a picture book based on an incident from their family's history, modeling their efforts on lessons learned from this author.

- Once a number of author studies are concluded, set up an interview show similar to the format of *The Barbara Walters Show.* Have students conduct interviews with other students, who assume the role of a specific author that they have come to know well.

- Ask the owners of local bookstores to display a few of your author displays in a safe but visually accessible place in their stores for a short period of time.

Suggested Titles for Independent Reading and Research

Polacco, Patricia. *Appelemandro's Dreams.* New York: Philomel, 1991.

———. *Aunt Chip and the Great Triple Creek Dam Affair.* New York: Philomel, 1996.

———. *Babushka Baba Yaga.* New York: Philomel, 1993.

———. *Babushka's Mother Goose.* New York: Philomel, 1994.

———. *The Bee Tree.* New York: Philomel, 1993.

———. *Boat Ride with Lillian Two Blossom.* New York: Philomel, 1988.

———. *Chicken Sunday.* New York: Putnam & Grosset, 1992.

———. *Firetalking.* Illustrated with photographs by Lawrence Migdale Katonah. New York: Owen, 1994.

———. *In Enzo's Splendid Gardens.* New York: Philomel, 1997.

———. *Just Plain Fancy.* New York: Bantam/Doubleday, 1990.

———. *The Keeping Quilt.* New York: Simon & Schuster, 1988.

———. *Meteor!* New York: Dodd, Mead, 1987.

———. *My Rotten Redheaded Older Brother.* New York: Simon & Schuster, 1994.

———. *Picnic at Mudsock Meadow.* New York: Putnam & Grosset, 1992.

———. *Pink and Say.* New York: Philomel, 1994.

———. *Rechenka's Eggs.* New York: Putnam & Grosset, 1988.

———. *Some Birthday!* New York: Simon & Schuster, 1991.

———. *Thank You, Mr. Falker.* New York: Philomel, 1998.

———. *Thunder Cake.* New York: Philomel, 1990.

———. *Tikvah Means Hope.* New York: Doubleday, 1994.

———. *The Trees of the Dancing Goats.* New York: Simon & Schuster, 1996.

Authors for Further Author Studies

Verna Aardema (Hispanic American)
Alma Flor Ada (Hispanic American)
George Ancona (Hispanic American)
Mitsumasa Anno (Japanese)

Jose Aruego (Hispanic)
Shonto Begay (Native American)
Joseph Bruchac (Native American)
Ashley Bryan (African American)
Lucille Clifton (African American)
Floyd Cooper (African American)
Donald Crews (African American)
Pat Cummings (African American)
Demi (Asian)
Tom Feelings (African American)
Nikki Giovanni (African American)
Eloise Greenfield (African American)
Sheila Hamanaka (Japanese American)
Virginia Hamilton (African American)
Joel Harris (African American)
Michael Lacapa (Native American)
Patricia McKissack (African American)
Nicholasa Mohr (Latino)
Pat Mora (Hispanic)
Walter Dean Myers (African American)
Brian Pinkney (African American)
Jerry Pinkney (African American)
Faith Ringgold (African American)
Cynthia Rylant (Appalachian)
Allen Say (Asian American)
Virginia Driving Hawk Sneve (Native American)
Gary Soto (Mexican American)
John Steptoe (African American)
Mildred D. Taylor (African American)
Joyce Carol Thomas (African American)
Yoshiko Uchida (Japanese American)
Baje Whitethorne (Native American)
Laurence Yep (Chinese American)
Yoshi (Chinese American)
Ed Young (Chinese American)
Song Nan Zhang (Chinese Canadian)

Lesson 38

Literature Circles—Reading and Discussing

SKILL: Fostering Comprehension and Response through Literature Circles

CULTURE OF FOCUS: Chinese

Materials

The Paper Dragon, by Marguerite W. Davol; illustrated by Robert Sabuda (Atheneum, 1997)

Copies of origami directions (see end of
lesson) and squares of colorful
paper (such as wrapping paper)
to make origami hearts

Questions to guide the discussion in
literature circles

Rubric for student performance (optional)

Lesson Motivator

1. Let students choose a square of colorful paper or one with a pattern
they like. Hand out the directions
for making the heart. Explain that
origami, or the art of paper folding, has long been practiced in
China and Japan but has become
popular in other cultures as well.

2. Following the directions, make an
origami heart as the students
work along with you. The heart
should be tied to the theme of the
book you will be reading aloud
and demonstrating in the model
literature circle. If possible, show
examples of some Chinese paper
cuts, intricate designs cut from
tissue-thin paper. This is the
beautiful art technique used in
The Paper Dragon.

Suggestions for
Teaching the Lesson

- Explain that students eventually will
be working in small groups, each
group reading a different book,
and that they will be spending
time sharing their reactions to that
book within their groups. Working
with a picture book the first time
through, they will be practicing
the routine involved with a literature circle. Literature circles are
important because they encourage
students to respond or react to a
book or a chapter they have read
together by talking about it.
Reading is a social process, and
students learn from one another as
they socialize and talk about
books. These circles are also important because they underscore
the fact that everyone has different
opinions and each one is valid.

- Model how a literature circle works
with a small group of students
first, then the students can break
into groups to read a book and
discuss it on their own. If this is
the first time you have used literature circles, it would be wise to divide the students up ahead of
time, integrating students into
groups where they will be the
most successful. The leader of
each group should be an individual who took part in the model literature circle and who has some
experience leading or engaging in
a good conversation about a book.

- Once the students are comfortable
working in these response groups,
they should have a choice about
which group and what book they
would like to work with in the future. Choice is a strong motivating
factor, and having a voice in what
they read is very important to the
reading process.

- When modeling with the first group,
reinforce how important it is that
there is no right or wrong when
it comes to people's opinions or
reactions. There is no room in a
literature circle for ridicule. Set
the rules clearly ahead of time
and put them in chart form if
necessary.

- Rather than reading the book aloud
yourself, reinforce the importance
of every student contributing in a
literature circle by putting students in the read-aloud role. Share
The Paper Dragon by letting each
member of the demonstration literature circle take a turn reading
and showing the illustrations in
the book so that the entire class is
familiar with the story and the
wonderful illustrations. Then, as a
temporary leader, start the discussion with a personal reaction,
inviting someone else in the group
to share his or her response. Ask
for further information after student responses by asking why
they think the way they do.

- A less intimidating follow-up is to
ask a student to tell you a little
more. Give each student in the

group a chance to express personal thoughts and then ask another question to get students to continue their interactions. For example:

1. They may discuss a part they didn't understand and ask others how they felt about that part.

2. They may talk about a favorite part and compare and contrast what each member of the group liked best.

3. They may discuss the illustrations, commenting about particularly interesting or clever artwork.

4. They may connect the story to something familiar in their own lives.

5. They may discuss why the author wrote the story, what the themes might be, and if the author accomplished the task. Be sure to address the role that the origami heart had as a motivator for this tale.

• Once the group has finished discussing *The Paper Dragon,* ask the class if they have reactions or responses to add. Encourage open conversation so that students feel safe expressing their opinions.

• Divide students into their groups. Book-talk a number of titles for the practice session. Each group should confer and write down their first and second choices. To make the selection fair, send one member of the group up to draw a number. Have students select their books based on the numbers they chose (number 1 picks first, and so forth). Explain to the class that in future literature circles, they will be able to select the group and book of their choice.

• Literature can often elicit some strong emotions, depending on the story. It is always wise to be especially sensitive to students and what you might know to be happening in their lives and to use your best judgment when matching readers and reading materials.

• You can give one student in each group the responsibility for being the group leader. Provide leaders with questions to guide the discussion the first time through and in future groups as is necessary, depending on the abilities of the class. Students quickly develop the desire to ask their own questions, so this type of prompt may not be needed beyond the initial practice grouping. The questions used in the modeling session are certainly appropriate, but others can be added at any time.

• Move from group to group as students read and then begin to discuss their books. Offer guidance and ask pertinent questions to keep the discussions moving.

• After all the groups have completed their responses, have them present their books to the rest of the class in a creative way.

• The next literature circle should be set up with small groups reading novels together. When working with longer reading selections, students need to decide how many pages must be completed before each gathering and how they will respond to what they read before they meet.

• They can keep a reading log, write short reactions in it, and then use the log as reference when the group meets. Or they may choose to complete character webs, adding characteristics and key items to the web as characters develop throughout the book. Then they can analyze changes each time the group meets. Meet with one group per day, circulating among the groups to monitor learning and group interactions. Again, students can extend their experiences with a novel by sharing it with the rest of the class in an appealing way.

Evaluation

• Prepare a simple rubric before literature circles begin. Share it with the students so that they know what kinds of behaviors you will be addressing. For example, one criterion could be coming to future literature circle sessions prepared, with the reading completed and with questions to ask. You could also include items such as working in a cooperative manner, listening politely and supporting everyone's ideas, giving responses that represent some quality thinking, and staying on task when the group is meeting. Ask for suggestions from the class and finalize the rubric.

- Fill in the rubric based on your observations and those of each student, who should reflect on his or her personal performance and then meet with you to compare results. A checklist and brief anecdotal write-up should be added to a student's ongoing reading portfolio. Looking over each literature circle evaluation should show you areas of growth that continue to need attention.

Extensions

- A class mural along the wall in the hallway would be a wonderful way to extend responses to the picture books read and entice others to read them. Each group should be in charge of a segment of the mural, with everyone contributing to the artwork. The title and author of the book being depicted should be displayed prominently.

- Pantomime or act out part of the story and then discuss with the class why that part was picked.

- Listen to Chinese music while extension activities are being completed. With only five notes in their musical scale instead of seven (as in the West), Chinese music will sound quite different initially.

- Have students research dragons and their place in Chinese mythology. Fill a bulletin board with pictures of mythological examples and stu-

dent-created dragons and retold or original stories to go with them. Two superb books to use as models for this activity, both by Demi, are *The Dragon's Tale and Other Animal Fables of the Chinese Zodiac* (New York: Henry Holt, 1996) and *Dragons and Fantastic Creatures* (New York: Henry Holt, 1993).

- Invite someone who is knowledgeable and qualified to teach the students about the Dragon Dance. Try it with a class-made dragon.

Suggested Titles for Use in Literature Circles

Barber, Antonia. *The Monkey and the Panda.* Illustrated by Meilo So. New York: Macmillan, 1995.

Demi. *The Magic Tapestry.* New York: Henry Holt, 1994.

———. *The Stonecutter.* New York: Crown, 1995.

Granfield, Linda. *The Legend of the Panda.* Illustrated by Song Nan Zhang. Plattsburgh, N.Y.: Tundra, 1998.

Hillman, Elizabeth. *Min-Yo and the Moon Dragon.* Illustrated by John Wallner. San Diego, Calif.: Harcourt Brace, 1992.

Lawson, Julie. *The Dragon's Pearl.* Illustrated by Paul Morin. New York: Clarion, 1993.

Louie, Ai-Ling. *Yeh-Shen: A Cinderella Story from China.* Illustrated by Ed Young. New York: Philomel, 1982.

Melmed, Laura Krauss. *Little Oh.* Illustrated by Jim LaMarche. New York: Lothrop, Lee & Shepard Books, 1997.

Meyer, Marianna. *Turandot.* Illustrated by Winslow Pels. New York: Morrow, 1995.

Pattison, Darcy. *The River Dragon.* Illustrated by Jean Tseng and Mou-sien Tseng. New York: Lothrop, Lee & Shepard Books, 1991.

Tan, Amy. *The Chinese Siamese Cat.* Illustrated by Gretchen Shields. New York: Simon & Schuster, 1994.

Wang, Rosalind C. *The Fourth Question: A Chinese Tale.* Illustrated by Ju-Hong Chen. New York: Holiday House, 1991.

Wolkstein, Diane. *White Wave: A Chinese Tale.* Illustrated by Ed Young. San Diego, Calif.: Gulliver/Harcourt Brace, 1996.

Yee, Paul. *Roses Sing on a New Snow: A Delicious Tale.* Illustrated by Harvey Chan. New York: Macmillan, 1991.

Yep, Laurence. *The Ghost Fox.* Illustrated by Jean Tseng and Mou-sien Tseng. New York: Scholastic, 1994.

Young, Ed. *Lon Po Po: A Red-Riding Hood Story from China.* New York: Philomel, 1989.

———. *The Lost Horse: A Chinese Folktale.* San Diego, Calif.: Silver Whistle/Harcourt Brace, 1998.

———. *Mouse Match.* San Diego, Calif.: Silver Whistle/Harcourt Brace, 1997.

Directions for Making an Origami Heart

You will need an 8-inch square piece of origami paper or gift wrap. The complete heart will look best if the paper has color or print on one side and is plain on the other. That contrast is important.

Remember to make sharp creases as you fold and refold the paper for best results.

Step 1: Fold the paper in half and then unfold it. Fold the top two corners into the middle, as shown.

Step 2: Turn the paper over so that you are working on the smooth back. Fold each edge to the center and crease.

Step 3: Fold the colored or patterned side down over the white section.

Step 4: Shape the heart by folding the four corners at the top edge to the back.

Step 1:

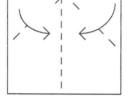

Step 2:

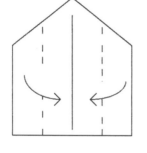

Step 3:

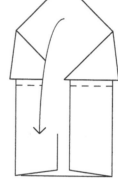

Step 4:

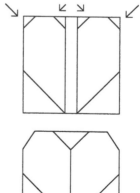

Lesson 39

Tales across Cultures

SKILL: Reading and Writing Trickster Tales

CULTURE OF FOCUS: African American

Materials

Anansi and the Talking Melon, by Eric A Kimmel; illustrated by Janet Stevens (Holiday House, 1994)

A variety of trickster tales representing numerous cultures (see list of suggested titles following lesson)

Copies of the "Trickster Tale Review and Planning Guide" (see end of lesson)

Sheets of newsprint for "dummy" copies of students' books

Pens and pencils

Quality paper for the final publication of a trickster tale

Art supplies for the illustrations

Chart paper or overhead projector

Video by a writer and/or the following titles for student reference: *How a Book Is Made,* by Aliki (Harper, 1986); *From Pictures to Words: A Book about Making a Book,* by Janet Stevens (Holiday House, 1995)

Lesson Motivator

1. Well before the lesson is to be presented, make several different puppets. Use paper plates for face puppets, colored socks for sock puppets, or simple construction paper shapes mounted on tongue depressors for stick puppets. Each puppet will represent a trickster from a different culture. Because Coyote, Raven, Spider, and Rabbit appear in the majority of trickster tales, these are sound choices.

2. On the day of the lesson, bring the puppets into class and introduce each one. You can either give a brief rundown of the kinds of adventures each one has had or retell a complete trickster tale using one puppet in particular. If you opt to retell an entire tale, stop periodically to involve the class.

3. When the trickster has a decision to make, ask class members what they would do. Respond to their replies with something like, "That may be so, but listen to what Anansi [or other appropriate character] did," and continue with the story. Between the puppets, the enjoyable nature of these tales, and the group involvement, students will be thoroughly hooked for the upcoming lesson.

Suggestions for Teaching the Lesson

- Tell the class that nearly every culture has trickster tales as a part of its literature. In these tales the main character must use cleverness, tricks, lies, deceit, and/or mischief to overcome challenges imposed by more powerful creatures. Sometimes the main characters are taught a lesson or two by the very creatures they seek to deceive. Sometimes these tricksters are human, at other times they are animals, but they are always male. In stories originating in Japan the trickster is often a badger or a hare, whereas Coyote and Raven assume this role in numerous Native American tales.

- As learners read through various tales closely, they will note the layer upon layer of human nature reflected in the actions of a trickster. For example, the particular main character in the focus book reflects the best and the worst in humanity in that sometimes he is the deceiver, at other times he can be easily deceived himself; he destroys in some tales but in others he creates. Like Iktomi in Paul

Goble's books, he is foolish and greedy. In other tales the trickster shows a more generous side. As students read and record information on the classroom chart, draw them into making these kinds of discoveries about the multi-faceted trickster.

- As part of a larger category of literature called folklore, these distinctive tales have a long history. They were often passed on to generation after generation of listeners through the oral tradition. Fortunately, a growing number of these tales are now being adapted and retold, recorded for fortunate readers in appealing picture books and anthologies.

- Students will learn that reading the folklore of a culture can be a pleasant educational experience. They will better understand the personal dimensions and standards of behavior that are accepted by a culture, reducing the possibility of stereotyping people within that culture.

- As they read and enjoy several tales students will be participating in cultural mini-lessons, noting values expressed, getting a glimpse of what members of the culture find humorous or what they ridicule, viewing things they might fear, and sensing how they might see themselves. An additional bonus is that these tales have been reproduced at various reading levels so that readers of different abilities and levels of maturity can all relish them without the frustration imposed by difficult text.

- Proceed with the lesson by reading *Anansi and the Talking Melon.* At the conclusion of the book, discuss what the students may have learned about the culture based on hearing the tale. Then work together to analyze how the tale is put together using a sample planning guide (included at the end of this lesson) on the overhead or by

writing the information on chart paper for the entire class to see. Focus on the following points:

Culture: What clues to the culture does the author or illustrator give you?

Setting: How does the author let you know when and where the story takes place?

Characters: How well do we get to know them? How many characters are in a tale? Do we come to know them as well as we come to know characters in a novel?

Challenge: What kinds of problems does the main character face? How long does it take to solve them?

Plot: How is the story told? Is the plot simple or complex?

Resolution: Does the ending make sense with the rest of the story?

Theme: Why do you think the author chose to retell this story?

- Devote an entire bulletin board covered with fresh butcher paper to a chart used for the recording of information about these tales. Include the following categories across the top of the paper: title of the tale, author, culture, main character (designating whether it is man, animal, or insect), main problem to solve, manner in which the problem was solved, solution, and cultural values depicted.

- Ask for volunteers to complete the information after discussing *Anansi and the Talking Melon.* As groups finish other titles, have one group at a time record and discuss their information. Eventually, a helpful visual summary of the critical ingredients in a trickster tale will be displayed for continued reference.

- Divide the class into groups of three or four. Have students select another trickster tale to read together. After discussing what they especially liked about the way it was retold and what might be learned from their particular tale, have them fill in a fresh copy of the planning guide. When work has been completed, share the gradually burgeoning knowledge in a large group again so that all students can benefit from each small group's discoveries.

- At this point, students should immerse themselves in the realm of trickster tales, reading a number of books from a variety of cultures to become as knowledgeable about this particular kind of folklore as possible. Their goal is to write a tale of their own representing a culture that is part of their background. They can continue to take notes on other planning guides, combining several tales on one sheet for future reference. An option is to jot additional information in their literature or writing journals as needed. During this time, you should be chatting with students as they work, monitoring their progress and their insights, clearing up confusion as it arises.

- When you feel the students have had enough exposure to the tales, have them plan out their personal trickster tales on fresh planning guides. They should include authentic bits from their culture as part of the story and as essential ingredients in the illustrations to add to the cultural flavor of the final product. They may consult parents, other relatives, members of the community, and you during this creative writing process. They may base the length of the finished product on the books they have read, but their goal is a standard 32-page picture book. Some of those pages will be devoted to title and copyright plus information about the author or notes on the research done to complete the story. The books they have used can serve as templates for their own products.

- Whenever you feel it fits best into the project, share Aliki's *How a Book Is Made* or Janet Stevens's *From Pictures to Words: A Book about*

Making a Book. Keep several copies of these titles or others like them for your writers to refer to. This is a great time to remind students of the value of the dictionary and the thesaurus as they search for just the right words to use in their stories.

- Have students follow your established classroom writing process for taking a piece of writing from rough draft to completed product, including careful editing. This is an opportune time to show a video of a writer at work so that students get the idea that a well-written story requires a great deal of time, effort, and editing. Check the resources listed in Appendix II for suggested titles. Sometimes words from an "expert" other than the teacher to whom students listen much of the time seem to carry more weight.

- When the draft of each story has been edited and polished, have students make a "dummy" copy of their books before beginning the final version. For this step they will need large sheets of newsprint that they can divide into squares representing the number of pages required for their book. The size of the newsprint and the personal preferences of the writer will dictate the number of sheets each writer requires. During this planning stage, students should decide how to divide the text of their story among the pages and do simple sketches of ideas for illustrations. By taking time to plan as real writers do, they should avoid a major catastrophe as they complete their polished versions. Be sure to preview each of these planning sheets before students continue.

- Offer several kinds of paper in varying sizes for the final copy. You can purchase blank books created just for this kind of activity or you can teach students how to bind a book, making it their own from cover to cover. If possible, enlist the aid of the art teacher as a consultant on the media to be used for illustrations. Students may enjoy illustrating their books using the folk art style popular in the culture in which their tales are rooted. Both the art teacher and the school librarian can help students accomplish this task. It would be wonderful if a local artist could join in the instruction at this point.

Evaluation

- Develop a rubric for assessing the final product and post it where all the students can see it. A rubric is most effective if the students have a say in what they think is important to their polished tales, so let them help to create the parameters for assessment.

- As students work, monitor progress by keeping brief anecdotal notes on how individuals worked in the group, the care they took in completing planning guides, the number and variety of books read in preparation, the effort that went into the drafts, and so forth. Watching a few students each day throughout the project and having short individual conferences periodically will yield helpful information upon which to base the final evaluation.

Extensions

- Students all need an opportunity to shine. Set up an "Author Day" during which each writer can read his or her tale. Divide up this "shine time" over several days to keep audience interest high and listeners fresh.

- Have student authors take their finished tales to other classrooms throughout the building and read to small groups of students.

- Give the stories a different kind of life by having the students present them in a reader's theater format both in and outside your classroom.

- As a grand finale when this reading and writing activity is done, have the students create a trickster quilt. Give them each an 8- or 9-inch square of light-colored muslin. After planning and sketching carefully, they should transfer their drawing from a favorite trickster tale onto the muslin using fabric crayons or markers. The title and author of the book and each student's name should be written neatly in the lower right-hand corner of the square. Upper-grade students and/or parent helpers can stitch the completed squares onto a large, colorful fabric background, which can then be attached to quilt batting and a muslin bottom cover. A parent volunteer can machine stitch the layers together. Students can then complete the quilting with simple yarn ties. Display this masterpiece in the front hall of the school for students and visitors to admire. Alternatively, put it in the library or learning center above a display of popular trickster tales.

Suggested Titles for Independent Reading and Research

Aardema, Verna. *Anansi Does the Impossible*. New York: Simon & Schuster, 1997.

Barber, Antonia. *The Monkey and the Panda*. Illustrated by Meilo So. New York: Macmillan, 1995.

Begay, Shonto. *Ma'ii and Cousin Horned Toad: A Traditional Navajo Story*. New York: Scholastic, 1992.

Bodkin, Odds. *The Crane Wife*. Illustrated by Gennady Spirin. San Diego, Calif.: Gulliver, 1998.

Brusca, Maria, and Tona Wilson. *The Cook and the King*. New York: Henry Holt, 1993.

———. *Pedro Fools the Gringo: And Other Tales of a Latin American Trickster*. Illustrated by Maria Brusca. New York: Henry Holt, 1995.

Chang, Margaret S. *The Beggar's Magic: A Chinese Tale*. Illustrated by David Johnson. New York: McElderry, 1997.

Czernecki, Stefan. *The Cricket's Cage: A Chinese Folktale*. New York: Hyperion, 1997.

Dwyer, Mindy. *Coyote in Love*. Seattle, Wash.: Alaska Northwest Books, 1997.

Goble, P. *Iktomi and the Ducks*. New York: Orchard, 1990.

Goldin, Barbara D. *Coyote and the Firestick: A Northwest Coast Indian Legend.* Illustrated by Will Hillenbrand. San Diego, Calif.: Harcourt Brace, 1996.

Hamilton, Virginia. *A Ring of Tricksters: Animal Tales from North America, the West Indies, and Africa.* Illustrated by Barry Moser. New York: Blue Sky, 1997.

Hausman, Gerald. *Coyote Walks on Two Legs: A Book of Navajo Myths and Legends.* Illustrated by Floyd Cooper. New York: Philomel, 1995.

Johnston, Tony. *The Tale of Rabbit and Coyote.* Illustrated by Tomie dePaola. New York: Putnam, 1994.

Kimmel, Eric A. *The Adventures of Hershel of Ostopol.* Illustrated by Trina Schart Hyman. New York: Holiday House, 1995.

———. *Hershel and the Hanukkah Goblins.* Illustrated by Trina Schart Hyman. New York: Holiday House, 1985.

———. *Ten Suns: A Chinese Legend.* Illustrated by YongSheng Xuan. New York: Holiday House, 1998.

Max, Jill. *Spider Spins a Story: Fourteen Legends from Native America.* Illustrated by various Native American artists. Flagstaff, Ariz.: Rising Moon, 1997.

Mayo, Gretchen W. *That Tricky Coyote!* New York: Walker, 1993.

McDermott, Gerald. *Coyote: A Trickster Tale from the Southwest.* San Diego, Calif.: Harcourt Brace, 1994.

———. *Papagayo, the Mischief Maker.* San Diego, Calif.: Harcourt Brace, 1992.

———. *Raven: A Trickster Tale from the Northwest.* New York: Scholastic, 1993.

———. *Zomo, the Rabbit: A Trickster Tale from West Africa.* San Diego, Calif.: Harcourt Brace, 1992.

McDonald, Margaret Reed. *The Girl Who Wore Too Much: A Folktale from Thailand.* Illustrated by Yvonne Lebrun Davis. Little Rock, Ark.: August House Little Folk, 1998.

McKissack, Patricia C. *Flossie and the Fox.* Illustrated by Rachel Isadora. New York: Dial, 1986.

Mollel, Tolowa M. *The King and the Tortoise.* Illustrated by Kathy Blankley. New York: Clarion, 1993.

———. *Rhinos for Lunch and Elephants for Supper! A Maasai Tale.* Illustrated by Barbara Spurll. New York: Clarion, 1991.

Morgan, Pierr. *Supper for Crow: A Northwest Coast Indian Tale.* New York: Crown, 1995.

Norman, Howard. *How Glooscap Outwits the Ice Giants and Other Tales of the Maritime Indians.* Illustrated by Michael McCurdy. Boston: Little, Brown, 1989.

Reed, M. Ann. *Raven Brings to the People Another Gift: A Story Based Upon Native American Legend.* Illustrated by Nakoma Volkman. Chamberlain, S.D.: Tipi Press, 1997.

Roberts, Moss. *Chinese Fairy Tales & Fantasies.* New York: Pantheon Books, 1979.

Rodanas, Kristina. *Follow the Stars.* Tarrytown, N.Y.: Marshall Cavendish, 1998.

Root, Phyllis. *Coyote and the Magic Words.* Illustrated by Sandra Speidel. New York: Lothrop, 1993.

Ross, Gayle. *How Rabbit Tricked Otter: And Other Cherokee Trickster Tales.* Illustrated by Murv Jacob. New York: HarperCollins, 1994.

San Souci, Robert D. *Cut from the Same Cloth: American Women of Myth, Legend, and Tall Tale.* Illustrated by Brian Pinkney. New York: Philomel, 1993.

Schwartz, Howard, and Barbara Rush. *The Diamond Tree: Jewish Tales from around the World.* Illustrated by Uri Shulevitz. New York: HarperCollins, 1991.

———. *The Wonder Child & Other Jewish Fairy Tales.* Illustrated by Stephen Fieser. New York: HarperCollins, 1996.

Sherman, Josepha. *Rachel the Clever & Other Jewish Folktales.* Little Rock, Ark.: August House, 1993.

Shetterly, Susan H. *Muwin and the Magic Hare.* Illustrated by Robert Shetterly. New York: Atheneum, 1993.

———. *Raven's Light: A Myth from the People of the Northwest Coast.* Illustrated by Robert Shetterly. New York: Atheneum, 1991.

Singer, Isaac Bashevis. "Shrewd Todie and Lyzer, the Miser." In *When Shlemiel Went to Warsaw and Other Stories.* Translated by the author and Elizabeth Shub. Illustrated by Margot Zemach. New York: Farrar, Straus & Giroux, 1968.

Snyder, Diane. *The Boy of the Three Year Nap.* Illustrated by Allan Say. Boston: Houghton Mifflin, 1988.

Stamm, Claus. *Three Strong Women.* Illustrated by Jean Tseng and Mou-sien Tseng. New York: Viking, 1990.

Stevens, Janet. *Coyote Steals the Blanket: A Ute Tale.* New York: Holiday House, 1993.

Strauss, Susan. *Coyote Tales for Children.* Illustrated by Gary Lund. Hillsboro, Oreg.: Beyond Words Publications, 1991.

Taylor, Harriet P. *Coyote and the Laughing Butterflies.* New York: Macmillan, 1995.

———. *Coyote Places the Stars.* New York: Aladdin Paperbacks, 1997.

Van Lann, Nancy. *In a Circle Long Ago: A Treasury of Native Lore from North America.* Illustrated by Lisa Desimini. New York: Knopf, 1995.

———. *Shingebiss: An Ojibwe Legend.* Illustrated by Betsy Bowen. Boston: Houghton Mifflin, 1997.

Wisniewski, David. *Rain Player.* New York: Clarion, 1991.

Yep, Laurence. *The Boy Who Swallowed Snakes.* Illustrated by Jean Tseng and Mou-sien Tseng. New York: Scholastic, 1994.

———. *The Man Who Tricked a Ghost.* New York: HarperCollins, 1993.

———. *The Rainbow People.* Illustrated by David Wiesner. New York: HarperCollins, 1989.

Young, Ed. *Lon Po Po: A Red Riding Hood Story from China.* New York: Philomel, 1989.

Trickster Tales—Trickster Tale Review and Planning Guide

Title: _____

Author: _____

Culture represented: _____

Setting (Where and when does this tale take place?): _____
_____

Characters (Who are the main characters in this story?): _____
_____
_____

Challenge (What is the main problem to be solved or challenge to be faced?):_____
_____

Plot (What events lead to solving the problem or facing the challenge?):

    1._____

    2._____

    3._____

    4._____

    5._____

    Others?_____

Resolution (How is the challenge faced or problem solved?): _____
_____

Theme or message in the tale (What do you think the author is trying to tell us?):_____
_____
_____

Cultural clues (What authentic elements are used in the text and illustrations to present the culture depicted in the tale?):_____
_____

Lesson 40

Strengthening the Language Arts with a Closer Look at Prejudice

SKILL: Integrating Reading, Writing, Listening, and Speaking

CULTURE OF FOCUS: Hungarian and Japanese

Materials

The Red Corduroy Shirt, by Joseph Kertes; illustrated by Peter Perko (Stoddard Kids, 1998)
Paper
Pens and pencils
Several books depicting Japanese traditional dress and artwork
Collection of other appropriate picture book titles and materials for group projects
Overhead projector or chalkboard
In Search of the Spirit: The Living National Treasures of Japan, by Sheila Hamanaka and Ayano Ohmi (Morrow Junior Books, 1999) (highlights Japanese art)

Lesson Motivator

1. Once the class is settled for the day's lesson, write the word *prejudice* in large letters on the board or an overhead transparency. Ask students to think about the word for a few minutes. Pose questions to foster their thinking.

2. As they organize their thoughts, have students focus on their reactions to the word in several different ways. For example, how did they feel when you first wrote the word on the board? Where do they think prejudice begins? How would they define it to someone who doesn't understand its meaning? Besides defining the word, have

they ever experienced prejudicial reactions themselves? Following an appropriate amount of time for thought, invite discussion.

3. After the class has completed the discussion of the word, take a different tack. Write the word *noun* on the board or overhead and ask students to refresh your memory on what a noun is (person, place, or thing).

4. Have students take out a piece of notebook paper and pen or pencil and brainstorm nouns that relate to prejudice. After a short time, encourage students to come up and write one of their words on the board or transparency, building a word bank from which to work on the next part of the activity.

5. Create an acrostic poem using the word *prejudice* and connecting meaningful nouns to each letter, one noun per letter. Give the students a few words to begin with, depending on the abilities of the class with which you are working. Students can pair up for this activity, combining their thoughts and their vocabulary to create a poem to be shared.

6. Once work is completed, encourage students to write their poems on the board or overhead to be viewed and discussed with the class as a whole. Suggested words follow:

    P — pride, peril, people, panic, protests
    R — races, riots, racism, renewal
    E — envy, egos, equality
    J — judgments
    U — ugliness, unrest
    D — defiance, destruction, differences, desegregation, discrimination
    I — injustice, inequality, immigration, inferiority
    C — courage, citizenship, concentration camps
    E — exclusion, ethnic groups

7. Share the results of the writing partnerships, then turn the students' attention to the read-aloud, *The Red Corduroy Shirt*.

Suggestions for Teaching the Lesson

- This is quite a small book, so the illustrations may be difficult for the entire class to see. You could hold the book up as you read anyway, or just have the students listen to the story and create their own pictures in their heads. Stop as you read to be sure the students understand the two cultures involved and how the story is unfolding. Students should take a few notes about the characters and interactions to aid them in the discussion following the book.

- When the story has been completed, ask students what they thought about it. Did they understand the reactions of the parents? What did they think about the friendship between the two boys? Have they ever experienced a similar situation between a friend and their parents? What might they say or do about the way Jerry's picture had mistakenly been given a place of honor in Jake's home?

- An understanding of the beautiful artwork will be enhanced if several books of Japanese art are available to share.

- Do the students have any other specific questions? Where does the story suggest that prejudice begins? Do classmates agree or disagree?

- Have students work with a partner or in small groups and read through several other picture books selected for this activity ahead of time. Students should look for evidence of prejudice or discrimination in each book, whether it was dealt with positively or negatively, writing down helpful comments, feelings, or ideas to be discussed with the larger group.

- After a general discussion session with the entire class, return to the first activity involving the acrostic poem. This time, switch to other parts of speech and rewrite the poems using adjectives or verbs. The reading activities should prompt the flow of new words, as will working with a partner. Write several of the resulting poems on the board or overhead. Talk about which words—nouns, adjectives, or verbs—were most powerful in communicating the feelings evoked by the word *prejudice.* Suggest that students remember the power that different kinds of words have when they return to future writing assignments.

Evaluation

- Develop a rubric for each project with the students who have chosen the project. Each one will look a little different because of the work involved. Areas to focus on include research skills, organizational skills, competence in presenting a final product to the class, and cooperation. Videotape group work for future reference and for parents to view.

Extensions

- Invite public speakers from different cultural backgrounds to talk about their unique cultures.

- Take a field trip to museums or cultural events to acquire more first-hand knowledge of another culture.

- Have students complete one of the following projects or activities and present the results to an interested audience:

  1. Move onto a larger project in an effort to integrate reading, writing, listening, and speaking. Emphasizing that prejudice and all its ramifications can lead to hardship and heartache for people of all ages, ask students how they feel about the existence

of prejudice in their lives and in their community.

2. Involve the class in some brainstorming. If they could play a small part in building multicultural understanding, what might they do? If they could develop an activity or a plan to help different races and cultures better understand each other, what might that look like? What are the simple things that could begin at the classroom level? List suggestions on the board and ask students which ones they want to work on over the next several class periods or several weeks (depending on the time to be devoted to this lesson).

3. Ask students what might happen if they moved beyond the classroom and into the school. Are there school projects, large or small, that could facilitate understanding and interaction? If students choose to pursue an idea in this area, they could approach the school or district administration. Ask students what would happen if they continued to work outside the classroom walls and extended their efforts into the community.

4. Students can talk to community leaders about how they try to celebrate cultural differences. What could they do at the community level? An art show in the public library, featuring art from different cultures; a poster show promoting friendship and understanding between cultures and displayed in the local mall; or a presentation of poetry, music, and dance from different cultures at the mall, cultural center, or library would be engaging projects.

5. Discuss the complexity and consequences inherent in broaching the topic of prejudice. Some of the ideas or projects may elicit negative reactions from surprising places. Be certain that students are aware of the fact that addressing prejudice touches the nerves of some adults, so they might get negative responses to some of their projects. Before embarking on any of the projects, enlist the aid and support of willing parents whenever possible. This is truly a sensitive topic.

6. Suggestions for individual student activities include:

Idea 1: Focus on the music of people who have endured prejudice in this country. Songs and their backgrounds would make a wonderful presentation. Students could begin their work with a picture book and a song that celebrates the diversity of this country and its people. (Such as, Bannerman, Helen. *The Story of Little Babaji.* Illustrated by Fred Marcellino. New York: HarperCollins, 1996.)

Idea 2: Gather a dozen or so picture books. Have students look for examples of books that represent cultures in a positive manner and those that are not as admirable. They should develop a list of criteria for quality multicultural literature using Web resources, the people and resources at the public library, the school media center director, and so forth. Have them present the project to the class and display it in the media center or the public library. A starting point is the original version of *Little Black Sambo*, by Helen Bannerman (HarperCollins,

1899). What about this book raised the ire of readers? How do the following two versions compare? Part of this project would be to rewrite another culturally insensitive book to show how people of that culture can be celebrated rather than denigrated. Jerry Pinkney illus170trated a version retold by Julius Lester, titled *Sam and the Tigers: A New Telling of Little Black Sambo* (Dial, 1996). Fred Marcellino's *The Story of Little Babaji* (Harper, 1996) closely follows the original tale.

Idea 3: Have students pursue an author study of an author from a parallel culture using websites and local library resources. They should present the author bio and short book talks of several of the author's books to the class and at scheduled times in the school media center for various classes to attend.

Idea 4: Investigate multicultural books that have caused a furor, such as *Nappy Hair,* written by Carolivia Herron and illustrated by Joe Cepeda (Alfred A. Knopf, 1997). Have students research the controversy on the Internet, look for other books about various cultures that have elicited angry responses from adults, and form an opinion about them. How far do people go when they are angry about a book and its content? Have the students present the books, opinions, and background information to the class. Ask them to think about how to prevent such strong community reactions, if that is even possible. Have them prepare a display for the library that will educate other readers in the school.

Idea 5: Upper-grade readers can create a selection of book partnerships to be displayed in the school media center or taken on book walks to different classrooms periodically throughout the year. Have them start with a picture book that covers a similar topic or has the same theme as a novel and tie them together through talk. They should read the picture book to a class and then briefly book-talk the novel for those readers who might be interested in pursuing the theme or issue in more depth.

Suggested Titles for Independent Reading and Research

Bannerman, Helen. *The Story of Little Babaji.* Illustrated by Fred Marcellino. New York: HarperCollins, 1996.

Bradby, Marie. *More Than Anything Else.* Illustrated by Chris K. Soentpiet. New York: Orchard, 1995.

Bunting, Eve. *Smoky Night.* Illustrated by David Diaz. San Diego, Calif.: Harcourt Brace, 1994.

Carnes, Jim. *Us and Them: A History of Intolerance in America.* Illustrated by Herbert Tauss, including photographs and prints. New York: Oxford University Press, 1999.

Cohen, Barbara. *Molly's Pilgrim.* Illustrated by Daniel Mark Duffy. 1983, Reprint. New York: Morrow, 1998.

Coles, Robert. *The Story of Ruby Bridges.* Illustrated by George Ford. New York: Scholastic, 1998.

Dorris, Michael. *Guests.* New York: Hyperion, 1994.

Howard, Elizabeth Fitzgerald. *Virgie Goes to School with Us Boys.* Illustrated by E. B. Lewis. New York: Simon & Schuster, 2000.

Johnston, Tony. *The Wagon.* Illustrated by James E. Ransome. New York: Tambourine, 1996.

Krull, Kathleen. *Gonna Sing My Head Off! American Folk Songs for Children.* Illustrated by Allen Garnes. New York: Alfred A. Knopf, 1992.

Lasky, Katherine. *True North: A Novel of the Underground Railroad.* New York: Blue Sky, 1996.

Leapman, Michael. *Witnesses to War: Eight True-Life Stories of Nazi Persecution.* Illustrated with photographs and maps. New York: Viking, 1998.

Lester, Julius. *From Slave Ship to Freedom Road.* Illustrated by Rod Brown. New York: Dial, 1998.

———. *Sam and the Tigers.* Illustrated by Jerry Pinkney. New York: Dial, 1996.

Lorbiecki, Marybeth. *Sister Anne's Hands*. Illustrated by K. Wendy Popp. New York: Dial, 1998.

Mochizuki, Ken. *Heroes*. Illustrated by Dom Lee. New York: Lee & Low, 1995.

Nerlove, Meriam. *Flowers on the Wall*. New York: McElderry, 1996.

Polacco, Patricia. *Chicken Sunday*. New York: Putnam & Grossett, 1992.

Ringgold, Faith. *If a Bus Could Talk: The Story of Rosa Parks*. New York: Simon & Schuster, 1999.

Sandler, Martin W. *Immigrants*. Illustrated with photographs and prints. New York: HarperCollins, 1995.

Savageau, Cheryl. *Muskrat Will Be Swimming*. Illustrated by Robert Hynes. Flagstaff, Ariz.: Northland Publishing, 1996.

Shrange, Ntozake. *White Wash*. Illustrated by Michael Sporn. New York: Walker, 1997.

Silverman, Jerry. *Just Listen to This Song I'm Singing: African-American History through Song*. Illustrated with photographs and prints. Brookfield, Conn.: Millbrook, 1996.

Smucker, Barbara. *Selina and the Shoo-Fly Pie*. Illustrated by Janet Wilson. New York: Stoddard Kids, 1998.

Surat, Michele Maria. *Angel Child, Dragon Child*. Illustrated by Vo-Dinh Mai. New York: Scholastic, 1983.

Tamar, Erika. *The Garden of Happiness*. Illustrated by Barbara Lambase. San Diego, Calif.: Harcourt Brace, 1996.

Wing, Natasha. *Jalapeño Bagels*. Illustrated by Robert Casilla. New York: Atheneum, 1996.

Lesson 41

Researching the Different Faces of Oppression across Cultures

SKILL: Integrating Reading and Social Studies, Fact and Fiction

CULTURE OF FOCUS: Japanese American

Materials

So Far from the Sea, by Eve Bunting; illustrated by Chris K. Soentpiet (Clarion, 1998)

Poetry sources:
Followers of the North Star: Rhymes about African American Heroes, Heroines, and Historical Times, by Susan Altman and Susan Lechner; illustrated by Byron Wooden (Children's Press, 1993)

The Dream Keeper and Other Poems, by Langston Hughes; illustrated by Jerry Pinkney (Knopf, 1994)

The Inner City Mother Goose, by Eve Merriam; illustrated by David Diaz (Simon & Schuster, 1996)

What Have You Lost? by Naomi Shihab Nye; photographs by Michael Nye (Greenwillow, 1999)

Music and Drum: Voices of War and Peace, Hope and Dreams, by Laura Robb; illustrated by Debra Lil (Philomel, 1997)

"I Never Saw Another Butterfly": Children's Drawings and Poems from Terezin Concentration Camp, 1942–1944, edited by Hana Volavkova (Schocken Books, 1993)

Spirit Walker, by Nancy Wood; illustrated by Frank Howell (Doubleday, 1993)

Variety of picture books depicting various kinds of oppression in different cultures

Paper
Pen or pencils
Posterboard
Overhead projector and transparencies
Video camera (optional)

Lesson Motivator

1. Begin class by asking students to sit quietly and listen to a selection of poems, from *"I Never Saw Another Butterfly,"* one of the suggested poetry resources, or others that you prefer. You are looking for samples of poems representing people of different cultures who have faced oppression at some time in history.

2. Invite students to think about what they heard in those poems. Then ask them to take out writing materials or their reflection journals and spend a few minutes doing a quickwrite.

3. As they write, students should define and explain the word *oppression*.

Tell them to specifically identify a culture and a period of history that had to endure oppression. The poetry you have read should prime the pump, so to speak, and give all writers something to say.

4. After a brief time, encourage students to engage in dialogue with one another in a large group discussion. How do they see oppression? What people do they see as being oppressed? Although obvious choices might be African Americans, who endured years of slavery, those Jews who experienced the horrors of the Holocaust, or the poor of many societies who struggle to survive, they might also think about women and children who worked in the mills early in this country's history, women and children who are abused, people who are homeless, and so forth. If questions are raised during this interaction, have the students write them down to be addressed in the upcoming research.

5. Explain that the project ahead will integrate reading, writing, social studies, picture books, novels, and numerous nonfiction materials as students research a people and the period of history in which they were oppressed. The focus book, *So Far from the Sea*, will introduce the class to a culture and a problem with which they may not be familiar.

Suggestions for Teaching the Lesson

• Show the cover of the book to the class, reading the title and author. Ask them to identify the culture and predict what the problem might be. Then read the story, which moves back and forth across the years, examining the internment of Japanese Americans during World War II and afterward.

• Stop as necessary to allow time to talk about the students' reactions to the story and pictures. Don't

omit the book's afterword, which contains important historical information. Once the book is completed, talk together about what listeners have learned about a culture and this particular kind of oppression.

• Connect this type of internment with that of the Jewish people in Europe in the same period. Do the students think it was internment when Native American tribes were rounded up and restricted to specific reservation lands? Why or why not? Invite students to spend some time with this book on their own because the text and pictures warrant a second visit.

• Take a few more minutes to think about other people who have suffered some form of oppression. Brainstorm ideas and list them on the board, adding them to the previous list developed from the quickwrite. Next, encourage students to work in pairs to talk about a group that they would like to research. Discuss whether there should be a core set of questions to answer for each project or if students would rather have their own individual questions drive the project.

• Introduce the collection of picture books gathered ahead of time for the students' perusal. Suggest that they read through them until they have a good idea of a direction of study. Tell them to jot down questions that arise as they read; those questions may guide their research.

• Once they have made a decision, each twosome should sign up on a class chart to be displayed in a convenient spot. If classmates come across a book or material that is of interest to another pair, they can consult the chart and share the information with the appropriate research team.

• Hand out an investigative guide to students as they delve into their research. The guide should include the parameters of the project as developed by you ahead of time or in cooperation with the students. In addition, students should list all the books and materials they use in a previously approved bibliographic format.

• Let the learning begin! Have students start with several picture books, both fiction and a short nonfiction title if one is available. This is the first step in gaining a better perspective on the people and their problems. Next, the members of each pair must both read the same novel set during the historical period depicting the lives of people at the time. As they read, they should write down insights, feelings, or any new information that they feel will guide them in understanding a people and their problems.

• During the reading process, the pairs should be talking, talking, talking about what they are reading. You should interact regularly with each team, answering questions and keeping brief anecdotal records while you monitor their progress.

• Finally, have students locate at least one nonfiction title, newspaper articles, and/or other nonfiction sources to provide the framework of facts about period, place, and people.

• Explain to the students that by integrating fiction and nonfiction, they will be getting a more realistic picture of the people and their problems. Fiction resources give the readers insight into human motives as they try to survive, their varying problems, and the consequences of the decisions they make or have made for them. Certainly these books will stimulate critical thinking and meaningful discussions. Later, nonfiction resources will provide the framework of facts upon which to build the students' understanding.

• Each member of the pair should read the same nonfiction materials as

well so that they can discuss them and share their opinions, learning from each other in the process. Then they should gather their notes and insights together and decide what kind of format they want to use to present what they have learned to the rest of the class. After organizing the materials, they should put their findings into a writing format determined by the direction of their presentation.

• Presentations can take a number of forms. Brainstorm options with the class so that there are a number of creative presentations upcoming. As they work on a project in which they share their knowledge with the class, the students will learn that this is an excellent way to synthesize the information gathered and to solidify learning. Ideas for presentations follow:

—Students can integrate fact and fiction and write their own picture books.
—Students can videotape an interview, taking the roles of different people who survived oppression. Another option is chatting with the key characters in the novel they read, comparing and contrasting their thoughts and experiences. The tape would become a part of the presentation.
—Students can prepare several pages representing a newspaper that might have been published at the time, including editorials, updates on local news, reports on government edicts, and so forth.
—Two groups who have researched the same problems can combine forces to present a more complete picture by writing a short skit that demonstrates the distress of people in a reader's theater segment from one of their novels or by creating a museumlike display depicting information on vividly illustrated posters.

• Students can create a visual display by wearing period dress as they lead the class through that era of history. Appropriate music from the period could be playing quietly in the background.

• Katherine Paterson says that she never ends a book without offering the readers some hope, even if the story has been filled with problems. Take that advice and ask that each group find a realistic element of hope to end their presentation on an honestly upbeat note.

Evaluation

• Collaborate with the class to develop a rubric to assess this major project. This should be completed before students begin their work so that they will always be aware of expectations and can work accordingly. Rubrics are a valuable tool because they enable students to see the relationship between quality and the processes they must complete to develop a product that meets quality criteria.

• Discuss the skills and knowledge that must be inherent in this project. What areas of the process are important? Careful note-taking? Quality resources? A practiced presentation? What criteria should be applied to the final product?

• Decide on the number of levels of the rubric. Do the students want criteria to gauge average, above average, and superior process and product? What does an acceptable job look like? What would a superior effort include? Prepare a checklist or chart containing the final parameters of the project and provide one for each student.

Extensions

• If possible, invite guest speakers who have experienced oppression or who can tell about relatives who endured hardships to speak to the class.

• Have the students take their presentations to other social studies classes in the school and share the wealth.

• Have students design and complete a mosaic capturing the feelings and experiences of those who have been oppressed.

• Visit a museum or other available sites in the area that have a display or present information on a people and a period of history in which they were oppressed.

• Encourage students to volunteer to work in a soup kitchen or food pantry or read books to children who are living in a shelter. Hold a fundraiser to get money for books that can be a permanent part of a shelter collection.

Suggested Titles for Independent Reading and Research

Alonso, Karen. *Korematsu v. United States: Japanese-American Internment Camps.* Illustrated with photographs. Springfield, N.J.: Enslow, 1998.

Bartoletti, Susan Campbell. *Growing Up in Coal Country.* Illustrated with various photographs. Boston: Houghton Mifflin, 1996.

Berck, Judith. *No Place to Be: Voices of Homeless Children.* Boston: Houghton Mifflin, 1992.

Bunting, Eve. *Train to Somewhere.* Illustrated by Ronald Himler. New York: Clarion, 1996.

Coleman, Penny. *Mother Jones and the March of the Mill Children.* Illustrated with various photographs. Brookfield, Conn.: Millbrook, 1993.

Dash, Joan. *We Shall Not Be Moved: The Women's Factory Strike of 1909.* New York: Scholastic, 1996.

Davis, Donlel S. *Behind Barbed Wire: The Imprisonment of Japanese Americans during World War II.* Illustrated with photographs. New York: Dutton, 1982.

Denenberg, Barry. *So Far from Home: The Diary of Mary Driscoll, an Irish Mill Girl, Lowell, Massachusetts, 1847.* Illustrated with various photographs, prints, and maps. New York: Scholastic, 1997.

DiSalvo-Ryan, DyAnne. *Uncle Willie and the Soup Kitchen.* New York: Morrow/Mulberry, 1991.

Fenner, Carol. *King of the Dragons.* New York: McElderry, 1998.

Fox, Paula. *Monkey Island.* New York: Orchard, 1991.

Freedman, Russell. *Kids at Work: Lewis Hine and the Crusade against Child Labor.* Illustrated with various photographs. New York: Clarion, 1995.

Hubbard, Jim. *Lives Turned Upside Down: Homeless Children in Their Own Words and Photographs.* New York: Simon & Schuster, 1996.

Kroll, Virginia. *Shelter Folks.* Illustrated by Jan Naimo Jones. Grand Rapids, Mich.: Eerdmans, 1995.

Levine, Ellen. *A Fence Away from Freedom: Japanese Americans and World War II.* New York: Putnam, 1995.

Littlefield, Holly. *Fire at the Triangle Factory*. Illustrated by Mary O'Keefe. Minneapolis, Minn.: Carolrhoda, 1995.

McCully, Emily Arnold. *The Ballot Box Battle*. New York: Knopf, 1996.

————. *The Bobbin Girl*. New York: Dial, 1996.

Nixon, Joan Lowry. *Aggie's Home*. Orphan Train series. New York: Delacorte, 1998.

————. *Circle of Love*. Orphan Train series. New York: Delacorte, 1997.

Parker, David L. *Stolen Dreams: Portraits of Working Children*. Illustrated with photographs. New York: Lerner, 1997.

Philbrick, Rodman. *The Fire Pony*. New York: Blue Sky, 1996. (novel)

Ruckman, Ivy. *In Care of Cassie Tucker*. New York: Delacorte, 1998.

Ryan, Pam Muñoz. *Riding Freedom*. New York: Scholastic, 1998.

Springer, Jane. *Listen to Us: The World's Working Children*. Illustrated with photographs. Toronto: Groundwood, 1998.

Stanley, Jerry. *Big Annie of Calumet: A True Story of the Industrial Revolution*. Illustrated with various photographs. New York: Crown, 1996.

Swain, Gwenyth. *The Road to Seneca Falls: A Story about Elizabeth Cady Stanton*. Illustrated by Mary O'Keefe. Minneapolis, Minn.: Carolrhoda, 1996.

Testa, Maria. *Someplace to Go*. Illustrated by Karen Ritz. Morton Grove, Ill.: Whitman, 1995.

Trottier, Maxine. *A Safe Place*. Illustrated by Judith Friedman. Morton Grove, Ill.: Whitman, 1997.

Tunnell, Michael O., and George W. Chilcoat. *The Children of Topaz: The Story of a Japanese Internment Camp*. New York: Holiday House, 1996.

Uchida, Yoshiko. *The Bracelet*. Illustrated by Joanna Yardley. New York: Philomel, 1993.

————. *Journey to Topaz*. Berkeley, Calif.: Creative Arts, 1985.

Warren, Andrea. *Orphan Train Rider: One Boy's True Story*. Illustrated with various photographs and prints. Boston: Houghton Mifflin, 1996.

Wilson, Jacqueline. *Elsa, Star of the Shelter!* Illustrated by Nick Sharratt. Morton Grove, Ill.: Whitman, 1996.

Lesson 42

Picture Books, Treasure Hunts, and Steppingstones

SKILL: Integrating Strategies to Promote Multicultural Understanding

CULTURE OF FOCUS: Native American (Navajo)

Materials

Sunpainters: Eclipse of the Navajo Sun, by Baje Whitethorne (Northland Publishing, 1994)

Navajo flute music

Large sheets of construction paper to be used to cut out steppingstone shapes in light gray or light tan (stone colors)

Markers

Collection of fiction and nonfiction picture books about the Navajo

Coordinating novels for extended reading

Copies of the "Clues to a Culture" worksheet (see end of lesson)

List of hunt activities for each team

Posted set of general rules for the "treasure hunt"

Lesson Motivator

1. Set the tone for this many-faceted lesson by playing a tape or CD of Navajo flute music quietly in the background. Tell the students that they will soon be visiting with the Navajo, a talented and fascinating tribe of Native Americans. If it is possible to get a speaker from a nearby museum to bring in some artifacts such as pots, pottery shards from ancestral tribes, Navajo weavings, or artwork, that would be a wonderful introduction to the treasure hunt. If speakers and music are not available, try to get a number of copies of current or back issues of *Arizona Highways* magazine. Some issues deal specifically with the Navajo and others provide breathtaking scenery and insights into the geographic region that these people call home.

2. Ask students if they have ever been on a treasure hunt. If so, have them explain their experiences. If not, tell them how a traditional hunt usually works.

3. Explain that they will be embarking on a variation of that hunt as a class as they learn about one specific culture. Later they will be involved in researching other

cultures on their own, if that is the direction this lesson takes in your classroom.

4. This particular hunt originates in the southwestern region of the United States and focuses on the Navajo, a fascinating Native American tribe. The suggestions incorporated within this demonstration treasure hunt illustrate how ripples of knowledge can move from one southwestern Native American culture to those in the same geographic region and then spiral outward in an ongoing hunt for cultural treasure.

5. The ideas suggested in this lesson for the investigation of one culture can be readily adapted to others. The approach discussed in the following pages could begin with any culture in any part of the United States depending on the choice of the teacher and learners involved.

6. When studying a culture from an area that is not well known to the class, a sound way to provide adequate background and also motivate learners is through a video. Videos provide sights and sounds, describe the location, and explain the everyday lives of a culture as a quick visit might do. One suggested video is *The Navajo* (Tellens, Flagstaff, Ariz.: Museum of Northern Arizona, 1984).

7. If the video becomes your motivator, set the stage for the upcoming assignment by telling the class that they are going to learn about another culture by taking a short trip to spend some time among the Navajo, many of whom live in the American Southwest.

8. You will be using a variety of books to embark on a multicultural treasure hunt to broaden their knowledge and understanding of these Americans. Tell students they will need to sharpen their wits and anticipate an exciting time of discovery. View the video, discuss observations by the class,

and write down any questions they may have as a result of their all-too-short visit.

9. A captivating start to studying the Navajo, as with other cultures, is with their colorful myths and legends. Rooted in a long oral tradition, at one time the only way these stories were passed down through the generations, a growing number of these Native American tales are finally being captured in writing. Although some were meant to entertain, they were frequently used to relay teachings from adults to children. Students should benefit from this background information if they are unaware of it.

10. Show the learners the focus book and invite them to listen to learn just a little more about the Navajo. The elders are usually the storytellers in a tribe, as Grandfather is in the focus book. What lesson do they think is being taught to Kii through *Sunpainters*?

Suggestions for Teaching the Lesson

• Read the story, stopping to remark on the scenery and how the geography of the area is similar to or different from where the students live. Continue the story. When you are done, wait for reactions, then answer any questions posed or write them down to be answered as part of the treasure hunt. Focus points to guide the discussion will tie into the topics driving the treasure hunt:

1. Can the students discern the lesson in this story?

2. Can students detect cultural values of importance in the tale?

3. Take a minute to talk about how lifestyle depends on the area in which one lives. What features of the area

would affect the life of the Navajo, as noted in the story or illustrations?

4. Are there any clues to the arts, crafts, or accomplishments distinctive to the Navajo people?

5. How is Kii's life similar to or different from the students' lives? Point out the distinctive hogan, the traditional dwelling of many Navajo families. Even if they live in a modern home, families often have a hogan on their property for religious ceremonies.

6. Do they have any other observations to make? What would they like to learn more about based on the video and the first picture book? Note areas of interest and be certain they are addressed before the end of the hunt.

- Before setting this book aside, draw the students' attention to something Baje Whitethorne does in all his books. In each illustration there is a tiny hogan and corral hidden among the black line drawings. Challenge the students to find them for themselves but not tell others so that they can enjoy the quest as well.

- The following example demonstrates how a treasure hunt would proceed and can serve as the model to follow in subsequent hunts. To begin, turn to a large classroom map. Locate Arizona, New Mexico, Colorado, and Utah, the "Four Corners" area in the Southwest that the Navajo have long called home. Explain that this first bit of geographic information should be remembered for steppingstone 1. It will be written on the stone as part of the publishing process a little later in the hunt.

- Next, model the completion of the "Clues to a Culture" worksheet. Hand out the data-gathering sheets and give students some processing time. Have each student fill in the sheet based on the reading and dis-

cussion of *Sunpainters* and information acquired from the video. When the work is finished, review the sheet. Begin with "Lessons taught" and talk about what students wrote down. Ask the students: "If we were going to record pertinent information on a steppingstone devoted to lessons, what could we write?" Check for accuracy and initial understanding before discussing the other categories on the sheet.

- Soon students will be able to work in teams on their own. Give them additional pointers for locating information in the books they will be using. Discuss the fact that accurately drawn illustrations, coupled with the text, extend the story within a distinctive picture book. Just what can they learn from those illustrations? Point out the valuable information that is often included in the author's note at the beginning or end of a picture book. In other words, advise students to scrutinize the entire book as they continue to learn about the Navajo.

- Following the read-aloud and discussion of student observations, direct students to a collection of tales gathered beforehand for classroom use. Students can break into triads or foursomes. Once the groups have been formed, discuss the general directions for the hunt. Write them on a posterboard and post them for quick review:

1. Each group will have a focus, one of the categories that will eventually go on a steppingstone. You will give that information to them as noted on each steppingstone later in the lesson, along with several fresh data-gathering forms.

2. Although they will read to fill in information for each category on a fresh data-gathering sheet, they should focus particularly on the one

they have been given. Eventually, it will be their responsibility to fill in a steppingstone of information on that specific category.

3. During the hunt, each group will read two other multicultural legends or myths plus two nonfiction picture books. As groups read, encourage them to compare their selections with the read-aloud, continually charting additional values or insights that they uncover. For example, they might support earlier observations with information from nonfiction titles such as Virginia Driving Hawk Sneve's *The Navajo: A First Americans Book* or Craig and Katherine Doherty's *The Apaches and Navajo* (see list of suggested titles following the lesson).

4. There will be a general time limit in which students must complete their work, but this is not a race to the finish as in a traditional treasure hunt. Caution students that insightful thinking and a growing knowledge base are the rewards of a hunt like this one.

- Turn the students loose and let them begin the treasure hunt for information.

- Move around the room as the groups work, guiding the hunt as necessary, clearing up any misconceptions, or sending readers to other sources for additional information when needed. Students will work across the curriculum with ease as boundaries dissolve between reading, language arts, social studies, science, and the arts. They will be integrating and polishing their skills in reading, writing, thinking, speaking, and listening effortlessly, totally engrossed as information is gathered, reported, recorded, and assimilated. This is a powerful learning process.

- Once the groups have read the required books, they should confer and organize their thoughts. What key observations should be written on their steppingstone? Meet with each group before the actual information is recorded to be certain that it is accurate. Initially, the work should be in rough draft form. Each triad or foursome should then polish their products.

- Finally, it is time to publish. Students may follow a pattern for designing the steppingstones or use shapes previously cut out by you. Stones need to fit closely together as in a flagstone path, so adjust the shapes accordingly.

- Have the students use markers to put their category at the top of their steppingstone-shaped paper and write down their "treasure," tidbits of knowledge about one aspect of the life of another culture. As a guideline for text size, the writing must be readable when the steppingstones are taped up on the wall. Depending on the amount of information they have to record, students may use more than one stone per category. On the back of each stone, students should list the complete bibliographic information for the books they used to find relevant information, then neatly finish the steppingstones and "publish" them.

- Tape up completed steppingstones at easy viewing level following the order of the data-gathering sheets. This is the beginning of a path to cultural understanding that will eventually encircle the room. Depending on how long this activity continues and the number of other cultures studied, that path might go right out the door and on down the hall as the year progresses.

- Regroup to share the completed stones in an effort to "publish" collective learning, with the first set of completed steppingstones displayed on the walls of the classroom. Students can read and reread what has previously been discovered about one culture, compare it with the one currently being investigated if the hunt continues, and readily see similarities and differences between groups of people across the country. As one steppingstone links another, so too is one culture linked to another.

- The hunt might go as follows: Moving from one steppingstone to the next, topics to be investigated as the hunt progresses include:

Stone 1—Focus: Lessons taught

Task: Does this story have a lesson to teach to its readers? What advice might the letter of the tale be trying to share.

Stone 2—Focus: Geographic observations

Task: Zero in on the general geographic location of the culture under study. For each culture, note where these people call home. What is it like there? Have they always lived there? If they have moved from somewhere else, where was that and why did they migrate? How does this location differ from where the students live? Two useful nonfiction titles are *Arizona A to Z* and *New Mexico A to Z*, both written by Dorothy Hines Weaver and illustrated by Kay Wacker, or *From Sea to Shining Sea: New Mexico*, by Judith and Dennis Fradin.

Stone 3—Focus: Values and beliefs

Task: Begin to learn about values and beliefs through reading at least two myths or legends. Triads may choose to read the books together or individually and then report back to teammates. Confirm early observations by reading two nonfiction resources. Along with the previous suggestions, students might enjoy "Four Worlds: The Diné Story of Creation" in *Keepers of the Earth*, by Michael Caduto and Joseph Bruchac, or *Eagle Boy—A Traditional Navajo Legend*, by Gerald Hausman. Consider the following kinds of information that might appear on the values steppingstone:

Unselfish actions are encouraged and rewarded.

Courageous and wise decisions are the best choice.

Religion is viewed as a natural phenomenon closely tied to nature.

Living in harmony with nature is an inherent belief.

Children respect the knowledge and wisdom of their elders.

Patience is a virtue.

Keeping one's word is important.

Emphasis is placed on group and extended family needs rather than on personal needs.

If any of these values are missed, address them before students move on to the next stone.

Stone 4—Focus: Distinctive arts

Task: Look at contributions of artists and musicians. Books to investigate are *The Goat in the Rug*, by Charles Blood and Martin Link; *The Magic Weaver of Rugs*, by Jerrie Oughton; *Songs from the Loom: A Navajo Girl Learns to Weave*, by Monty Roessel; or *Forbidden Talent*, by Redwing Nez.

Stone 5—Focus: Notable leaders and accomplishments

Task: Are there leaders to emulate in addition to talented artisans? One title to start the search is *The Unbreakable Code*, by Sara Hoagland Hunter, a book that relates information about the Navajo Code Talkers and their remarkable contributions during World War II. A supportive nonfiction title is *Navajo Code Talkers*, by Nathan Aaseng.

Stone 6—Focus: Current lives

Task: Students research what daily lives are currently like for the Navajo, beginning with a catalyst like *Building a Bridge*, by Lisa Shook Begaye. *To Live in Two Worlds—American Indian Youth Today*, by Breant Ashabranner; and *Katie Henio: Navajo Sheepherder*, by Peggy Thompson are excellent nonfiction choices. Don't miss the unique cuisine, either.

Stone 7—Focus: Comparison and contrast

Task: Students should look at how these particular values and lifestyles compare to those of their own culture, reflect, and then summarize their thoughts. Later, the question of how the values and lifestyles compare or contrast with other cultures that have been studied can be addressed in a class discussion.

Stone 8—Focus: Personal reflection

Task: Each student notes one particularly interesting fact that he or she discovered about the culture and reflects on it briefly in writing. Reflections could take a poetic form, such as adapting an autobiographical/biographical poem format like that in the following formula:

> **Title:** Name of the culture
> **Line 1:** First name of an individual or repeat name of the culture
> **Line 2:** Four traits that describe the culture or an individual from the culture
> **Line 3:** Brother/sister of … (may substitute Son/daughter of … or Descendants of …)
> **Line 4:** Lover of … (give names of three people or ideas)
> **Line 5:** Who feels … (give three feelings)
> **Line 6:** Who fears … (give three items)
> **Line 7:** Who would like to see … (give three places or things)
> **Line 8:** Resident of … (give area)
> **Line 9:** Last name of the individual or repeat name of the culture

Evaluation

- To evaluate the learning process and the products produced, involve the students. The results are more likely to reflect the actual learning occurring as a result of this approach.

- Use a clipboard and teacher-designed checklist to monitor students' processing of information and group performance. As suggested in previous lessons, brief notes can be jotted down in squares next to a student's name. Sticky notes or self-adhesive address labels are also useful. Once comments are recorded, those notes can be attached to a sheet designated for each learner.

- To avoid the possibility of a student opting to sit back and let teammates do all the work, an intra-group evaluation should be used. Each member of the learning triad or foursome rates the productivity of other group members, self-evaluating as well.

- For overall evaluation of the final product, the steppingstones, stu-

dents should develop a rubric, setting the criteria for quality performance in a class planning session before the first hunt. Careful critical thinking, cooperation, and active involvement in learning should be included. Obviously, speed is not a key factor in this type of treasure hunt because understanding is of the utmost importance.

Extensions

- Bring drama into the curriculum by having the students perform a skit based on one of the Navajo myths.

- If possible, invite a Native American flute player to play his or her music and explain the role of the flute in the culture.

- Corn is vital to the lives and culture of the Navajo. Extend learning into science and investigate this multipurpose vegetable. Have students research growing conditions, kinds, the uses within the Navajo culture, and the myriad of products that use corn in the mass market today.

- Navajo legends often are used to explain natural phenomena such as the occurrence of the eclipse in *Sunpainters*. Have students investigate the eclipse as explained in science textbooks and other nonfiction resources and then present a poster session about this phenomenon with pictures and explanations neatly displayed on several posters.

- A weaver would be a wonderful guest. Ask him or her to talk about the loom, where the fibers come from, and how the yarn is created, and then show some of his or her crafts. If a Navajo weaver is available, have him or her discuss the entire process, from sheep to finished rug. Check for understanding and see if students remember that both men and women are responsible for some weaving activities in the Navajo culture.

- Have students make triaramas illustrating three different aspects of the life of a Navajo child or adult that particularly appeal to them.

- If the art teacher is well-versed in pottery, ask him or her to teach a lesson in coil pot making. Getting one's hands messy and being totally involved in creating something from scratch is quite a rewarding experience. A potter visitor would be an excellent extension of the basic art lesson.

Spiraling Onward and Outward

- As they embark on their next small group treasure hunt, students could randomly choose from index cards listing other cultures or sign up for another Native American culture of personal interest based on a listing on the chalkboard. Ripples may move to the Apache, Hopi, Zuni, or other Pueblo Indian tribes in the Southwest, onward to the Plains Indians or any number of different Native American tribes. Perhaps multicultural study will refocus entirely and center in a city like Los Angeles, New York, or Chicago.

- The students will have an enticing array of cultures to learn about in any large metropolitan area. Although the preceding example focuses on the Navajo for the purpose of modeling how this particular approach to studying a culture works, remember that multicultural understanding grows from the study and understanding of many cultures.

- Let the hunt for multicultural treasure begin! Let students choose the location to start the study and gather wonderful materials. They should select a genuinely captivating picture book and drop that multicultural "pebble" into the classroom milieu.

- Get set to guide learners on a journey of discovery moving across the curriculum and into cultures on a quest that will widen their personal worlds. The integration of picture books, treasure hunts, and steppingstones should move students toward increased multicultural understanding in pleasing and surprising ways.

Suggested Titles for Independent Reading and Research

Aaseng, Nathan. *Navajo Code Talkers.* New York: Walker, 1992.

Ashabranner, Brent. *To Live in Two Worlds—American Indian Youth Today.* New York: Dodd & Mead, 1984.

Begay, Shonto. *Ma'ii and Cousin Horned Toad: A Traditional Navajo Story.* New York: Scholastic, 1992.

———. *Navajo Visions & Voices across the Mesa.* New York: Scholastic, 1995.

Begaye, Lisa Shook. *Building a Bridge.* Illustrated by Libba Tracy. Flagstaff, Ariz.: Northland Publishing, 1993.

Bland, C. *Peter MacDonald: Former Chairman of the Navajo Nation.* Illustrated with photographs. New York: Chelsea, 1995.

Blood, C. L., and M. Link. *The Goat in the Rug.* Illustrated by Nancy Winslow Parker. New York: Aladdin, 1990.

Bonvillain, N. *The Navajos: People of the Southwest.* Illustrated with photographs. Brookfield, Conn.: Millbrook, 1995.

Browne, Vee. *Monster Slayer.* Illustrated by Baje Whitethorne. Flagstaff, Ariz.: Northland Publishing, 1991.

Caduto, Michael J., and Joseph Bruchac. *Keepers of the Earth: Native American Stories and Environmental Activities for Children.* Golden, Colo.: Fulcrum Publishing, 1989.

Carter, A. R. *The Apache and Navajos.* Danbury, Conn.: Franklin Watts, 1989.

Chanin, Michael. *The Chief's Blanket.* Illustrated by Kim Howard. Tiburon, Calif.: H. J. Kramer, 1998.

Cohlene, Terri. *Turquoise Boy: A Navajo Legend.* Illustrated by Charles Reasoner. Vero Beach, Fla.: Watermill Press, 1990.

Dailey, Robert. *The Code Talkers: American Indians in World War II.* New York: Franklin Watts, 1995.

Doherty, Craig A., and Katherine M. Doherty. *The Apaches and Navajo.* New York: Franklin Watts, 1989.

Emery, N. *Day and Night.* Illustrated by V. Clinton. Flagstaff, Ariz.: Salina Bookshelf, 1996.

Fradin, Dennis B. *Arizona.* Minneapolis, Minn.: Learner, 1993.

———. *Utah.* Chicago: Children's Press, 1993.

Fradin, Judith, and Dennis Fradin. *From Sea to Shining Sea: New Mexico.* Chicago: Children's Press, 1994.

Franklin, Kristine L. *The Shepherd Boy.* Illustrated by Jill Kastner. New York: Atheneum, 1994.

Hausman, Gerald. *Coyote Walks on Two Legs: A Book of Navajo Myths and Legends.* Illustrated by Floyd Cooper. New York: Philomel, 1995.

———. *Eagle Boy—A Traditional Navajo Legend.* Illustrated by Cara Moser and Barry Moser. New York: HarperCollins, 1996.

Hayden, C. D., ed. *Venture into Cultures: A Resource Book of Multicultural Materials and Programs.* Chicago: American Library Association, 1992.

Hunter, Sara Hoagland. *The Unbreakable Code.* Illustrated by Julia Miner. Flagstaff, Ariz.: Northland Publishing, 1996.

Keams, Gerri. *Snail Girl Brings Water: A Navajo Story.* Flagstaff, Ariz.: Rising Moon, 1998.

Max, Jill. *Spider Spins a Story: Fourteen Legends from Native America.* Flagstaff, Ariz.: Northland Publishing, 1997.

Miles, Miska. *Annie and the Old One.* Illustrated by Peter Parnell. Boston: Little, Brown, 1971.

Neil, Philip, ed. *Earth Always Endures: Native American Poems.* Illustrated with photographs by Edward S. Curtis. New York: Viking, 1996.

Nez, Redwing T. *Forbidden Talent.* Flagstaff, Ariz.: Northland Publishing, 1995.

Oughton, Jerrie. *How the Stars Fell into the Sky: A Navajo Legend.* Illustrated by Lisa Desimini. Boston: Houghton Mifflin, 1992.

———. *The Magic Weaver of Rugs: A Tale of the Navajo.* Illustrated by Lisa Desimini. Boston: Houghton Mifflin, 1994.

Rochman, Hazel. *Against Borders: Promoting Books for a Multicultural World.* Chicago: American Library Association, 1993.

Roessel, Monty. *Kinaalda: A Navajo Girl Grows Up.* Illustrated with photographs. Minneapolis, Minn.: Lerner, 1993.

———. *Songs from the Loom: A Navajo Girl Learns to Weave.* Minneapolis, Minn.: Lerner, 1995.

Rucki, Ani. *Turkey's Gift to the People.* Flagstaff, Ariz.: Northland Publishing, 1992.

Schick, Eleanor. *My Navajo Sister.* New York: Simon & Schuster, 1996.

———. *Navajo Wedding Day: A Diné Wedding Ceremony.* Tarrytown, N.Y.: Marshall Cavendish, 1999.

Slapin, B., and D. Seale, eds. *Through Indian Eyes: The Native Experience in Books for Children.* Philadelphia, Pa.: New Society Publishers, 1992.

Sneve, Virginia Driving Hawk. *The Navajo: A First Americans Book.* Illustrated by Ronald Himler. New York: Holiday House, 1993.

Tapahonso, Luci, and Eleanor Schick. *Navajo ABC: A Dine Alphabet Book.* Illustrated by Eleanor Schick. New York: Simon & Schuster, 1999.

Thompson, Peggy. *Katie Henio: Navajo Sheepherder.* Illustrated with photographs by Paul Conklin. New York: Cobblehill Books, 1995.

Tiedt, P., and I. M. Tiedt. *Multicultural Teaching: A Handbook of Activities, Information, and Resources.* 3d ed. Needham Heights, Mass.: Allyn and Bacon, 1990.

Van Laan, Nancy. *In a Circle Long Ago: A Treasury of Native American Lore from North America.* Illustrated by Lisa Desimini. New York: Scholastic, 1995.

Weaver, Dorothy H. *Arizona A to Z.* Illustrated by Kay Wacker. Flagstaff, Ariz.: Northland Publishing, 1994.

———. *New Mexico A to Z.* Illustrated by Kay Wacker. Flagstaff, Ariz.: Northland Publishing, 1996.

Westridge Young Writers Workshop. *Kids Explore the Heritage of Western Native Americans.* Santa Fe, N.Mex.: John Muir, 1995.

Internet Sites for Native American Information

- American Indian Heritage Foundation: http://indians.org/tribes/idxcity2.html

- Index of Native American Resources on the Internet: http://hanksville.phast.umass.edu/misc/naresources.html

- Multicultural Bibliography: http://falcon.jmu.edu/~ramseyil/mulnativ.html

- Native American Indian Art, Culture, Education, History, and Science:

  http://indy4.fdl.cc.mn.us/~ish/books/bookmenu.html

- Native American Sites Home Pages:

  http://www1pitt.edu/~lmitten/indians.html

- The North American Native Authors Catalog:

  http://nativeauthors.com

- Smithsonian Institute National Museum of the American Indian:

  http://www.si.edu/cgi-bin/nav.cgi

Clues to a Culture: _____

Title of resource book: _____

Author: _____

Lessons taught: _____

_____

_____

_____

Geographic observations (What is it like there?): _____

_____

_____

Values and beliefs: _____

_____

_____

Distinctive arts: _____

_____

_____

Notable leaders and accomplishments: _____

_____

_____

Current lives: _____

_____

Comparison and contrast (use the back of the sheet to compare and contrast cultures):

_____

_____

Personal reflection: _____

_____

_____

Appendix I

Novels, Nonfiction, and
Poetry Celebrating Diverse Cultures

· ·

General Books

Birdseye, Debbie Holsclaw, and Tom Birdseye. *Under Our Skin: Kids Talk about Race.* Illustrated with photographs by Robert Crum. New York: Holiday House, 1997.

Six students in their early teens from different cultures discuss their pride in their own culture, the difficulties they face as they interact with peers from different races, and their feelings of acceptance across cultural groups.

Caduto, Michael J. *Earth Tales from around the World.* Illustrated by Adelaide Murphy Tyrol. Golden, Colo.: Fulcrum Publishing, 1997.

These Earth tales represent more than 40 countries and include suggestions for lessons and activities to further explore the wealth of the Earth.

Caduto, Michael J., and Joseph Bruchac. *Keepers of the Animals: Native American Stories and Wildlife Activities for Children.* Illustrated by John Kahionhes Fadden. Golden, Colo.: Fulcrum Publishing, 1991.

This book relates Native American tales focused on animals and provides engrossing extension activities for each tale.

———. *Keepers of the Earth: Native American Stories and Environmental Activities for Children.* Illustrated by John Kahionhes Fadden and Carol Wood. Golden, Colo.: Fulcrum Publishing, 1989.

This book focuses on tales about the Earth and is enriched by accompanying activities for students.

Carnes, Jim. *Us and Them: A History of Intolerance in America.* Illustrated by Herbert Tauss plus photographs and prints. New York: Oxford University Press, 1999.

Beginning in Boston in 1660 and moving across places and time to Brooklyn in 1991, a painful side of American history is analyzed. A list for further reading is included.

Cohn, Amy L., comp. *From Sea to Shining Sea: A Treasury of American Folklore and Folk Songs.* New York: Scholastic, 1993.

This interesting collection begins with Native American folklore and moves to tales from more contemporary times.

Duvall, Lynn. *Respecting Our Differences: A Guide to Getting Along in a Changing World.* Illustrated with prints, photographs, and drawings by Paul Palnik. Minneapolis, Minn.: Free Spirit, 1994.

This book presents points of conflict between different cultures and suggests possible solutions to move people toward tolerance rather than violence.

Fleischman, Paul. *Seedfolks.* Illustrated by Judy Pedersen. New York: Colter/HarperCollins, 1997.

Readers meet 13 different characters who illustrate a variety of cultures and perspectives as they relate short stories filled with hope and pride. The stories are set against the backdrop of a neighborhood project that changes a vacant lot into a garden through cooperative efforts.

Keenan, Sheila. *Scholastic Encyclopedia of Women in the United States.* New York: Scholastic, 1997.

The strength, achievements, and contributions of women from the 1500s to the 1990s are highlighted through brief biographies.

Krull, Kathleen. *Lives of the Athletes: Thrills, Spills (and What the Neighbors Thought).* San Diego, Calif.: Harcourt Brace, 1997.

Included here are 20 biographical sketches of famous athletes from around the world. They share what it takes to make them world-class competitors plus some insights into themselves as human beings.

Leavy, Una. *Irish Fairy Tales & Legends.* Illustrated by Susan Field. Boulder, Colo.: Roberts Rinehart Publishers, 1996.

Readers will revel in these rich tales filled with leprechauns, fairies, giants, druids, and strong heroes and heroines.

McCaughrean, Geraldine. *The Bronze Cauldron: Myths and Legends of the World.* Illustrated by Bee Willey. New York: McElderry, 1998.

This excellent collection of tales rooted in the art of storytelling reveals stories of everyday people who were changed by a deed or a mysterious event.

Meltzer, Milton. *Ten Queens: Portraits of Women of Power.* Illustrated by Bethanne Andersen. New York: Dutton, 1998.

Ester, Cleopatra, Elizabeth I, Catherine the Great, and others are described, including both their accomplishments and their ruthlessness as they wielded tremendous power. Maps, notes, bibliography, and an index provide additional information.

———. *Who Cares? Millions Do ... A Book about Altruism.* New York: Walker, 1994.

This book moves from early civil rights efforts to modern times, showing how young adults have made a difference in working against social injustice and striving to make the world a better place for everyone.

Taylor, Maureen. *Through the Eyes of Your Ancestors: A Step-by-Step Guide to Uncovering Your Family's History.* Boston: Houghton Mifflin, 1999.

A black-and-white photo can start a reader wondering about the life of that relative and begin a search into interesting ancestors. This excellent book gets readers started and makes helpful suggestions about how to proceed with an investigation into one's past.

Walker, Richard. *The Barefoot Book of Pirates.* Illustrated by Olwyn Whelan. New York: Barefoot Books, 1998.

Would you believe that pirates abound in so many cultures? These seven brightly illustrated tales will make great silent reading or read-aloud selections.

———. *The Barefoot Book of Trickster Tales.* Illustrated by Claudio Muñoz. New York: Barefoot Books, 1998.

These delightful trickster tales from nine different cultures are appealing read-alouds and excellent for an introduction to a unit on trickster tales.

African Americans

Aardema, Verna. *Misoso: Once Upon a Time Tales from Africa.* Illustrated by Reynold Ruffins. New York: Alfred A. Knopf, 1994.

Misoso refers to African tales that are told primarily to entertain. This book contains 12 tales from a variety of African cultures that will both enlighten and entertain readers.

Armstrong, Jennifer. *Steal Away*. New York: Orchard Books, 1992.

In 1955 orphaned Susannah arrives from Vermont to live with slave-holding relatives. Bethlehem is a "gift" given to Susannah. A strong bond forms between the courageous teenagers as they escape from an unhappy life and journey north.

Avi. *Encounter at Easton*. New York: Morrow, 1994.

In this sequel to *Night Journeys*, the two runaway indentured servants, Robert and Elizabeth, try to find sanctuary. The text is presented in the form of the court testimony of Robert and three others, making interesting reading.

———. *Night Journeys*. New York: Morrow, 1994.

This is a suspenseful story set in colonial Pennsylvania involving an orphan, Peter, and two runaway indentured servants. As part of the search party, Peter both helps and hinders one of the runaways.

Barboza, Steven. *Door of No Return: The Legend of Goree Island*. Illustrated with photographs. New York: Cobblehill, 1994.

Goree Island has not received much attention in history textbooks, but it was a place of pain and suffering as a holding site for captured Africans destined for lives of slavery in the New World.

Bentley, Judith. *"Dear Friend": Thomas Garrett and William Still: Collaborators on the Underground Railroad*. New York: Dutton, 1997.

This true story is about Thomas Garrett, a white Quaker man, and William Still, a free black man. They worked together to provide a safer escape route for slaves on the Underground Railroad. Excerpts from some of their correspondence are included.

Berry, James. *Ajeemah and His Son*. New York: HarperCollins, 1992.

In this story set in the early 1800s, Ajeemah and his son, Atu, are captured by slave traders as they travel to a neighboring village with a dowry for Atu's bride. Landing in Jamaica after a six-week voyage, they are sold to separate sugar plantation owners and never meet again.

Bial, Raymond. *The Strength of These Arms: Life in the Slave Quarters*. Illustrated with photographs. San Diego, Calif.: Houghton Mifflin, 1997.

Readers note the distinct contrast between the lives of the slaves in the slave quarters and the lives of luxury enjoyed by their plantation owners. Both nonfiction text and moving photographs are testimony to the courage of those who lived out their lives in slavery.

Birchman, David Frances. *A Green Horn Blowing*. Illustrated by Thomas B. Allen. New York: Lothrop, Lee & Shepard Books, 1997.

Set during the Great Depression, this is the story of the friendship of a young white boy and an African-American farm worker who plays the trumpet.

Burns, Khephra, and William Miles. *Black Stars in Orbit: NASA's African American Astronauts*. Illustrated with photographs. San Diego, Calif.: Gulliver/Harcourt Brace, 1994.

African Americans struggle to become an important part of America's space program, as evidenced by vivid black-and-white photographs and engrossing text.

Chambers, Veronica. *Amistad Rising: The Story of Freedom*. Illustrated by Paul Lee. San Diego, Calif.: Harcourt Brace, 1998.

Based on the factual account of the *Amistad* revolt, this fictionalized story describes the interactions between Joseph Cinque and his captors.

Charbonneau, Eileen. *Honor to the Hills*. New York: Tor, 1996.

A number of cultures clash as complex ancestry and issues surrounding the Underground Railroad underscore a struggle over slavery in the 1850s in the remote Catskill Mountains.

Cooper, Floyd. *Mandela: From the Life of the South African Statesman*. New York: Philomel, 1996.

The author relates how Mandela applied lessons learned from his father to the fight against injustice and to end apartheid.

Curtis, Christopher. *The Watsons Go to Birmingham—1963*. New York: Delacorte, 1995.

This award-winning book begins with light-hearted humor as the "Weird Watsons" head from Flint, Michigan, south to Birmingham for a vacation. Quickly the tone shifts as the family witnesses attitude-altering, tragic events evolving from the civil rights movement.

The Estate of Langston Hughes. *The Dream Keeper and Other Poems*. Illustrated by Brian Pinkney. New York: Alfred A. Knopf, 1994.

This is poetry with power and inspiration that depicts the essence of our nation and its people.

Farmer, Nancy. *A Girl Named Disaster*. New York: Puffin Books, 1996.

A Newbery Honor Book and an American Library Association's Best Book for Young Adults, this is an outstanding survival story about Nhamo, a resilient and courageous 14-year-old who escapes from an arranged marriage to a cruel man and lives through experiences in the wilds of South Africa and Zimbabwe.

Feelings, Tom. *The Middle Passage: White Ships, Black Cargo*. New York: Dial, 1995.

This absolutely riveting, wordless picture book depicting the capture and transfer of West Africans to the United States to be sold as slaves is a moving experience not easily forgotten. The author's note and the introduction by Dr. John Henrik Clarke are stories in themselves.

Fleischner, Jennifer. *I Was Born a Slave: The Story of Harriet Jacobs*. Illustrated by Melanie K. Reim. Brookfield, Conn.: Millbrook Press, 1997.

At age six, Harriet learned that she was a slave. The book recounts her seven years in hiding, her escape to the North, and her life as a free black.

Forrester, Sandra. *My Home Is over Jordan*. New York: Lodestar, 1997.

Readers who enjoyed *Sound the Jubilee* will quickly be caught up in the life and struggles of Maddie Henry and her family, who find that freedom is more difficult than they envisioned.

———. *Sound the Jubilee*. New York: Lodestar Books, 1995.

Set in 1861 on Roanoke Island, the story introduces strong-willed Maddie, an 11-year-old slave. After being freed from slavery she and her family struggle to achieve economic security over a 14-year period.

Hamilton, Virginia. *The Bells of Christmas*. Illustrated by Lambert Davis. San Diego, Calif.: Harcourt Brace, 1989.

It is 1890, and 12-year-old Jason is impatiently awaiting Christmas in this carefully researched story about life in a middle-class black family in Ohio.

———. *Cousins*. Illustrated by Jerry Pinkney. New York: Philomel, 1990.

This award-winning story relates how Cammy deals with missing her Gran and with the antagonism and rivalry between her and her cousin Patricia Ann. Strong family ties pull Cammy through when her cousin tragically dies.

———. *Drylongso*. Illustrated by Jerry Pinkney. San Diego, Calif.: Harcourt Brace, 1992.

Drylongso is a young boy filled with human kindness. Somewhat mythical, he has talent as a dowser and represents hope and fate to folks in drought-affected lands west of the Mississippi.

———. *Her Stories: African American Folktales, Fairy Tales, and True Tales*. Illustrated by Leo Dillon and Diane Dillon. New York: Scholastic, 1995.

This beautifully illustrated book contains a wonderful collection of tales rooted in the African-American world that are both instructional and inspirational.

———. *A Ring of Tricksters: Animals Tales from North America, the West Indies, and Africa*. Illustrated by Barry Moser. New York: Scholastic/Blue Sky, 1997.

Eleven enduring trickster tales retold by a gifted author and illustrated with lively full-page pictures make this an entertaining read.

Hansen, Joyce. *The Captive*. New York: Scholastic, 1994.

Masterful writing entwines history and fiction as the life of a young Ashanti boy is revealed, beginning with his capture in West Africa and continuing through the Middle Passage across the Atlantic Ocean to his life as a slave in Salem, Massachusetts. The book ends on a positive note with his freedom serving with Captain Paul Cuffe, an African-American ship captain.

Hansen, Joyce, and Gary McGowan. *Breaking Ground, Breaking Silence: The Story of New York's African Burial Ground*. Illustrated with photographs and maps. New York: Henry Holt, 1998.

A 1999 King Author Honor Book, this carefully researched book gives the reader an insight into how history is uncovered.

Haskins, Jim. *Black, Blue & Gray*. New York: Simon & Schuster, 1998.

Readers come face-to-face with African-American soldiers and sailors who fought for this country during the Civil War. An interesting author's note, a helpful bibliography, and a timeline are included.

Hearne, Betsy. *Listening for Leroy*. New York: McElderry, 1998.

Set in rural Alabama in the 1950s, this story centers around 11-year-old Alice, who develops a friendship with Leroy, a black farmhand. When the family moves to Tennessee, Alice takes invaluable lessons with her: the trust and acceptance taught to her by her friend Leroy.

Hudson, Cheryl, and Wade Hudson, comps. *In Praise of Our Fathers and Mothers: A Black Family Treasury by Outstanding Authors and Illustrators*. Orange, N.J.: Just Us Books, 1997.

Authors and illustrators pay tribute to many experiences through essays, stories, and beautiful art.

Hurmence, Belinda. *Slavery Time: When I Was Chillum*. New York: Putnam, 1998.

Hurmence has selected 12 stories from a collection of 2,000 narratives gathered by the Federal Writers Project that vividly portray the reality of a life in slavery. For interested readers, the remaining narratives are currently housed in the Library of Congress.

Johnson, Angela. *The Other Side: Shorter Pieces*. New York: Orchard Books, 1998.

"Shorter poems" relate a family's everyday experiences on the road from Shorter, Alabama, to Cleveland, Ohio.

Jurmain, Suzanne. *Freedom's Sons: The True Story of the Amistad Mutiny*. New York: Lothrop, Lee & Shepard Books, 1998.

The only successful slave revolt aboard ship in American history is detailed in this fascinating book about the unfailing courage of a crew who faced phenomenal odds and savored the joy of success.

Klass, David. *Danger Zone*. New York: Scholastic, 1996.

This book deals with the clash of cultures faced by Jim Doyle, the only white player on the U.S. Dream Team. He learns of another kind of life from the predominantly black inner-city and then faces issues of nationalism when the team plays in Rome.

Kramer, Barbara. *Toni Morrison: Nobel Prize–Winning Author*. Springfield, N.J.: Enslow, 1996.

Learn about this Nobel Prize winner from her childhood in Lorain, Ohio, to becoming a prize-winning author.

Krull, Kathleen. *Wilma Unlimited: How Wilma Rudolph Became the Fastest Woman in the World*. Illustrated by David Diaz. San Diego, Calif.: Harcourt Brace, 1996.

Winning three gold medals in the 1960 Olympics, a phenomenal achievement, came only after incredible determination on the part of this remarkable woman. Disabled by polio as a child, Wilma remained undaunted in spirit and persevered to reach her dreams. Certainly an inspiration to readers and a woman to emulate.

Lasky, Kathryn. *True North: A Novel of the Underground Railroad*. New York: Blue Sky Press, 1996.

Fourteen-year-old Lucy takes over her grandfather's role in the Underground Railroad movement and saves a young girl her own age. The story is told in alternating stories, and the reader follows the paths of the girls until they meet and then on into old age.

Lester, Julius. *From Slave Ship to Freedom Road*. Illustrated by Rod Brown. New York: Dial, 1998.

This is a memorable look at the issue of slavery set against the backdrop of compelling oil paintings.

Lisandrelli, Elaine S. *Maya Angelou: More Than a Poet*. Springfield, N.J.: Enslow, 1996.

Maya Angelou reminds her readers that we are more alike than unalike as they read about her successes in the face of many obstacles. Her hard work, belief in herself, and perseverance are the underpinnings of her accomplishments as a writer, dancer, singer, and actress.

Lowery, Linda. *Wilma Mankiller*. Illustrated by Janice Lee Porter. Minneapolis, Minn.: Carolrhoda, 1996.

Wilma became the first woman chief of the Cherokee Nation despite prejudice and racism. She believed in herself and her ability to help her people, earning the right to her distinguished office.

Lyons, Mary E. *Letters from a Slave Girl: The Story of Harriet Jacobs*. New York: Scribner, 1992.

Harriet Jacobs is a slave who is attractive and intelligent. She avoids her master and turns to another white man in hopes of being freed. Pursued by her owner, she hides in her grandmother's attic for seven years before she can escape to the North. Her life is revealed through letters that she writes to different family members.

———. *Master of Mahogany: Tom Day, Free Black Cabinetmaker*. Illustrated with photographs. New York: Scribner, 1994.

Tom Day is a free black man who lives in the time when slavery is dominant. His life as a talented cabinetmaker is traced in well-written text and excellent photographs.

McKissack, Patricia C. *A Picture of Freedom: The Diary of Clotee, a Slave Girl*. New York: Scholastic, 1997.

This is a book in the Dear America series. Clotee is a 12-year-old Virginia slave who has taught herself to read and write. If caught, she could be severely beaten or face an even worse punishment.

———. *Run Away Home*. New York: Scholastic, 1997.

Living in rural Alabama, Sarah Jane and her family help a runaway Apache boy. Their story shows the hardships both blacks and Native Americans faced in the 1880s as they work together to fight off white supremacists who threaten the farm and their very lives.

McKissack, Patricia C., and Frederick McKissack. *Black Diamond: The Story of the Negro Baseball Leagues*. Illustrated with photographs. New York: Scholastic, 1994.

This is an outstanding history of Negro Baseball leagues before desegregation. Filled with colorful quotes and anecdotes, it showcases talented players against a background of poor living and playing conditions.

———. *Red-Tail Angels: The Story of the Tuskegee Airmen of World War II.* Illustrated with photographs. New York: Walker, 1995.

This book relates the background and experiences of the only African-American pilots to serve their country in the battle raging overseas.

———. *Sojourner Truth: Ain't I a Woman?* New York: Scholastic, 1992.

Sojourner Truth was an advocate for freedom for her people. Born Belle, she renamed herself and became a strong abolitionist and advocate for women's rights. Tragic personal losses marked her life but didn't deter her as a strong leader.

Mead, Alice. *Junebug and the Reverend.* New York: Farrar, Straus & Giroux, 1998.

Moving always presents challenges, but they are especially difficult for the main character as he struggles to find new friends after moving from a housing project to a nearby city.

Medearis, Angela Shelf. *Princess of the Press: The Story of Ida B. Wells-Barnett.* New York: Lodestar, 1998.

Ida B. Wells-Barnett was an energetic black journalist who used her pen to wage a battle for equality and freedom. A writer, speaker, and editor of periodicals for African Americans in her adult years, she also assumed the responsibility of caring for her younger siblings at a young age.

Merriam, Eve. *The Inner City Mother Goose.* Illustrated by David Diaz. New York: Simon & Schuster, 1996.

Recently released after being censored, these poems are filled with the despair of inner city life, presented in a familiar format that makes them even more chilling.

Meyer, Carolyn. *Jubilee Journey.* San Diego, Calif.: Harcourt Brace, 1997.

In this contemporary novel, readers are introduced to several tolerance issues, such as regional diversity, preservation of family history, and reverse discrimination, as Emily Rose and her family celebrate Juneteenth with her great-grandmother in Texas. Life on the East Coast did not prepare her for the reception she and her brother received in the Texas community.

———. *White Lilacs.* San Diego, Calif.: Gulliver/Harcourt Brace, 1993.

The black community of Freedomtown is leveled to create a park for the city's white residents. All that remains are memories of residents who once called the area home and the drawings that Rose Lee makes in an effort to celebrate the community.

Myers, Walter Dean. *Amistad: A Long Road to Freedom.* New York: Dutton, 1998.

This book contains the historical account of the 1839 revolt on the Amistad, a ship carrying slaves to the United States. Details of the journey, the mutiny led by Sengbe, and the ensuing trials in the United States are described, as are the survivors' struggles to return home.

———. *The Glory Field.* New York: Scholastic, 1994.

The reader can follow five generations of the Lewis family's lives on Curry Island, South Carolina, beginning with the landing of the first slave boat on the island.

———. *One More River to Cross: An African American Photograph Album.* San Diego, Calif.: Harcourt Brace, 1995.

A simple narrative and marvelous photographs pair up to create an inspiring history of African Americans and their diverse lives in the United States.

———. *Slam!* New York: Scholastic, 1996.

Greg "Slam" Harris is in control on the basketball court but not in his daily life. His dream is to get into the NBA because of his phenomenal basketball skills, but he learns that it takes more than basketball skills to succeed in life.

———. *Somewhere in the Darkness.* New York: Scholastic, 1992.

Jimmy travels across the country with Crab, a father he barely knows, a man who has recently escaped from prison. Father and son learn some painful lessons about what it means to be a family as they travel to Crab's old haunts.

Parks, Rosa, with Gregory J. Reed. *Dear Mrs. Parks: A Dialogue with Today's Youth.* Illustrated with various photographs. New York: Lee & Low, 1996.

This is a collection of letters between Rosa Parks and a number of children. Parks's honest reactions are encouraging to her correspondents and to today's readers. A short biographical sketch is also included.

Paulsen, Gary. *Nightjohn.* New York: Doubleday, 1993.

In this story set against the backdrop of the Civil War era, Nightjohn risks his life to teach slaves to read and write, a personal mission to help his people understand what is being done to them.

———. *Sarny: A Life Remembered.* New York: Delacorte, 1997.

This sequel to *Nightjohn* is about a slave girl who gets her freedom and a new life following the Civil War. Sarny tells a tale of trails, tragedies, and hopes for change. It is a thrill when she can open a school for black children later in her life.

Paye, Won-Ldy, and Margaret H. Lippert. *Why Leopard Has Spots: Dan Stories from Liberia.* Illustrated by Ashley Bryan. Golden, Colo.: Fulcrum Publishing, 1998.

Discover the universal values held by the Dan culture in western Africa through the tales they tell for entertainment, while working in the fields, and at celebration time.

Rees, Douglas. *Lightning Time.* New York: DK Ink, 1997.

This fascinating piece of historical fiction tells the story of young Theodore Worth, who sneaks away to join John Brown's Invisibles as they gather to attack Harper's Ferry. John Brown's struggle against slavery and his place in "loosening the lightning" in the inevitable war make for engrossing reading.

Rinaldi, Ann. *Hang a Thousand Trees with Ribbons: The Story of Phillis Wheatley.* San Diego, Calif.: Gulliver/Harcourt Brace, 1996.

Phillis Wheatley was kidnapped from her home in Senegal and sold into slavery in 1760. Her eager mind and life with the wealthy Wheatley family enabled her to have successes few others in her place might have had. She became America's first published black poet.

Robinet, Harriette G. *Forty Acres and Maybe a Mule.* New York: Atheneum, 1998.

Winner of the Scott O'Dell Award for Historical Fiction, this powerful story involves a family of freed slaves who began farming in 1865 with hopes focused on a better life, only to have those hopes dashed when the government took the land away from them.

———. *Washington City Is Burning.* New York: Simon & Schuster/Atheneum, 1996.

Virginia is a young slave who comes to Washington, D.C., to work for James and Dolley Madison just before the War of 1812. Trustworthy, she is quickly involved in secret activities to help slaves to freedom. One careless mistake results in an unforgettable loss, as readers learn about events surrounding the War of 1812 from a slightly different perspective.

Rosen, Michael J. *A School for Pompey Walker.* Illustrated by Aminah Brenda Lynn Robinson. San Diego, Calif.: Harcourt Brace, 1995.

Slaves can have dreams, and Pompey Walker has one: He wants to go to school. When Jeremiah Walker, son-in-law of a wealthy plantation owner, buys him, the two devise a plan to get money to found a school for black children. The story is based on the recollections of some former slaves and a newspaper account of an Ohio man's experiences.

Ruby, Lois. *Steal Away Home*. New York: Macmillan, 1994.
Two stories are interwoven in this intriguing volume, one about the Underground Railroad in the 1850s and the other about a young girl in Lawrence, Kansas, in the 1990s. Readers will be treated to a history lesson filled with mystery and drama as they turn the pages of this well-written book.

Sachar, Louis. *Holes*. New York: Farrar/Frances Foster, 1998.
Stanley Yelnets is accustomed to bad luck, so ending up in Camp Green Lake, a boys' detention center, doesn't surprise him. What does is that each boy must dig a five-foot-deep and five-foot-wide hole every single day, battling the packed earth and intense heat. He befriends a homeless boy from the multicultural mix and unravels the truth behind the warden's punishment in this creative Newbery winner.

Schulman, Arlene. *Muhammad Ali: Champion*. Illustrated with photographs. Minneapolis, Minn.: Lerner, 1996.
Heavyweight boxing champion Muhammad Ali has given people much to talk about. He is outspoken but also charismatic. Black-and-white photographs extend an interesting text that takes readers through events in his childhood and into his adult years.

Spinelli, Jerry. *Maniac Magee*. Boston: Little, Brown, 1990.
Spinelli takes the reader from one social issue to another in this book about the interactions of two cultures. The love of reading is reinforced through the story as well.

Stolz, Mary. *Go Fish*. Illustrated by Pat Cummings. New York: HarperCollins, 1991.
Thomas and Grandfather share a special companionship as they fish and end the day with Grandfather's stories, passed down from generation to generation.

Taylor, Mildred D. *Mississippi Bridge*. Illustrated by Max Ginsburg. New York: Dial, 1990.
This story hits the reader hard as Jeremy Sims, a white boy, tells the events that transpire when the weekly bus arrives at his family store. Set in rural Mississippi in the 1930s, the story reveals the extent to which racism ruled the lives of all too many people, with disastrous results.

———. *The Well: David's Story*. New York: Dial, 1995.
This is a thoughtful novel about a hardworking African-American family in Mississippi and how they are willing to share their bounty with all neighbors, black or white.

Tillage, Leon Walter. *Leon's Story*. Illustrated by Susan L. Roth. New York: Farrar, Straus & Giroux, 1998.
Leon's life was filled with hatred and cruelty, as recounted through memories of his everyday life. Because of the despair depicted, this book should be counterbalanced with those about more hopeful experiences of African Americans.

Turner, Glennette T. *Follow in Their Footsteps*. New York: Cobblehill, 1997.
This inspiring book contains the biographies of 10 successful African Americans who achieved acclaim despite the adversities they faced. Note that there are also skits included in this book.

Walter, Mildred Pitts. *Second Daughter: The Story of a Slave Girl*. New York: Scholastic, 1996.
This book, based on a true story, tells how two sisters dreamed of being free from slavery. It is told through the eyes of the younger sister. Readers learn how Mum Bett sued for her freedom under the Massachusetts Constitution in 1781.

Woodson, Jacqueline. *I Hadn't Meant to Tell You This*. New York: Delacorte, 1994.
This powerful story for older readers recounts the interracial friendship of two eighth grade girls who buoy each other up in the face of difficult home situations. Both girls have lost their mothers, but Lena's life is further complicated because she is being sexually abused by her father.

Wright, Richard. *Rite of Passage*. New York: HarperCollins, 1994.
Johnny Gibbs teaches readers a powerful story about racism, violent crime, juvenile delinquency, and life in the black urban ghetto.

Yarbrough, Camille. *The Little Tree Growin' in the Shade*. Illustrated by Tyrone Geter. New York: Putnam, 1996.
While attending a concert in the park, Sister and Brother learn about their African roots through a story Daddy tells about the Tree of Life in Africa and the broken branch that took root in America with the beginning of slavery.

Zemser, Amy Bronwen. *Beyond the Mango Tree*. New York: Greenwillow, 1998.
When her mother isn't well or thinking clearly, she ties Sarina to the mango tree. Life has changed drastically since the family moved from Boston to Africa. When a young Liberian boy cuts her free, the twosome flee into the new world beyond the mango tree.

Asian Cultures

Alonso, Karen. *Korematsu v. United States: Japanese-American Internment Camps*. Illustrated with photographs. Springfield, N.J.: Enslow, 1998.
The text explains the plight of Fred Korematsu and the disgraceful internment of Japanese Americans during World War II. Titles for further reading are included.

Blakeslee, Ann R. *A Different Kind of Hero*. New York: Marshall Cavendish, 1997.
Renny is having difficulty pleasing his father as he faces the rigors of life in a mining camp in 1881. Life is also complicated by racial issues, and he finds courage when he needs it as he defends a Chinese friend.

Brown, Tricia. *Konnichiwa! I Am a Japanese American Girl*. Illustrated with photographs by Kazuyoshi Arai. New York: Henry Holt, 1995.
Lauren introduces readers to her life in San Francisco, reflecting her Japanese heritage including dancing traditional dances, learning the Japanese language, and playing taiko drums and bamboo flutes.

Choi, Sook Nyul. *Year of Impossible Goodbyes*. Boston: Houghton Mifflin, 1991.
Sookan lives in Japanese-occupied North Korea during World War II. Her father and brothers are fighting in the resistance and her grandfather dies as a result of the cruelty of Japanese soldiers. This 10-year-old, her mother, and a brother plan to escape to American-occupied South Korea as the harshness of war permeates their lives.

Coerr, Eleanor. *Mieko and the Fifth Treasure*. New York: Putnam, 1993.
The bombing of Nagasaki is nearly catastrophic to a young girl who nearly loses her gift for drawing when her hand is badly cut.

Dalkey, Kara. *The Heavenward Path*. San Diego, Calif.: Harcourt Brace, 1998.
In this sequel to *Little Sister*, Mitsuko finds herself attempting to complete a number of seemingly impossible tasks to placate an angry spirit. Again she gets help from an impish shape-shifter as they travel through a legendary world in twelfth-century Japan.

———. *Little Sister*. San Diego, Calif.: Jane Yolen Books, 1996.
In the aftermath of an attack on her village, Mitsuko ventures into the netherworld to search for her sister's wandering spirit. A shape-shifter and other magical creatures from Japanese myths come to

her aid as she gathers her courage in a legendary world.

Goldin, Barbara D. *Red Means Good Fortune: A Story of San Francisco's Chinatown.* Illustrated by Wenhai Ma. New York: Viking, 1994.

Jin Mun leaves China in 1868 with plans to join his father in San Francisco. Working in the laundry business, Jin Mun delivers laundry each day and studies English each night. When he meets Wai Hing and learns that she has been sold as a slave to a Chinese family in the city, he resolves to help her gain her freedom.

Gollub, Matthew. *Cool Melons—Turn to Frogs! The Life and Poems of Issa.* Illustrated by Kazuko G. Stone. New York: Lee & Low, 1998.

This is a beautifully illustrated biography of one of Japan's best-loved masters of haiku. Readers get a sense of Japanese culture through the blending of art, text, and poetry in this book.

Hamanaka, Sheila, and Ayano Ohmi. *In Search of the Spirit: The Living National Treasures of Japan.* New York: Morrow, 1999.

This is a beautiful book that honors masters who have devoted their lives to traditional Japanese crafts and performing arts. Six highly talented people are featured; they explain the hard work and dedication that goes into preserving traditions that have existed in Japan since medieval times.

Haugarrd, Erik Christian. *The Revenge of the Forty-Seven Samurai.* Boston: Houghton Mifflin, 1995.

When their master is ordered to commit ritual suicide for an unjust reason, 47 of his samurai decide to avenge his death. Jiro, a 14-year-old servant, relates this exciting tale.

Hoobler, Dorothy, and Thomas Hoobler. *The Ghost in the Tokaido Inn.* New York: Penguin/Putnam/Philomel, 1999.

Seikei and his father are on a trip to open a branch of his thriving tea firm. Resting for the night at an inn, Seikei finds himself in the midst of a mystery involving a stolen jewel, a beautiful young girl, and a cast of fascinating characters.

Jiang, Ji-li. *Red Scarf Girl: A Memoir of the Cultural Revolution.* New York: HarperCollins, 1997.

Jiang's story reveals her life as a young girl in China, caught up in the Cultural Revolution that swept the country into chaos in 1966.

Kidd, Diana. *Onion Tears.* Illustrated by Lucy Montgomery. New York: Orchard Books, 1991.

Nam Huong has lost her entire family and is at a loss as she tries to adjust to life in Australia. Miss Lily, an eccentric teacher, teaches Nam to trust again and to cry real tears of sorrow over her losses.

Kim, Helen. *The Long Season of Rain.* New York: Henry Holt, 1996.

Tradition and culture placed demands on Korean women during the 1960s, and 11-year-old Junelee sees the negative impact they have had on her mother. She has much to think about as she contemplates her own future and the changes she might make.

Kuklin, Susan. *Kodomo: Children of Japan.* Illustrated with photographs. New York: Putnam, 1995.

Color photographs and personal narratives of seven children give the reader a glimpse into the contemporary lives of elementary school–age children living in Japan, including some of the traditional activities that are a part of their lives.

Levine, Ellen. *A Fence Away from Freedom: Japanese Americans and World War II.* New York: Putnam, 1995.

This book tells of the internment of Japanese Americans from a variety of perspectives and through young voices. Their words are filled with pain, humor, and courage. Maps, timelines, and pertinent biographies are included.

Meissel, Chris. *Hakeem and Yoshi.* Nashville, Tenn.: Winston-Derek, 1996.

Hakeem, a nine-year-old New York City boy, travels to Japan with his mother. There he makes a Japanese friend and learns a great deal about the culture of the country.

Namioka, Lensey. *The Coming of the Bear.* New York: HarperCollins, 1993.

In this story set in the sixteenth century, Zenta and Matsuzo are unemployed samurai who are saved from drowning during a terrible storm at sea. Saved by a culture much different than that of the Japanese, they reach a point where they must choose between their own culture and that of their rescuers.

———. *Den of the White Fox.* San Diego, Calif.: Harcourt/Browndeer, 1997.

Readers follow two unemployed samurai through sixteenth-century feudal Japan to a remote village, where a gang is using the legend of the white fox to fight off encroaching military occupation.

———. *Yang the Youngest and His Terrible Ear.* Illustrated by Kees de Kiefte. Boston: Little, Brown/Joy Street Books, 1992.

Yingtao is the youngest in the musical Yang family. Unfortunately, his talents run more in the direction of baseball than playing a violin. A humorous scheme is devised to prove that he is different from his siblings.

Reeder, Carolyn. *Foster's War.* New York: Scholastic, 1998.

This is a sad story set against the backdrop of the bombing of Pearl Harbor. It relates the impacts of internment, racism, and the war on a soldier's family.

Salisbury, Graham. *Under the Blood-Red Sun.* New York: Delacorte, 1994.

Tomi and his family are Japanese Americans living in Hawaii. They are subjected to prejudice and hatred following the attack on Pearl Harbor. Father is taken to an internment camp and Grandfather disappears. Readers learn through Tomi how the Japanese Americans were treated during wartime.

Say, Allen. *The Ink-Keeper's Apprentice.* Boston: Houghton Mifflin, 1994.

This is a reissue of Say's autobiography, which focuses on his adolescent years and the development of the young artist's talent when apprenticed to a famous cartoonist.

Soto, Gary. *Pacific Crossing.* San Francisco, Calif.: Harcourt Brace, 1992.

Lincoln Mendoza and Tony Contreras are in Japan for the summer. They are foreign exchange students studying the martial arts. They learn to appreciate their own culture as they explain it to their Japanese hosts, and they realize just how much they have in common with another culture.

Stanley, Jerry. *I Am an American: A True Story of Japanese Internment.* Illustrated with family photographs. New York: Crown, 1994.

This is a nonfiction book relating the story of a Japanese-American family as they struggled through days of internment in the United States during World War II.

Tunnell, Michael O., and George W. Chilcoat. *The Children of Topaz: The Story of a Japanese-American Internment Camp.* Illustrated with photographs. New York: Holiday House, 1996.

Based on entries in a diary of a third grade teacher who taught in an internment camp, readers are informed about a difficult time for Japanese Americans during World War II. Photographs and drawings enhance the text.

Uchida, Yoshiko. *The Invisible Thread.* New York: Morrow, 1991.

In this book the author relates touching stories of her childhood and her unhappiness at being a prisoner of war in her own country during World War II.

———. *Journey Home*. Illustrated by Charles Robinson. New York: Atheneum, 1978.

In this sequel to *Journey to Topaz*, Yuki and her parents return to California and face adjustments.

———. *Journey to Topaz*. Illustrated by Donald Carrick. New York: Scribner, 1971.

The life of a Japanese family held in an internment camp in Utah is related, enabling readers to get a sense of the despair a situation like this involves.

Watkins, Yoko Kawashima. *My Brother, My Sister, and I.* New York: Bradbury, 1994.

In this sequel to *So Far from the Bamboo Grove,* the author relates the story of living as refugees with her older brother and sister in postwar Japan while searching for their father.

Wong, Janet S. *A Suitcase of Seaweed and Other Poems.* New York: McElderry/Macmillan, 1996.

Wong displays her deep pride in her Korean, Chinese, and American ancestry through her poems that show the differences among these three cultures.

Wu, Priscilla. *The Abacus Contest: Stories from Taiwan and China.* Illustrated by Xiao-Jun Li. Golden, Colo.: Fulcrum Publishing, 1996.

An engaging collection of short stories from Taiwan and China.

Yee, Paul. *Tales from Gold Mountain: Stories of the Chinese in the New World.* Illustrated by Simon Ng. New York: Macmillan, 1990.

Eight original tales about the difficult times Chinese immigrants faced in the New World are interwoven with folklore in a book that provides insight into a heritage that included the building of transcontinental railroads, the gold rush, and the settling of the West Coast.

Yep, Laurence. *The Case of the Goblin Pearls.* New York: HarperCollins, 1997.

Set in the heart of Chinatown, this story presents the reader with a mystery that must be solved.

———. *Dragon's Gate.* New York: HarperCollins, 1993.

Young Otter's dreams of life in America are cruelly destroyed when he joins his father and the uncle who has always been his hero. Enduring inhumane conditions while working on the transcontinental railroad, a death, and disillusionment push Otter to take some desperate measures.

———. *Hiroshima.* New York: Scholastic, 1995.

Even though more than 50 years have passed since the bombing of Hiroshima, families in Japan are still dealing with the results of radiation.

———. *The Lost Garden.* New York: Julian Messner, 1991.

In his autobiography, Yep compares his life to a jigsaw puzzle. As he matured, more puzzle pieces fell into place. Readers of his novels will recognize snippets about his life in San Francisco and his Chinese-American heritage.

———. *Ribbons.* New York: Putnam, 1996.

Robin Lee's life changes drastically when her elderly Chinese grandmother comes to live with her family. Although ribbons represent Robin's love of ballet, they remind her grandmother of her deformed feet, long ago bound by the ribbons of tradition.

Yumoto, Kazumi. *The Friends.* New York: Farrar & Straus, 1996.

In this contemporary story three sixth-grade boys try to understand death because of a recent loss of one of their grandmothers. They stalk an old man in their neighborhood in hopes of learning about death, but end up forming a friendship with the man, who teaches them about aging, dying, and growing up. A Batchelder Award winner.

Cuban/Hispanic/Latino Cultures

Ada, Alma Flor. *Where the Flame Trees Bloom.* Illustrated by Antonio Martorell. Translated from the Spanish by Rosalma Zubizarreta. New York: Atheneum, 1994.

Ada re-creates memories of her childhood in Cuba in an entertaining recounting of her life and the loving people who were so much a part of it.

Aldana, Patricia, ed. *Jade and Iron: Latin American Tales from Two Cultures.* Illustrated by Luis Gaaray. Translated by Hugh Hazelton. Toronto: Groundwood, 1996.

Readers will enjoy this collection of myths and legends from Central and South America, some gathered from the indigenous peoples of the area and others of European origin. Because some are violent in nature, this collection is best suited for more mature readers.

Anastos, Phillip, and Chris French. *Illegal: Seeking the American Dream.* New York: Rizzoli International Publications, 1991.

Written by two high school students, this informative book discusses Hispanic immigrant children and is set in Brownsville, Texas, a port of entry for many seeking a better life.

Anaya, Rudolfo. *The Farolitos of Christmas.* Illustrated by Edward Gonzales. New York: Hyperion, 1995.

Ingenuity is required when Abuelo cannot cut the wood for the traditional Christmas luminarias. Luz creates small lanterns of her own by placing candles in paper bags, which are held in place with sand. Set in New Mexico during World War II, this family story explains the tradition of farolitos.

Ancona, George. *Mayeros: A Yucatec Maya Family.* Illustrated with photographs. New York: Lothrop, 1997.

This photodocumentary depicts the life and customs of Mayan descendants.

Atkin, S. Beth, ed. *Voices from the Fields: Children of Migrant Farmworkers Tell Their Stories.* Boston: Little, Brown, 1993.

Nine children of migrant workers tell about their daily lives.

Bernardo, Anilu. *Fitting In.* Houston, Tex.: Piñata, 1996.

The five short stories in this book are drawn from the author's own Cuban immigrant experiences. Her adolescent characters conquer new challenges in a positive, courageous manner.

Braun, Barbara. *A Weekend with Diego Rivera.* Illustrated with photographs. New York: Rizzoli International Publications, 1994.

Illustrated with reproductions of the artist's work, the life and work of this great Mexican painter and muralist are explained. Insight into the history and traditions of Mexico can be gleaned from this book.

Buss, Fran Leeper, with Daisy Cubias. *Journey of the Sparrows.* New York: Lodestar Books, 1991.

In a book written for mature readers, the horrors faced by 15-year-old Maria and her two siblings are related as they are smuggled into the United States from El Salvador. In Chicago they suffer from starvation and cruel working conditions. The terrors faced by illegal aliens are clearly depicted. Maria's strong hope of being reunited with her family ends the story on an upbeat note.

Carlson, Lori M., ed. *Cool Salsa: Bilingual Poems on Growing Up in the United States.* New York: Henry Holt, 1994.

The Latino culture is celebrated through poetry in this bilingual book. It covers a variety of topics and illuminates what it is like for Latinos who grow up in the United States.

Collins, David R. *Farmworkers' Friend: The Story of Cesar Chavez.* Minneapolis, Minn.: Carolrhoda, 1996.

This is an informative book about the farmworkers' labor movement, highlighting the work of a contemporary hero.

Cumpian, Carlos. *Latino Rainbow: Poems about Latino Americans.* Illustrated by Richard Leonard. Chicago: Children's Press, 1994.

An illustration and a poem depict various occupations of Latino Americans such as Chavez, Ronstadt, and Valens.

Delacre, Lulu. *Arroz Con Leche: Popular Songs and Rhymes from Latin America.* New York: Scholastic, 1989.

A variety of poems and songs celebrating the culture are included in this book.

Garland, Sherry. *Indio.* New York: Gulliver/Great Episodes, 1995.

Indio is caught up in the brutal conquest by the Spaniards in the late 1500s, which led to the eventual birth of the Mexican people.

Hesse, Karen. *The Music of Dolphins.* New York: Scholastic, 1996.

Mila is orphaned when her parents are shipwrecked while trying to flee from Cuba. She is raised by a pod of dolphins until she is discovered as an adolescent and taken to a research center to be studied. The ending will certainly provoke discussion.

Hurwitz, Johanna. *Class President.* Illustrated by Sheila Hamanaka. New York: Scholastic, 1991.

Julio Sanchez quickly realizes that fifth grade may not be quite what he planned when he meets the new teacher, Ernesto Flores. The year's lessons include learning to be proud of his heritage, that he can be a fine leader, how to help a friend, and even how to make brownies.

Lasky, Kathryn. *Days of the Dead.* Illustrated with photographs by Christopher G. Knight. Boston: Hyperion, 1994.

Poetic text filled with details combines with excellent photographs to show a Mexican family preparing for and celebrating the Days of the Dead, a special celebration to honor their ancestors.

Madrigal, Antonio Hernandez. *The Eagle and the Rainbow: Timeless Tales from Mexico.* Illustrated by Tomie de Paola. Golden, Colo.: Fulcrum Publishing, 1998. Ancient Mexico comes to life in the pages of this collection of enduring tales about the lives of members of the Aztec, Tarascan, and Tarahumaran cultures.

Martin, Patricia Preciado. *El Milagro and Other Stories.* Tucson: The University of Arizona, 1996.

Positive and upbeat, this book is filled with family stories and memories from the life of the author.

Martinez, Victor. *Parrot in the Oven: Mi Vada.* New York: Joanna Cotler, 1996.

A book for mature readers, this award winner touches on the miscarriage of a teenage pregnancy, the anger of a father, and the brutality of gang involvement in an honest approach to some tough problems.

Mikaelsen, Ben. *Sparrow Red Hawk.* Boston: Hyperion/Little, Brown, 1993.

This engrossing story is about a 13-year-old boy who seeks to avenge his mother's death at the hands of drug smugglers.

O'Dell, Scott. *The Amethyst Ring.* Boston: Houghton Mifflin, 1983.

This is the story of Julian Escobar. It is the third book in a chronicle based upon the legend of Kuhulan, god of the Maya Indians.

———. *Carlota.* Boston: Houghton Mifflin, 1981.

Set in early California, this is an exciting story about a high-spirited Spanish-American girl who chooses to fight alongside her father during the Mexican American War.

———. *The Feathered Serpent.* Boston: Houghton Mifflin, 1981.

For readers who liked *Carlota,* this is a sequel to be enjoyed.

Orozco, Josè-Luis, trans. *Diez Deditos and Other Play Rhymes and Action Songs from Latin America.* Illustrated by Elisa Leven. New York: Dutton, 1997.

This is a delightful addition to the classroom routine. Students can enjoy finger rhymes and action songs in an appealing bilingual collection.

Paulsen, Gary. *Sisters/Hermanas.* San Diego, Calif.: Harcourt Brace, 1993.

This story is told in both English and Spanish. It relates the stories of Rosa, a 14-year-old illegal immigrant from Mexico City, and Traci, also 14, who lives in the Houston suburbs. Adolescent values and real-life pressures make this engrossing reading.

Poynter, Margaret. *The Uncertain Journey: Stories of Illegal Aliens in El Norte.* New York: Atheneum, 1992.

In a moving manner, 12 illegal immigrants share their experiences trying to survive as undocumented workers in the United States.

Reeve, Kirk. *Lolo and Red-Legs.* Flagstaff, Ariz.: Rising Moon Press, 1998.

Three Mexican-American friends fill their summer days with action in Las Lomitas, California. A tarantula named Red-Legs and their fort are the focus of their activities.

Soto, Gary. *Canto Familiar.* Illustrated by Annika Nelson. San Diego, Calif.: Harcourt Brace, 1995.

Touching and also filled with a few smiles, this beautifully written and illustrated volume celebrates Mexican-American childhood in a lively and memorable manner.

———. *Neighborhood Odes.* Illustrated by David Diaz. San Diego, Calif.: Harcourt Brace, 1992.

Filled with moments from childhood that often get forgotten, this poetry book takes a fresh look at life.

———. *Novio Boy.* San Diego, Calif.: Harcourt Brace, 1997.

This is a play about adolescent puppy love that involves the trials faced by ninth grade Rudy when Patricia, an eleventh grader, agrees to go out on a date.

———. *Off and Running.* Illustrated by Eric Velasquez. New York: Delacorte, 1996.

This book relates the events that surround an election in the fifth grade.

———. *Petty Crimes.* San Diego, Calif.: Harcourt Brace, 1998.

Manuel, Josè Luis, and Alma are three gutsy Mexican-American youths who tackle life head on in this collection of short stories.

Temple, Frances. *Grab Hands and Run.* New York: Orchard Books, 1993.

Felipe tells about his family's attempts to leave El Salvador after their father's disappearance.

Walker, Paul Robert. *Pride of Puerto Rico: The Life of Roberto Clemente.* San Diego, Calif.: Harcourt Brace/Gulliver Books, 1988.

A wonderful role model, this talented right-fielder for the Pittsburgh Pirates is proud of his country, his family, and his achievements as a baseball player.

Native Americans

Allen, Paula Gunn, and Patricia Clark. *As Long as the Rivers Flow: The Stories of Nine Native Americans.* New York: Scholastic, 1996.

This collective biography contains the stories and accomplishments of Native Americans in a variety of areas: Weetanmoo (woman warrior), Geronimo (tribal leader), Will Rogers (humorist), Jim Thorpe (athlete), Maria Tallchief (ballet dancer), Ben Nighthorse Campbell (U.S. Senator), Wilma Mankiller (tribal leader), Michael Naranjo (artist), and Lousie Erdrich (writer).

Armstrong, Nancy M. *Navajo Long Walk.* Illustrated by Paulette Livers Lambert. Niwot, Colo.: Roberts Rinehart Publishers, 1994.

Kee and his family are forced to make an arduous journey beyond the spiritual boundaries of their Arizona lands when a U.S. government decree moves the Navajo to New Mexico in 1864.

Ayer, Eleanor H. *The Anasazi*. New York: Walker, 1993.
     An appealing and informative nonfiction account of the Anasazi, where they came from, how the pueblo dwellers lived, and speculations about what might have happened to them.

Baron, T. A. *The Ancient One*. New York: Tom Doherty Associates, 1992.
     Set in the dying logging town of Blade, Oregon, this time-travel tale sets young Kate and Aunt Melanie against a determined group of loggers bent on destroying an ancient grove of redwood trees. Wrapped in Indian lore, magic, and a respect for nature, this book points out that some things in nature should never be destroyed.

Begay, Shonto. *Navajo: Visions and Voices across the Mesa*. New York: Scholastic, 1995.
     This gifted writer and artist depicts numerous aspects of the life of the Navajo through paintings and poetry.

Bierhorst, John. *The Dancing Fox: Arctic Folktales*. Illustrated by Mary K. Okheena. New York: Morrow, 1997.
     Age-old stories from the American Arctic are distinctive and reveal rich, powerful images of life in the Arctic to appreciative readers.

Bouchard, Dave. *The Elders Are Watching*. Illustrated by Roy Henry Vickers. Vancouver, B.C.: Eagle Dance/Raincoast Books, 1990.
     Revival, culture, heritage, environment, and the importance of instilling respect for all of them are addressed when a young boy goes to live with his grandfather to learn about his heritage.

Brown, Tricia. *Children of the Midnight Sun: Young Native Voices of Alaska*. Illustrated with photographs by Roy Corral. Seattle, Wash.: Alaska Northwest, 1998.
     Eight native Alaskan children are highlighted along with the cultural differences that make them unique. One cultural thread that ties these children to those in other Native American tribes is the important role that grandparents play.

Bruchac, Joseph. *The Arrow over the Door*. Illustrated by James Watling. New York: Dial, 1998.
     This historically based story relates a touching encounter between Algonquin Indians and Quakers at the Friends' Meetinghouse in Saratoga, New York, in 1777.

———. *Bowman's Store: A Journey to Myself*. New York: Dial, 1997.
     Joseph Bruchac relates his life as he was raised by grandparents in Maine, only learning about his Abenaki heritage later in his life. Each chapter begins with an intriguing Abenaki legend.

———. *The Boy Who Lived with the Bears and Other Iroquois Stories*. Illustrated by Murv Jacob. New York: HarperCollins, 1995.
     This is an appealing collection of six traditional Iroquois tales that would have been retold around campfires by elders wishing to entertain and to educate the young.

———. *Dog People: Native Dog Stories*. Golden, Colo.: Fulcrum Publishing, 1995.
     Readers of these tales slip back in time as they experience a number of outdoor adventures, learning how to survive along with Abenaki children and their dogs.

———. *Eagle Song*. Illustrated by Dan Andreasen. New York: Dial, 1997.
     A move from the Mohawk Reservation to Brooklyn subjects Danny Bigtree to intolerance and teasing from his classmates until his father and teacher work together to teach the children about the Iroquois, underscoring traditional values, storytelling, and family support.

———. *The Heart of a Chief*. New York: Dial, 1998.
     Sixth grader Chris Nicola worries about fitting in when he leaves the Penacook Indian Reservation to attend school in town. Much to his relief, he fits in well, but he must face bigger issues back home, including his father's alcoholism and the possibility that a casino will be built on his special piece of land.

Bruchac, Joseph, and Gayle Ross. *The Girl Who Married the Moon: Tales from Native North America*. Illustrated by S. Burrus. New York: BridgeWater, 1994.
     This volume contains 16 tales that celebrate the coming of age of young women in a number of traditional Native American cultures. It is an excellent choice that reinforces the importance of Native American women and their deeply rooted wisdom.

Burks, Brian. *Runs With Horses*. San Diego, Calif.: Harcourt Brace, 1995.
     Runs With Horses is a 16-year-old member of a small band of Apaches who are struggling to survive in 1886. He is trying to complete the training for manhood as a Chiricahua Apache before they must surrender to the U.S. Army.

———. *Walks Alone*. San Diego, Calif.: Harcourt Brace, 1998.
     The strong human instinct for survival driven by self-determination is what enables an Apache girl to survive in the face of tremendous hardship and loss.

Cornelissen, Cornelia. *Soft Rain: A Story of the Cherokee Trail of Tears*. New York: Delacorte, 1998.
     A tragic decision by the U.S. government forces the Cherokee from their homes. Readers glimpse the courage of a people under oppression in this tale told from nine-year-old Soft Rain's viewpoint.

Cossi, Olga. *Fire Mate*. Illustrated by Paulette Livers Lambert. Niwot, Colo.: Roberts Rinehart Publishers, 1995.
     Yvonne is a nine-year-old Pomo contemporary American Indian girl living on the California reservation. She is on a quest to find her Fire Mate, a person or thing necessary to ignite her Soul Fire, as related through tribal myths and legends.

Dewey, Jennifer Owings. *Navajo Summer*. Honesdale, Pa.: Boyds Mills Press, 1998.
     In an effort to cope with her parents' impending divorce and her anger over her father's mental and physical abuse, 12-year-old Jamie buys a one-way ticket to Navajo country. She feels safe with the Navajo family she has known for many years and hopes time with them in Canyon de Chelly will help heal her personal sadness.

Dorris, Michael. *Morning Girl*. New York: Hyperion, 1992.
     This story relates the life of a Native American tribe in the Bahamas in 1492.

———. *Sees Behind Trees*. New York: Hyperion, 1996.
     Native Americans are noted for using their senses. This tale describes the life of a partially sighted boy who must rely on his even more.

Durant, Lynda. *The Beaded Moccasins: The Story of Mary Campbell*. New York: Clarion, 1998.
     Mary Campbell was taken captive by the Delaware Indians in the mid-1700s. This book relates her interactions with the tribe as she tried to learn their beliefs, traditions, and daily routines.

———. *Echohawk*. New York: Clarion, 1996.
     In the early 1730s four-year-old Jonathan Starr is taken from his family to live with the Mohawks who massacred his family. Raised as their own, Jonathan must eventually make a choice between the world he knows and the world from which he was taken.

Eckert, Allen W. *Return to Hawk's Hill*. Boston: Little, Brown, 1998.
     This is a sequel to *Incident at Hawk's Hill*. Although it doesn't deal directly with a Native American protagonist, it is filled with details about Native American culture and survival techniques.

Ellison, Suzanne Pierson. *The Last Warrior*. Flagstaff, Ariz.: Northland Publishing, 1997.

Solito, a teenage Apache brave, is unable to complete his warrior training before his band is captured by the U.S. Army. Forced to adapt to the white man's ways and stripped of his culture, he eventually finds himself at odds with the world into which he has been thrust. This coming-of-age story is based on the true story of Geronimo's Chiricahua Apaches.

Erdrich, Louise. *The Birchbark House*. New York: Hyperion, 1999.

Omakayas takes the reader through her days on an island in Lake Superior and shares many details of her traditional Ojibwa life and the effects of the white man on it.

Finley, Carol. *Art of the Far North: Inuit Sculpture, Drawing, and Printmaking*. Minneapolis, Minn.: Lerner, 1998.

This book looks at three major forms of Inuit art. Although the Inuit have changed with time, they remain a distinctive culture with their own unique customs, beliefs, and legends.

Fox, Mary Virginia. *Chief Joseph of the Nez Perce Indians: Champion of Liberty*. Chicago: Children's Press, 1992.

The author relates the carefully researched story of Chief Joseph, a courageous man who led his people on a long journey to escape the injustices of the U.S. government.

Freedman, Russell. *Buffalo Hunt*. New York: Holiday House, 1988.

Freedman uses text and illustrations to teach the reader about the importance of the buffalo hunt to the Great Plains Indians.

———. *Indian Chiefs*. New York: Holiday House, 1987.

This is an excellent volume of short biographies to use to research the lives of six Indian chiefs.

———. *An Indian Winter*. Illustrated by Karl Bodmer. New York: Holiday House, 1992.

This book gives a detailed description of the Mandan and Hidasta tribes, based on accounts of two European explorers who were befriended by the two tribes.

———. *The Life and Death of Crazy Horse*. Illustrated by Amos Bad Heart Bull. New York: Holiday House, 1996.

This is a wonderful book about a fascinating Teton Sioux warrior, illustrated by authentic sketches that were found in 1926.

Gates, Viola. *Journey to Center Place*. Illustrated by Paulette Livers Lambert. Niwot, Colo.: Roberts Rinehart Publishers, 1996.

Research on the ancient Anasazi is interwoven throughout this story of Neekah and her people as they journey to a new home in Chaco Canyon. Key issues running through the story are friendship, love, and survival.

Green, Rayna. *Women in American Indian Society*. Broomall, Pa.: Chelsea, 1992.

Great for interested readers and those pursuing research, this book presents the history of Native American women from a time before contact with Europeans up through contemporary times.

Green, Timothy. *Twilight Boy*. Flagstaff, Ariz.: Rising Moon /Northland Publishing, 1998.

When Carolyn flies in from the East Coast to spend time with her parents, who have just purchased a trading post, she expects to be bored. Her first night at Standing Rock Trading Post is filled with horror when a nightmarish skinwalker peers in at her. Her days on the Navajo Reservation are filled with both suspense and warm friendship.

Hamm, Diane Johnston. *Daughter of Suqua*. Morton Grove, Ill.: Whitman, 1997.

Ida is a 10-year-old member of the Suquamish tribe. It is through her eyes that readers learn how the tribe members' lives change as the government takes the lands through treaties and forces them to endure policies of assimilation. The author's notes depict careful research.

Harrah, Madge. *My Brother, My Enemy*. New York: Simon & Schuster, 1997.

Robert is proud of his ties with his blood brother, a Susquehannock Native American boy. Those ties are stretched when Robert's whole family is massacred by the tribe. An informative author's note adds additional interest to a fast-paced story.

Hobbs, Will. *Beardance*. New York: Avon/Camelot Books, 1993.

In this sequel to Bearstone, Cloyd watches a trophy hunter purposely kill a grizzly, an endangered species. When he sees a mother grizzly buried in an avalanche, Cloyd assumes the responsibility for saving the cubs, a task that becomes an adventure in survival.

———. *Bearstone*. New York: Atheneum, 1989.

Cloyd has failed school and run away from home, seeking some semblance of family life. A blue stone bear and an attempt to save the last grizzly reunite him with his grandfather in this coming-of-age novel.

———. *Far North*. New York: Morrow, 1996.

Gabe Rogers and his Navajo roommate survive a plane crash in the Northwest Territories. An elderly Dene Indian provides wisdom and support, but only for a short time. Then they must survive their wilderness ordeal through cooperation and common sense.

———. *Kokopelli's Flute*. New York: Atheneum, 1995.

This is an imaginative but informative fantasy about Tepary Jones, the Ancient Ones, plundering pot hunters, and a supernatural event that occurs at Picture House, the "last best" cliff dwelling in the Southwest.

Hucko, Bruce. *A Rainbow at Night: The World in Words and Pictures by Navajo Children*. San Francisco, Calif.: Chronicle, 1997.

Insight into the lives of Navajo children is presented through 23 illustrations and children's writing.

Hudson, Jan. *Dawn Rider*. New York: Philomel, 1990.

Kit Fox, a 16-year-old Blackfoot Indian girl, dreams of being the first in her tribe to own a horse. Life in the tribe is revealed through Kit as preparations are made for a buffalo run, the upcoming marriage of her older sister, battles that ensue with the enemy Snake Indians, and her romance with Found Arrow. The book is based on information gleaned from Blackfeet Nation records.

———. *Sweetgrass*. New York: Philomel, 1989.

Sweetgrass proves her capability and maturity to her father when she saves her family from a devastating smallpox epidemic. The story is filled to the brim with information about the Blackfeet Indians' way of life.

Jacobs, Paul S. *James Printer: A Novel of Rebellion*. New York: Scholastic, 1997.

James Printer is a Nipmuck Indian and a master apprentice printer in Cambridge. He battles divided loyalties as he carries out his role of translator and scribe for the Indians, but feels the necessity to warn colonists of an upcoming attack in King Philip's War.

MacGregor, Rob. *Prophecy Rock*. New York: Simon & Schuster, 1995.

Spending a summer with his father, a police chief on a Hopi reservation, helps Will to better understand his Native American heritage. While there, he becomes involved in solving a mystery involving a killer who is obsessed with an ancient prophecy.

Manitonquat. *The Children of the Morning Light*. Illustrated by Mary F. Arquette. New York: Macmillan, 1994.

Stories of creation and migration gathered from the oral tradition of the mainland Wampanoag Indians in southeastern Massachusetts are preserved for future generations.

Martin, Nora. *The Eagle's Shadow.* New York: Scholastic, 1997.

In this story set in Alaska in the summer of 1946, 12-year-old Clearie learns about her Tlingit roots. There is a story behind her mother's disappearance and the reasons her father is so bitter.

Matcheck, Diane. *The Sacrifice.* New York: Farrar, Straus & Giroux, 1998.

Readers follow a courageous young Crow woman who sets out on a trek to prove herself to her people, but only to discover that she has been designated the "Morningstar" sacrifice.

Meyer, Carolyn. *In a Different Light: Growing Up in a Yup'ik Eskimo Village in Alaska.* Illustrated with photographs by John McDonald. New York: McElderry/Macmillan, 1996.

Here is a close look at the life of the Yup'ik Eskimo people struggling to retain their lifestyle and traditions as Westernized cultures encroach upon their world.

———. *Where the Broken Heart Still Beats.* San Diego, Calif.: Gulliver/Harcourt Brace, 1992.

Cynthia Ann Parker was captured during an Indian raid when she was only nine years old. After 24 years she is the wife of a chief and mother of a young warrior. When she is recaptured by the Texas Rangers and returned to a white settlement, she struggles with her identity in this new social structure.

Morris, Juddi. *Tending the Fire: The Story of Maria Martinez.* Flagstaff, Ariz.: Rising Moon, 1997.

Maria Martinez is a world-famous potter who learned her craft from her Tewa family. Southwestern life is the backdrop for the life story of this talented artisan.

Norman, Howard. *The Girl Who Dreamed Only Geese and Other Tales of the Far North.* Illustrated by Leo Dillon and Diane Dillon. San Diego, Calif.: Gulliver/Harcourt Brace, 1997.

Based on extensive research with Inuit storytellers, these 10 retellings take readers on a journey from Siberia and Alaska to the Canadian Arctic and Greenland. Dramatic artwork by the Dillons heightens the immediacy of these tales.

Normandin, C., ed. *Echoes of the Elders: The Stories and Paintings of Chief Lelooska.* Illustrated by Chief Lelooska. New York: DK Publishing, 1997.

Before he died, Chief Lelooska was determined to preserve some of the stories long shared through the oral tradition. This is a collection of five beautifully retold stories that relate the traditions of the Northwest Coast Indians. A compact disc containing the same stories is included with the book.

———. *Spirit of the Cedar People: More Stories and Paintings of Chief Lelooska.* New York: DK Publishing, 1998.

Chief Lelooska's legacy continues through bold pictures and wonderful tales of spirits, tricksters, and the magic surrounding the lives of the Kwakuitl peoples.

O'Dell, Scott. *Sing Down the Moon.* Boston: Houghton Mifflin, 1988.

This is an award-winning book about the forced march of the Navajo people in 1864, as related by a young Navajo girl.

O'Dell, Scott, and Elizabeth Hall. *Thunder Rolling Down the Mountain.* New York: Dell, 1993.

The daughter of Chief Joseph, Sound of Running Feet, relates the story of the Nez Perce Wars of 1988. Completing the book after the author's death, O'Dell's wife fills out the story of a daughter's respect for her father; her strong love for a warrior, Swan Necklace; and her grief over the changing lives of her people.

Osborne, Mary Pope. *Standing in the Light: The Captive Diary of Catherine Carey Logan.* New York: Scholastic, 1998.

This is part of the Dear America series. It relates the fictionalized account of an adolescent Quaker girl's capture by the Lenape Indians in the Delaware Valley of Pennsylvania. The conflict involves the struggle to retain Quaker ways while growing to like her captors and their kind ways.

Paulsen, Gary. *Canyons.* New York: Bantam Doubleday Dell, 1990.

A mystical link across time unites 15-year-old Brennan Cole and Coyote Runs, an Apache boy on the brink of adulthood. A skull with a bullet hole and the search for an ancient sacred place change Brennan's life.

Philip, Neil. *Earth Always Endures: Native American Poems.* Illustrated with photographs by Edward S. Curtis. New York: Viking, 1996.

This collection depicts the traditions of numerous Native American cultures as the poets write about their reverence for nature, their dreams, and their fears.

Purdy, Carol. *Nesuya's Basket.* Niwot, Colo.: Roberts Rinehart Publishers, 1997.

Set in the Sacramento Valley in the 1800s, this is a tale about 12-year-old Nesuya, who is weaving a basket to honor her late grandmother. In the process, she learns a memorable lesson about the power of forgiving others.

Rappaport, Doreen. *The Flight of Red Bird: The Life of Zitkala-Sa.* New York: Dial, 1997.

Readers meet a courageous young girl who was taken from her family and raised in a Quaker boarding school. Red Bird continued her education, becoming a writer and a Native American activist.

Russell, Sharman Apt. *The Humpbacked Fluteplayer.* New York: Alfred A. Knopf, 1994.

May has recently moved to Phoenix and is homesick. When she gently touches a cave drawing of a humpbacked flute player, she and a classmate are transported into a parallel world, where they become slaves of a harsh, magical desert tribe.

Sewell, Marcia. *People of the Breaking Day.* New York: Atheneum, 1990.

This is a nonfiction account of the Wampanoag Nation, located in the southeastern portion of Massachusetts.

———. *Thunder from the Clear Sky.* New York: Atheneum, 1995.

In these two intertwining stories, a Pilgrim and a Wampanoag Indian relate their first encounters and the troubles that ensued as more and more immigrants arrived.

Speare, Elizabeth. *The Sign of the Beaver.* Boston: Houghton Mifflin, 1983.

This book won the Newbery Committee's attention. It recounts the story of a young boy who survives when his father returns home to gather his family, but he does so only with the help of a new Native American friend.

St. George, Judith. *To See with the Heart: The Life of Sitting Bull.* New York: Putnam, 1996.

This is a compelling story of a wise and courageous leader, Sitting Bull. His compassion and understanding set him apart from leaders who ruled by fear. A readable biography about a warrior who counted coup at age 14 and lost his life in a tragic struggle many years later.

Thomasma, Ken. *Naya Nuki: Shoshoni Girl Who Ran.* Charlotte, N.C.: Baker & Taylor, 1992.

Naya Nuki is kidnapped by a rival tribe and must walk alone through the wilderness for more than a month to attempt to return to her people. This tale of courage is a winner of the Wyoming Children's Book Award.

———. *Pathki Nana: Kootenai Girl Solves a Mystery.* Charlotte, N.C.: Baker & Taylor, 1992.

A reserved and shy Kootenai girl goes into the mountains to seek a guardian spirit, as is the tribal custom. Her quest results in an exciting life-and-death struggle in this Wyoming Children's Book Award winner.

Valgardson, W. D. *Sarah and the People of Sand River.* Illustrated by Ian Wallace. Toronto: Douglas & McIntrye, 1996.

This is a literary folktale in which a young girl is helped by a magic raven and a Cree man and woman.

Vick, Helen Hughes. *Shadow: The Courage of the Stone.* Niwot, Colo.: Roberts Rinehart Publishers, 1998.

In this story set in 1180 in the Sinagua culture, 13-year-old Shadow finds herself outside the safety of her pueblo, searching for her father, Stone Carrier, and her twin brother, Sun. She surpasses the expectations for a woman in a male-dominated society, jeopardizing her life in the process.

———. *Walker of Time.* Niwot, Colo.: Roberts Rinehart Publishers, 1994.

Two teenage boys, one a Hopi and the other the son of an area archeologist, are zapped back in time, into Walnut Canyon and the lives of the Sinagua culture. Learning to survive under bleak conditions and facing strong superstition and animosity, the boys become the hope of this dwindling band of ancient people.

———. *Walker's Journey Home.* Niwot, Colo.: Roberts Rinehart Publishers, 1995.

In the sequel to *Walker of Time,* Walker must lead his people across the desert to the Hopi Mesas, a danger-filled, 90-mile journey. For readers who want to know what happens to Tag in his efforts to travel back to the present century, Hughes has written *Tag Against Time,* a lively look at Flagstaff, Arizona, in the 1880s.

Viola, Herman J. *It Is a Good Day to Die: Indian Eyewitnesses Tell the Story of the Battle of Little Bighorn.* New York: Crown, 1998.

A compelling view of history unfolds as the reader learns of the Battle of Little Bighorn from Native Americans who were there.

———. *North American Indians.* Illustrated by Bryn Barnard. New York: Crown, 1996.

This excellent resource on a number of Native American tribes contains personal essays, informative text, and appealing illustrations and photographs.

Von Ahnen, Katherine. *Heart of Naosaqua.* Illustrated by Paulette Livers Lambert. Niwot, Colo.: Roberts Rinehart Publishers, 1996.

Events in far-away St. Louis trigger a dramatic change of life for Naosaqua and her people, the Mesquakie, as they flee the Missouri lands that have long been a part of their lives. Change, painful losses, young love, and the depth of friendship are explored in this interesting tale.

Wood, Nancy, ed. *Many Winters: Prose and Poetry of the Pueblos.* Illustrated by Frank Howell. New York: Doubleday, 1974.

The lives of the Native Americans at the Taos Pueblo and the impact of the world around them are addressed in this thought-provoking volume.

———. *The Serpent's Tongue: Prose, Poetry, and Art of the New Mexico Pueblos.* New York: Dutton, 1997.

This treasure of art and lore from the New Mexico Pueblos is organized into eight segments that begin, logically, with "Creation," and conclude with "Two Worlds." This book offers insights into the values, rituals, and institutions of the Pueblo people.

———. *Spirit Walker.* Illustrated by Frank Howell. New York: Doubleday, 1993.

This volume is a celebration of the determination, courage, and strong spiritual faith of Native Americans.

Jewish Culture

Ayer, Eleanor. *Parallel Journeys.* New York: Atheneum, 1995.

Alternating chapters compare and contrast the lives of two young Germans: Waterford, who is a prisoner in a concentration camp, and Heck, a member of Hitler's youth. The book is composed primarily of excerpts from these two men's autobiographies, which describe life before, during, and after the Holocaust.

Bat-Ami, Miriam. *Dear Elijah.* New York: Farrar, Straus, 1995.

After her father suffers a heart attack, Rebecca and her Jewish Orthodox family must prepare for Passover without him. Frightened for her father, Rebecca writes to the prophet Elijah, confiding her worries and hopes.

Bergman, Tamar. *Along the Tracks.* Translated by Michael Swirsky. Boston: Houghton Mifflin, 1991.

This is a true story about a Jewish boy who is on the run in Russia during World War II.

Bierman, Carol. *Journey to Ellis Island: How My Father Came to America.* Illustrated by Laurie McGraw. New York: Hyperion, 1998.

Julius Weinstein is 12 when he sails from Russia with his mother and sister. He relates their experiences at Ellis Island, where the adventure is just beginning.

Britton-Jackson, Livia. *I Have Lived a Thousand Years: Growing Up in the Holocaust.* New York: Simon & Schuster, 1997.

This is a riveting memoir illuminating a teenager's horrendous experiences in Auschwitz. She endures because of unfailing faith, perseverance, and some miraculous twists of fate.

Brooks, Philip. *Extraordinary Jewish Americans.* Chicago: Children's Press, 1998.

Students researching famous Jewish Americans will find 60 short biographies of people who excelled in numerous professions and who lived between the American Revolution and the present day.

Douglas, Kirk. *The Broken Mirror.* New York: Simon & Schuster, 1997.

Set during the Holocaust, this is a story of human loss and human gain as a young man finds his way back to happiness, personal identity, and pride in his religion.

Giff, Patricia Reilly. *Lily's Crossing.* Delacorte, 1997.

This award-winning book tells of the friendship between a young girl whose father goes off to war and a young boy who has had to leave his family behind to escape persecution.

Hausman, Gerald. *Night Flight.* New York: Philomel, 1996.

Twelve-year-olds Jeff and Max are best friends. That friendship is severely tested when both of their dogs are poisoned and Max is convinced that Jews in the area are responsible. Jeff is half Jewish and must face his friend's hatred of Jewish people and his plans for vengeance against them.

Hautzig, Esther. *The Endless Steppe: A Girl in Exile.* New York: HarperCollins, 1968.

This is a true story that depicts the life of a young Jewish girl and her parents when they are exiled to Siberia during World War II.

Hesse, Karen. *Letters from Rifka.* New York: Henry Holt, 1992.

In this story set in 1919, Rifka flees Russia with her family to avoid the impending persecution of the Jews. Reaching out to what is familiar as the family travels to America, Rifka writes to her cousin using the only paper she has, the margins in her much-loved poetry book.

Hoestlandt, Jo. *Star of Fear, Star of Hope.* Translated from the French by Mark Polizzotti. Illustrated by Johanna Kang. New York: Walker, 1995.

Nine-year-old Helen recounts the story of the disappearance of her good friend during the war.

Hoobler, Dorothy, and Thomas Hoobler. *The Jewish American Family Album.* New York: Oxford University Press, 1995.

Relying on first-person narratives, the difficulties and joys of Jewish immigrants arriving in America between the 1840s and the turn of the century are detailed.

Hurwitz, Johanna. *Faraway Summer.* Illustrated by Mary Azarian. New York: Morrow, 1998.

A young Jewish girl is given the opportunity to spend a summer on a Vermont farm, where she makes new friends, including Snowflake Bentley, and helps those around her develop cultural understanding.

Krantz, Hazel. *Look to the Hills.* Philadelphia, Pa.: Jewish Publication Society, 1995.

In this story set in Denver's Jewish community during the 1880s and 1890s, Sally falls in love with an immigrant involved in social issues, including women's suffrage.

Leapman, Michael. *Witnesses to War: Eight True-Life Stories of Nazi Persecution.* New York: Viking, 1998.

Personal stories recounted by eight youngsters who lived in Europe during the 1930s and 1940s illustrate how so many lives could be affected by the deadly events of this historical period.

Leder, Jane Mersky. *A Russian Jewish Family.* Illustrated with family photographs. Minneapolis, Minn.: Lerner, 1996.

Readers can relive a family's 14-year struggle to emigrate from Leningrad to Chicago and their adjustment as political refugees through the photographs and text in this eye-opening book.

Lobel, Anita. *No Pretty Pictures: A Child of War.* New York: Greenwillow, 1998.

Award-winning author Anita Lobel shares the horrors of the early years of her life as she, her brother, and her nanny tried to stay one step ahead of the Nazis. She and her family were miraculously reunited at the end of the war, a rare happy ending for those who lived under Hitler's edicts.

Matas, Carol. *Greater Than Angels.* New York: Simon & Schuster, 1998.

Anna Hirsch is a Jewish girl, part of a group being helped to safety by the American Red Cross. Based on actual events, this story reinforces the courage shown by so many people in communities large and small during World War II.

Meyer, Carolyn. *Gideon's People.* San Diego, Calif.: Gulliver/Harcourt Brace, 1996.

Isaac, an Orthodox Jew, helps 16-year-old Gideon leave his Amish family to seek a less restrictive way of life. Set in 1911, this book depicts the rich heritage of two cultures, similar because of their traditions and regulations.

Miklowitz, Gloria D. *Masada: The Last Fortress.* Grand Rapids, Mich.: Eerdmans, 1998.

Simon Ben Eleazar is the 17-year-old son of the Jewish leader of the Zealots. It is through his eyes that readers follow the siege of the Romans and the Jews' last stand on Masada.

Novac, Ana. *The Beautiful Days of My Youth: My Six Months in Auschwitz and Plaszow.* Translated by George L. Newman. New York: Henry Holt, 1997.

Ana's secret journal is a historical record of the grim days of the Holocaust. It is also a mesmerizing personal memoir filled with determination to grow even under the most horrifying of circumstances.

Perl, Lila, and Marion Blumenthal Lazan. *Four Perfect Pebbles: A Holocaust Story.* New York: Greenwillow, 1996.

This is the true story of Marion Blumenthal, her brother, and her parents as they struggled to survive the brutal Holocaust. Waiting for papers that will enable them to leave the country, they are transported from one camp to another, eventually ending up in Auschwitz. Marion carries four perfect pebbles, believing that they will help keep the family together.

Rabinovici, Schoschana. *Thanks to My Mother.* New York: Dial, 1998.

It is never completely possible to walk in another's shoes, but readers can try to do so as they imagine being a young Jewish child who loses her home to live in one work and concentration camp after another. Amazingly, it is Susie's mother who keeps her alive.

Rochman, Hazel, and Darlene Z. Campbell, selectors. *Bearing Witness: Stories of the Holocaust.* New York: Orchard Books, 1995.

The compilers of this work have chosen memorable excerpts from a number of resources to bear witness to the events of the Holocaust.

Rose, Deborah Lee. *The Rose Horse.* Illustrated by Greg Shed. San Diego, Calif.: Harcourt Brace, 1995.

It is 1909 and Lily's father has a job carving carousel animals on Coney Island. A nearby clinic for premature babies houses Lily's new sister. This loving family of Eastern European immigrants is shown as they pass their heritage on to their children.

Schur, Maxine Rose. *When I Left My Village.* Illustrated by Brian Pinkney. New York: Dial, 1996.

Menelik and his family are Ethiopian Jews who must flee to Israel to enjoy a life free from political oppression.

Vos, Ida. *Hide and Seek.* Translated by Terese Edelstein and Inez Smidt. Boston: Houghton Mifflin, 1991.

Dutch neighbors hide a Jewish family when the Germans occupy the Netherlands.

Wassiljewa, Tatjana. *Hostage to War: A True Story.* New York: Scholastic, 1997.

Tatjana must leave her Russian family to serve as a forced laborer for Nazi Germany. She survives the ordeal, but her future is bleak. An insightful book on what Russian citizens had to endure during World War II.

Yolen, Jane. *The Devil's Arithmetic.* New York: Viking, 1988.

Hannah has had it with her Jewish heritage. When she opens the door to symbolically let Elijah into her family's home during a religious celebration, she travels back in time to a small Jewish village in Nazi-occupied Poland. Once there, she suffers the atrocities of incarnation in a concentration camp.

———. *Milk and Honey: A Year of Jewish Holidays.* Illustrated by Louise August. New York: Putnam, 1996.

This appealing book is filled with customs and history for a year of holy days, including stories, poems, and songs of celebration.

Appendix II
Additional Materials
for Reference

Helpful teacher resources have been integrated throughout this book. In addition to those already mentioned, the following journals, addresses, and books may fill a niche as the preceding lessons are taught and adapted to meet the specific needs of your class from year to year.

Journals and Review Sources to Keep You Up-to-Date on Multicultural Literature and Possible Classroom Activities

The ALAN Review. National Council of Teachers of English, 1111 W. Kenyon Rd., Urbana, IL 61801-1096.

This journal is published three times a year and contains articles and book reviews relating to young adult literature.

Book Links. 434 W. Downer, Aurora, IL 60506.

Thematic bibliographies, ways to use literature in the classroom, and articles of interest to teachers, librarians, and parents fill this excellent resource on a bi-monthly basis.

Book Links: Connecting Books, Libraries, and Classrooms. Booklist Publications/American Library Association, 50 E. Huron St., Chicago, IL 60611. Subscription information: (630) 892-7465, $29.95/year.

A magazine directed at adults who are interested in connecting children with books. Issues are theme related.

Bookbird: World of Children's Books. P.O. Box 3156, West Lafayette, IN 47906.

Published quarterly by the International Board of Books for Young People (IBBY), it includes articles about authors and addresses trends in book publishing around the world.

Horn Book Magazine. Horn Book, Inc., 14 Beacon St., Boston, MA 02108-3704.

Published six times a year, this magazine contains numerous book reviews, interviews with authors and illustrators, and excellent articles related to children's literature.

Language Arts. National Council of Teachers of English, 1111 W. Kenyon Rd., Urbana, IL 61801-1096.

Ideas for teaching literature and language arts plus annotations of children's books and reviews of professional resources make this a useful journal.

New Advocate. Christopher-Gordon Publishers, Inc., 480 Washington St., Norwood, MA 02062.

This quarterly journal includes articles and book reviews by teachers and scholars pertaining to the world of children's literature.

The Reading Teacher. International Reading Association, 800 Barksdale Rd., P.O. Box 8139, Newark, DE 19714-8139.

This journal focuses on teaching reading. It offers a thematic review of children's books and suggestions for teaching reading through quality literature. Professional book reviews and timely research appear in the issues from September through May.

School Library Journal. P.O. Box 1978, Marion, OH 43305-1978.

In this monthly journal readers can find information and reviews of books for children and young adults. The "Best Books" issue in December is particularly interesting with its list of outstanding books.

The United States Board on Books for Young People Newsletter. USBBY Secretariat, c/o International Reading Association, P.O. Box 8139, Newark, DE 19714-8139.

This newsletter highlights international children's literature. It comes out twice a year.

Various publishers have a variety of free materials available. Check websites for current information. Write to the address below to get on the mailing list for three annual issues of *Puffin Papers*. It contains reviews of books, ideas for using books in the classroom, and sources for free materials:

Puffin Papers
Peggy Guthart
Penguin Putnam Inc.
345 Hudson St.
New York, NY 10014

General Multicultural Resources

Helbig, Althea K., and Agnes R. Perkins. *This Land Is Our Land: A Guide to Multicultural Literature for Children and Young Adults.* Westport, Conn.: Greenwood, 1994.

This is a resource of more than 600 titles published since 1985 about African, Native American, Hispanic, and Asian cultures.

Kruse, Ginny Moore, Kathleen T. Horning, and Megan Schliesman. *Multicultural Literature for Children and Young Adults: A Selected Listing of Books by and about People of Color, Volume 2, 1991–1996.* Madison, Wis.: Friends of the CCBC, 1998.

Presented by subject matter, fine literature by and about people of color is included in this volume. Books were selected with an eye to authenticity and accuracy.

Kuipers, Barbara J. *American Indian Reference Books for Children and Young Adults.* Englewood, Colo.: Libraries Unlimited, 1991.

An especially practical feature of this book is the detailed evaluation criteria, handy for teachers wanting only the best in their classrooms.

McCabe, Alyssa. *Chameleon Readers: Teaching Children to Appreciate All Kinds of Good Stories.* New York: McGraw-Hill, 1996.

The point of this book is to teach children to better understand children of other cultures and more easily find similarities between cultural traditions through reading and storytelling.

Thomas, Rebecca. *Connecting Cultures: A Guide to Multicultural Literature for Children.* New Providence, N.J.: R. R. Bowker, 1996.

This is an extensive bibliography, indexed by grade level, title, subject, culture, and author.

Williams, Helen E. *Books by African-American Authors and Illustrators for Children and Young Adults*. Chicago: American Library Association, 1991.

This volume includes books with an African-American focus published in the twentieth century.

Books That Connect Readers with Authors and Illustrators

Cummings, Pat. *Talking with Artists I*. New York: Simon & Schuster, 1992.

Victoria Chess, Pat Cummings, Leo Dillon and Diane Dillon, Richard Egielski, Lois Ehlert, Lisa Campbell Ernst, Tom Feelings, Steven Kellogg, Jerry Pinkney, Amy Schwartz, Lane Smith, Chris Van Allsburg, and David Wiesner are included in this volume.

———. *Talking with Artists II*. New York: Simon & Schuster, 1995.

Thirteen artists are presented in two-page spreads: Thomas B. Allen, Mary Jane Begin, Floyd Cooper, Julie Downing, Denise Fleming, Sheila Hamanaka, Kevin Henkes, William Joyce, Maira Kalman, Deborah Norse Lattimore, Brian Pinkney, Vera B. Williams, and David Wisniewski.

Ehrlich, Amy, ed. *When I Was Your Age: Original Stories about Growing Up*. Cambridge, Mass.: Candlewick Press, 1999.

This book contains stories from Norma Fox Mazer, Rita Williams-Garcia, Paul Fleischman, Jane Yolen, Howard Norman, E. L. Konigsburg, Michael J. Rosen, Kyoko Mori, Karen Hesse, and Joseph Bruchac.

———. *When I Was Your Age: Original Stories about Growing Up*. Cambridge, Mass.: Candlewick Press, 1996.

Contains stories from Mary Pope Osborne, Laurence Yep, James Howe, Katherine Paterson, Walter Dean Myers, Susan Cooper, Nicholasa Mohr, Reeve Lindbergh, Avi, and Francesca Lia Block.

Gallo, Donald R., ed. *Speaking for Ourselves: Autobiographical Sketches by Notable Authors of Books for Young Adults*. Urbana, Ill.: National Council of Teachers of English, 1990.

Brief snippets of information and a list of books written by 88 authors are included in this volume.

———. *Speaking for Ourselves, Too: Autobiographical Sketches by Notable Authors of Books for Young Adults*. Urbana, Ill.: National Council of Teachers of English, 1993.

In this continuation of his first book, Gallo introduces readers to more authors via interesting facts about them plus a list of their writings.

Smaller Publishers of Interest

Barefoot Books
37 W. 17th St.
4th Floor East
New York, NY 1011-5512
(212) 604-0505
fax: (888) 346-9138
e-mail: sales@barefoot-books.com
website: www.barefoot-books.com
Publishes quality picture books for children of all ages with a focus on folktales and fairy tales, wonderful myths and legends, and appealing poetry offerings. Barefoot Books promotes work of artists and writers from many cultures.

Ninos
P.O. Box 1603
Secaucus, NJ 07096-1603
(800) 634-3304
An excellent resource for bilingual products including books, tapes, videos, CDs, and games in both English and Spanish.

Northland Publishers/Rising Moon
P.O. Box 1389
Flagstaff, AZ 86002
(800) 346-3257
fax: (800) 257-9082
Although this publisher has a superb collection of books for the adult reader, its growing collection of award-garnering children's books should not be missed. The company focuses on many cultures and has appealing picture books and novels about African-American, Native American, and Hispanic heroes and heroines.

Lee & Low Books
website: www.leeandlow.com
Classroom orders:
Lee & Low Books
95 Madison Avenue
New York, NY 10016
(212) 779-4400, ext. 20
fax: (212) 683-1894
An excellent resource for truly fine multicultural literature.

Books and Materials on Japan

Makino, Yasuko. *Japan through Children's Literature: An Annotated Bibliography*. 2d ed.: Greenwood, 1985.

U.S. Sources for Obtaining Books from and about Japan

Charles E. Tuttle Company
28 S. Main St.
P.O. Box 410
Rutland, VT 05702

Kinokuniya Book and Gallery
123 Astronaut Ellison Onizuka, Suite 205
Los Angeles, CA
(888) 454-6692

Mexican/Mexican-American Resources

Vigil, Angel. *Una Linda Raza: Cultural and Artistic Traditions of the Hispanic Southwest*. Golden, Colo.: Fulcrum Publishing, 1997.

Native American Resources

Erickson, Bonnie O. "At Home with Multicultural Literature." *The ALAN Review* 23, no. 1 (Fall 1995): 44–46.

McCann, Donnarae. "Native Americans in Books for the Young." In *Teaching Multicultural Literature in Grades K–8*, edited by Violet J. Harris. Norwood, Mass.: Christopher-Gordon Publishers, 1993.

Slapin, B., and D. Seale. *Through Indian Eyes: The Native Experiences in Books for Children*. Philadelphia, Pa.: New Society, 1992.

Stott, J. C. *Native Americans in Children's Literature*. Phoenix, Ariz.: Oryx Press, 1995.

Useful Poetry Resources

Brown, Bill, William Stafford, and Malcolm Glass. *Important Words: A Book for Poets and Writers.* Portsmouth, N.H.: Heinemann, 1991.

Carey, Michael A. *Poetry: Starting from Scratch: A Two Week Lesson Plan for Teaching Poetry Writing.* Foundation Books, 1989.

Copeland, Jeffrey S. *Speaking of Poets: Interviews with Poets Who Write for Children and Young Adults.* Urbana, Ill.: National Council of Teachers of English, 1993.

Copeland, Jeffrey S., and Vickly L. Copeland, eds. *Speaking of Poets 2: More Interviews with Poets Who Write for Children and Young Adults.* Urbana, Ill.: National Council of Teachers of English, 1994.

Dunning, Stephen, and William Stafford. *Getting the Knack: 20 Poetry Writing Exercises.* Urbana, Ill.: National Council of Teachers of English, 1992.

Graves, Donald H. *Explore Poetry: The Reading/Writing Teacher's Companion.* Portsmouth, N.H.: Heinemann, 1992.

Heard, Georgia. *For the Good of the Earth and the Sun: Teaching Poetry.* Portsmouth, N.H.: Heinemann, 1989.

Janeczko, Paul B., selector. *Poetspeak: In Their Work, about Their Work.* New York: Simon & Schuster, 1983.

Lewis, J. Patrick. *Doole Dandies: Poems That Take Shape.* Images by Lisa Desimini. New York: Atheneum, 1998.

Livingstone, Myra Cohn. *Poem-Making: Ways to Begin Writing Poetry.* New York: HarperCollins, 1991.

McClure, Amy, with Peggy Harrison and Sheryl Reed. *Sunrises and Songs: Reading and Writing Poetry in an Elementary Classroom.* Portsmouth, N.H.: Heinemann, 1990.

Working across the Curriculum

Angell, Carole S. *Celebrations around the World: A Multicultural Handbook.* Golden, Colo.: Fulcrum Publishing, 1996.

Barchers, Suzanne, and Peter J. Rauen. *Holiday Storybook Stew: Cooking through the Year with Books Kids Love.* Illustrated by Darcie Clark Frohardt. Golden, Colo.: Fulcrum Publishing, 1998.

———. *Storybook Stew: Cooking with Books Kids Love.* Illustrated by Darcie Clark Frohardt. Golden, Colo.: Fulcrum Publishing, 1996.

Fuhler, Carol J. *Discovering Geography of North America with Books Kids Love.* Illustrated by Audra Loyal. Golden, Colo.: Fulcrum Publishing, 1998.

Haven, Kendall. *New Year's Kwanzaa: Original Stories of Celebration.* Golden, Colo.: Fulcrum Publishing, 1999.

Appendix III
Websites to Investigate

··

Because the World Wide Web is in constant flux, be sure to check these sites periodically. They seem to change, move, and disappear on short notice. Even if there is a change, you may still be able to find a site by typing in the first part of the address and letting your search engine go to work.

- Aaron Shepard's RT Page
  (http://www.aaronshep.com/rt/)

This is a useful site for readers of all ages who are interested in reader's theater scripts.

- The Academy of American Poets
  (http://www.poets.org/index.cfm)

This academy is the largest organization in the country dedicated specifically to poetry. It supports poets in all stages of their writing. During National Poetry Month, April, it is a source of excellent ideas on how to celebrate poetry.

- Amazon Books
  (http://www.amazon.com)

What a way to spend several hours and several dollars! Search by title or browse by subject in a catalog with more than 2.5 million titles. You can also order directly (books are shipped promptly if they are in stock), read author interviews, and learn about new books. There is an endless array of children's books, many titles discounted between 10 and 30 percent.

- Ask the Author
  (http://ipl.sils.umich.edu/youth/ask author/)

This is part of the Internet Public Library. Its focus is biographies and interviews with well-known authors and illustrators.

- Author! Author!
  (http://www.greyware.com/authors/)

A resource about authors of children's books.

- Bantam Doubleday Dell: The Teacher's Resource Center
  (http://www.bdd.com/teachers)

Here you can find teacher's guides for novels appropriate for grades 4–8. You can also listen to interviews with authors.

- Book-a-Minute
  (http://www.rinkworks.com/bookaminute)

Browse through condensed book summaries that include children's books.

- Book Nook
  (http://isite.on.ca/isite/education/bk_report/booknook/default.html)

Here is a site where children have the opportunity to publish and to read reviews of a specific book that someone else has reviewed. Then they can select a title from a list of books awaiting review.

- Carol Hurst's Children's Literature Newsletter
  (http://www.crocker.com/-rebotis/newsletters.html)

Carol Hurst shares her expertise as a storyteller, lecturer, author, columnist, and language arts consultant via book reviews, teaching ideas, links to author interviews, professional topics, and more.

- Children's Author Directory
  (http://www.inkspot.com/author/directory)

- Children's Book Council
  (http://www.cbcbooks.org)

Exploring the four major categories will provide a wealth of information: "Publishers," "Teachers and Librarians," "Booksellers," and "Parents' Authors and Illustrators." For example, the "Publishers" category includes listings of all the publishers that are members along with their website addresses, information about newly released or upcoming books, and resources for teachers.

- Children's Literature Authors and Illustrators
  (http://www.ucet.ufl.edu/~jbrown/chauth.html)

Here is a specialized website that provides direct links to pages of information about historic and contemporary children's authors and illustrators.

- Children's Literature Home Page
  (http://www.parentsplace.com/readroom/index)

A site that reviews thousands of books.

- Children's Literature Sampler
  (http://funnelweb.utcc.utk.edu/~estes/estes2.html)

A teacher can obtain lists of critical reading that have been carefully organized into thematic groupings, suggested curricular connections to various themes, and other miscellaneous material.

- Children's Literature Web Guide/Tell Me More
  (http://www.acs.ucalgary.ca/~dkbrown/authors.html)

Offers a wealth of information to teachers; it includes links to selected author sites and is updated on a regular basis.

• Cinderella Project *and* Little Red Riding Hood
Project
(http://www.usm.edu/usmhburg/lib_art
/english/cinderella/cinderella.html *and*
http://www-dept.usm.edu/~engdept/
lrrh/lrrhhome.htm)

Both of these sites give the user direct access to online texts and reproductions of pages from numerous print versions of these tales, which are contained in the deGrummond Collection housed at the University of Southern Mississippi.

• Cooperative Children's Book Center
(http://www.soemadison.wisc.edu/
ccbc/index.htm)

The CCBC is located in the School of Education at the University of Wisconsin–Madison and offers a myriad of resources, including online bibliographies of children's books. Book discussions among staff members can also be accessed.

• *Cyberkids*
(http://www.cyberkids.com/)

Cyberkids is an enticing magazine for students that publishes children's writing, art, and musical compositions and offers a fine option for free reading time.

• The deGrummond Children's Literature Collection
(http://www.lib.usm.edu/degrum)

A wealth of books old and new can be located here. For author biographies for more than 170 authors, access this site specifically:
http://www.lib.usm.edu/~degrum/newreg.htm#index

• Global Heinemann Keypals
(http://www.reedbooks.com.au/
heinemann/global/global1.html)

Here is a great resource for locating penpals via the computer. It can be used by individuals or by the entire class. Rules for etiquette when being a penpal are included with the site. They can be printed out and located near the computers for easy reference.

• HarperCollins Publishers
(http://www.harpercollins.com)

Watch this site for teaching ideas, information about authors and books, special discounts, and promotional materials.

• Houghton Mifflin Publishers
(http://www.homco.com/trade)

As do other publishers, Houghton Mifflin has much to offer the teacher in the line of free and educational materials.

• ICONnect
(http://www.ala.org/iconn/index.html)

The American Library Association offers this site, which includes links to additional sites involving authors, illustrators, and books. Includes Kids Connect for students K–12.

• The Internet Public Library
(http://www.ipl.org/_=_i;l@ipl.org)

A trip to this site is like a trip to the library to do research, get reading and teaching ideas, polish your math, and more. An extensive, continually updated site.

• Internet School Library Media Center's Index
to Author and Illustrator Internet Sites
(http://falcon.jmu.edu/~ramseyil/
biochildhome.htm)

James Madison University hosts this metasite. It provides easy access to curriculum-related Web resources for school librarians, teachers, parents, and interested students.

• ISLMC Poetry for Children
(http://falcon.jmu.edu/%7eramseyil/
poechild.htm)

The Internet School Library Media Center sponsors this site, packed with resources for teachers and librarians. Three poetry bibliographies are available.

• Kathy Schrock's Guide for Educators
(http://www.capecod.net/schrockguide)

This popular site enables teachers to use search engines and directories to locate important educational information on the Internet.

• Kay Vandergrift's Learning about the Author
and Illustrator Pages
(http://www.scils.rutgers.edu/special/
kay/author.html)

Attractive and simply packed with enticing information, this site links learners to more than 500 author pages, including personally designed and publisher-created pages. There is also a list of 60 excellent author biographies and autobiographies and a second list citing more than 40 author videos.

• KidPub
(http://www.kidpub.org/kidpub/)

Here is another outlet for readers and writers from grades K–12 who would like to be published. Thousands of stories have already been published and are available to be enjoyed by other aspiring writers.

• Library of Congress
(http://lcweb.loc.gov/homepage/lchp.html)

An invaluable site for materials to use across the curriculum to motivate readers and writers alike.

• North American Native Authors Catalog
(http://nativeauthors.com)

For teachers who want to read books written in an authentic Native American voice.

• Random House Publishers
(http://www.randomhouse.com/teachers/)

A resource center with teacher's guides, author and illustrator biographies, and thematic and interdisciplinary indexes.

• Robert G. Shubinski's Glossary of Poetic Terms
(http://shoga.wwa.com/~rgs/glossary.html)

What a great resource! Users will find definitions of poetry terms, examples, poetic quotations from well-known writers, and more.

• Scholastic Publishers
(http://www.scholastic.com)

A wealth of information, and you can buy books here too!

- The Scoop
  (http://www.friendly. net/scoop/)

This site provides an online newsletter, author and illustrator information, teaching ideas, book reviews, and activities for children.

- Semantic Rhyming Dictionary
  (http://www.cs.cmu.edu/~doughb/rhyme.html)

A handy reference for three types of research: perfect rhymes, partial rhymes, and homophones from a selection of more than 115,000 words.

- Smithsonian Institute National Museum of the American Indian
  (http://www.si.edu/cgi-bin/nav.cgi)

A wealth of information awaits investigation here for students who want to research specific topics involving Native Americans and their history.

- *Stone Soup*
  (http://www.stonesoup.com/)

Stone Soup is an international magazine for ages 8–13. Poems and stories written by children can be enjoyed at this site. Instructions for submitting work are also included.

- Tales of Wonder
  (http://www.ece.ucdavis.edu/~darsie/tales.html)

A fabulous resource of folktales and fairy tales from around the world. Tales are arranged by country or region of origin and include a list of related print resources.

- Virginia Hamilton
  (http://www.virginiahamilton.com)

This attractive website can engross readers for quite some time as they follow threads of information from one page to another in the process of learning about this wonderful, award-winning African-American author. For specific biographical information, try:
http://www. virginiahamilton.com/pages/biostuff.htm

- Webtime Stories
  (http://www.kn.pacbell.com/wired/kidlit/kid.html)

This is an annotated collection of websites. The printed word, graphics, sounds, interactivity, and animation make this a site difficult to resist. You will find a story time where you can read books and participate in activities, scout for "Great Books," listen to fables, myths, or legends, find craft ideas, and get tips for choosing quality children's literature.

- *Wordsmiths: Teen Voices @ Teen Link*
  (http://www.nypl.org/branch/teen/vox.html)

Teen Link is the New York Public Library's website for young adults. *Wordsmiths* offers 12- to 18-year-olds the opportunity to publish original poetry and short stories on the Internet. Instructions on how to submit work can be found at the site. In addition, other Internet sources for young writers are available.

Electronic Journals That Focus on Children's Literature

- *The ALAN Review*
  (http://scholar.lib.vt.edu/ejournals/alan/alan-review.html)
- *Booklist*
  (http://www.ala.org/booklist/index.html)
- *The Bulletin of the Center for Children's Books*
  (http://edfu.lis.uiuc.edu/puboff/bccb/)
- *Horn Book*
  (http://www.hbook.com)
- *Publishers Weekly*
  (http://www.book wire.com/pw/childrens.articles)

Print Resources

Burgstahler, Sheryl, and Laurie Utterback. *New Kids on the Net: Internet Activities in Elementary Language Arts.* Boston: Allyn and Bacon, 2000.

Look for this excellent resource for general information on the Internet and classroom teaching ideas galore involving Internet activities. Internet etiquette, where to go for different kinds of information, and answers to questions like "What is a search engine?" are but a few of the tidbits available here. The text focuses on the subject area of language arts but would work with ease across the curriculum.

Index